Geography,
Postmodern
...tics of Place

Literature, Geography, and the Postmodern Poetics of Place

Eric Prieto

palgrave
macmillan

First published in 2013 by PALGRAVE MACMILLAN® in the United States—a division of St. Martin's Press LLC, 175 Fifth Avenue, New York, NY 10010.

Where this book is distributed in the UK, Europe and the rest of the world, this is by Palgrave Macmillan, a division of Macmillan Publishers Limited, registered in England, company number 785998, of Houndmills, Basingstoke, Hampshire RG21 6XS.

Palgrave Macmillan is the global academic imprint of the above companies and has companies and representatives throughout the world.

Palgrave® and Macmillan® are registered trademarks in the United States, the United Kingdom, Europe and other countries.

ISBN: 978-1-137-03111-2

Library of Congress Cataloging-in-Publication Data

Prieto, Eric, 1966–
    Literature, geography, and the postmodern poetics of place / Eric Prieto.
        p. cm.
    ISBN 978-1-137-03111-2 (hardback)
    1. Place (Philosophy) in literature. 2. Literature—20th century—History and criticism. 3. Literature—21st century—History and criticism. 4. Liminality in literature. 5. Postmodernism (Literature) I. Title.

    PN56.P49P75 2013
    809'.93358—dc23   2012031254

A catalogue record of the book is available from the British Library.

This book is printed on paper suitable for recycling and made from fully managed and sustained forest sources. Logging, pulping and manufacturing processes are expected to conform to the environmental regulations of the country of origin.

Design by Scribe Inc.

First edition: January 2013

10 9 8 7 6 5 4 3 2 1

For Kim, Sofie, and Charlie

Contents

Acknowledgments

The origins of this book go back a long way. I have, for as long as I can remember, had a particular fascination with transitional neighborhoods and in-between places of various kinds. And for most of my adult life I have, through an inextricable mix of necessity, preference, and good luck, lived and worked in neighborhoods (Fort Green, Shepherd's Bush, Créteil, Belleville, and Schoelcher) that enabled me to partake in the life of some of the world's great cities while also discovering the particularities that give life on the margins its distinctive flavor. I would like to thank all the friends met along the way who helped me to get to know and love these places. I would also like to thank all the friends and colleagues who helped me to develop and test the ideas put forth in this book. My UC Santa Barbara colleagues Porter Abbott, Peter Bloom, Catherine Nesci, and Sydney Lévy were particularly generous with their time and advice, reading early drafts of the manuscript and helping me to strengthen the book considerably. Other colleagues have also been generous in exchanging ideas with me at various stages in the genesis of this project: Alec Hargreaves, Martin Munro, Nick Nesbitt, Rob Tally, Richard Watts, Bertrand Westphal, and many others. The students in my "Space and Place" seminars challenged me to open up new and unforeseen windows onto the subject—as did the doctoral research of Claudio dell'Oca and Lachelle Hannickel. I am grateful to the University of California at Santa Barbara for facilitating my research in various ways: notably through a Regents' Humanities Faculty Fellowship, a travel grant from the Interdisciplinary Humanities Center, and a Faculty Career Development Award. And I'm thankful above all for my wife and family, who do indeed make our house a home.

Acknowledgment of Previous Publications

Portions of chapter 6 were published in "Landscaping Identity in Contemporary Caribbean Literature," in *Francophone Post-Colonial Cultures: Critical Essays*, ed. Kamal Salhi (Lanham, MD: Lexington Books, 2003), 141–52, and in "Edouard Glissant, *Littérature-monde*, and *Tout-monde*," *Small Axe* 14, no.3 33 (2010): 111–20. They are reprinted by permission.

Excerpts from "These Also Once Under Moonlight" are used by kind permission of Jane Hirshfield. This poem was published in Hirshfield's *Come, Thief* (New York: Knopf, 2011) and also appeared in *The American Poetry Review* 38, no. 5 (September–October 2009): 38.

Introduction

But let a suburb stand a generation or so and, in literature as in life, it is perceived as a Real Place.

—Gillian Tindall, *Countries of the Mind*

Ours, too, a transitional species,
chimerical, passing,
what is later, always, called monstrous—
no longer one thing, not yet another.

—Jane Hirshfield, "These Also Once Under Moonlight"

This is a book about making it onto the map. It studies some of the ways in which emergent geographical spaces come to be recognized as full-fledged, autonomous places with their own identities and internal dynamics. More specifically, it focuses on the role that literature and the other imaginative arts play in that process, emphasizing the ability of fictional representations to shape our attitudes about the actual environments through which we move. Within this field of inquiry, I deploy my analyses around a concept that has taken on particular importance in the current, transitional (postmodern, postcolonial, globalizing) moment of world history—that of the *entre-deux*, or in-between. The term *entre-deux* designates the many different kinds of sites that fall between the established categories that shape our expectations of what a place should be and that often tend, therefore, to be misunderstood, maligned, or simply ignored. Such places, because they deviate from established norms, are all too often thought of in terms of what they lack or what is wrong with them—as defective variants of more-established, better-understood places. However, as recent reappraisals of interstitial geographical entities like American suburbia and third-world squatter cities have emphasized, such places, despite their very real problems and inadequacies, may also prove to be unexpectedly resourceful loci of innovation and development—provided that we know how to look. By emphasizing the overlooked productive potential of in-between places—like the "borderlands," "edge-cities," and "non-places" theorized respectively by Gloria Anzaldúa, Joel Garreau, and Marc Augé—I treat them not as symptoms of today's social pathologies but as laboratories for the ways of life of tomorrow.

It is the underappreciated dynamic potential of such interstitial places that suggests the need for a study that brings the particular kinds of knowledge generated by works of imaginative literature into contact with the social and spatial sciences—an approach that might be termed "geocritical."[1] Although a geographer, sociologist, or urban planner might consider the hypothetical or counterfactual status of fictional and metaphorical language a liability, I emphasize the ways in which its relative freedom from documentary concerns and from the scientific test of falsifiability enhances its ability to generate new spatial concepts and attitudes. It is precisely the imaginative dimension of fictional representation that gives it its peculiar form of power over the real, making it more sensitive to those qualities of emergent spatial and geographical formations that are most difficult to detect from within established explanatory frameworks. This is not, of course, to suggest that scientific discourse has no interest in developing new concepts or insights. It is, rather, to propose that the scientific search for new concepts pushes it in the direction of literature, requiring the use of the kinds of hypothetical modes of representation associated here with fiction.[2] The *indirect referentiality* (Paul Ricoeur) of fictional representation enables it to act as a kind of midwife, drawing emergent spatial intuitions out of the conceptual purgatory of the *entre-deux*, a critical phase in the process of concept formation.[3]

My purpose in this book, then, is to examine the ways in which literary representations help us to understand the often misunderstood properties of emergent forms of place. I focus on texts that provide new insights into the changing experience of place in the late twentieth and early twenty-first centuries. Some of them are highly experimental, while others belong to more mainstream genres like the coming-of-age novel or buddy film, but all of them deploy innovative representational strategies that enable them to help us understand what is most significant and productive about the kinds of places they depict.

Historically, much of the writing on the emergence of new and unfamiliar place types has tended to oscillate between utopianism and nostalgia or mourning. We have, on the one hand, the messianism of the prophet (one thinks of Fourier's *phalanstères* or Le Corbusier's *cités radieueses*) and, on the other hand, a stubborn clinging to the status quo. When new modes of spatial organization threaten to displace the familiar patterns, it seems that they often awaken a kind of conservative impulse—even among the most forward looking thinkers. Laments for what is being lost often compete with interest in what is emerging. Charles Baudelaire, for example, responding to the changes wrought by Haussmann's mid-nineteenth-century renovation of Paris, memorably captured the nostalgic impulse in his poem *Le cygne*: "The form of a city changes faster, alas, than the human heart."[4] This poem, an elegy about being exiled in one's own city, clearly expresses the poet's regret for the loss of the old Paris—the still essentially medieval Paris immortalized by Balzac, Rétif de la Bretonne, Eugène Sue, and Victor Hugo (to whom the poem is dedicated). But Baudelaire was also among the first self-consciously modernist thinkers and, as such, was aware that new forms of life were springing up around him even as he wrote those lines. These changes, both exhilarating and threatening, were necessarily difficult to put into context for those living through them, and a significant part of the genius of Baudelaire was to have grappled with them in his poetic work.[5] The profound changes that were reshaping Baudelaire's Paris were examined in some of his best texts, and his attunement to the ever-evolving complexity of his urban environment appears to have inspired what may be his greatest poetic innovation: the prose poem. In the preface to his *Petits poèmes en prose*, he writes of his search for a poetic form "supple enough and jagged enough" to express his modernist sensibility, and he explains the origins of that quest in terms of his urban environment: "The notion of such an obsessive ideal has its origins above all in our experience of the life of great cities, the confluence and interactions of the countless relationships within them" (*The Poems in Prose* 25).

Today, as in the period of urban renewal/destruction that Baudelaire lived through in the 1860s, it has become commonplace to lament the irreparable damage that modernity (and *a fortiori* postmodernity) has wrought on our environments. The ecocritical movement, for example, has given powerful expression to worries about our changing relationship with the natural environment. But the fear of environmental degradation is also linked to the more general fear that any significant changes to our environment, whether natural or built, might fundamentally undermine our relationship with the places we inhabit. Urban sociologists like Richard Sennett and Jane Jacobs, for example, have deplored the threats to urban communities posed by insensitive urban renewal, suburbanization, and the like.[6] Of course the modes of urban sociability defended by these writers would have been impossible without the previous history of industrialization and urbanization that gave rise to the modern city. And those developments had been resisted with just as much vigor by previous generations of writers, giving rise, for example, to the kind of city/country pastoral myth critiqued by Raymond Williams.[7] That kind of myth, with its nostalgia for an idyllic past that most likely never existed, is in no danger of going away. On the contrary, it seems to have undergone a renaissance in recent years that is due in part to the ongoing urbanization of the global landscape characteristic of modernism and is due also to a perceived acceleration in the pace of change that is linked to postmodernism and globalization.[8] Thus one way to understand the somewhat apocalyptic laments of recent books like Howard Kunstler's *The Geography of Nowhere* might be to think of them as postmodern urban variants of the pastoral myth, projecting all that is good into a receding past.[9]

My point here is simply that we must learn to resist the dualist tendency to oscillate between reactionary conservatism and utopian futurism. Every new development—even those that hold out the promise of a bold new future—is bound to bring about regret for what is lost. Conversely, just as life springs from decay, new forms of place arise from the demise of their predecessors and it is possible to make something good in even the most inhospitable environments. Baudelaire knew that this was true of Haussmann's Paris, and it stands to reason that similar dynamics might be operating in many of today's most characteristic geographical transformations—even those that are hardest to understand and/or accept. Success in navigating and controlling these transformations will require sorting through the spurious arguments on both sides, identifying bedrock values, and reconciling them with the material and social challenges of our era—all without losing sight of the question of what is possible politically and economically.

At the center of this maelstrom of competing priorities and needs is a deceptively simple concept: that of place. This is a concept that had largely disappeared from the field of geography by the middle of the twentieth century but has been revived in recent years, in large part because of the many perceived threats to the qualities that have traditionally ensured a strong affective bond between humans and the places they inhabit. The humanistic geography movement, spearheaded by Yi-Fu Tuan and Edward Relph in the 1970s, played a notable role in reviving this concept, making the study of place a central focus of its activities.

For some, although by no means all, members of this school, the transformations that technological modernity has wrought on the landscape pose a series of threats to the bonds of affection and identification that have traditionally linked peoples to the places they inhabit. A list of such transformations, which are in many ways definitive of our era, would include the following: industrial modernism's tendency toward standardization and homogenization, buttressed by ideologies of technical and economic efficiency; ongoing migration from the country to the city (with attendant phenomena like rural depopulation and urban squatter cities); migration from the third world to the first (with accompanying cultural shocks); the trend toward suburbanization in both its (sprawling, middle-class) American and (starker, proletarian) European senses; geographical redistribution due to the digital revolution and the information-age economy; the effects of environmental degradation and climate change; and shifting cultural allegiances caused by globalization and the various (often fundamentalist and exclusionary) reactions against it.

Fearing that these forces have significantly undermined the geographical and cultural cues that help us to orient ourselves meaningfully in the world, the humanistic geographers nonetheless recognize that there can be no simplistic response to such developments. The central question posed by humanist geography is how best to respond to such threats in a world that seems to be changing at an ever-more-rapid pace, following the principle of space-time compression identified by David Harvey. This question has also been asked by many others who recognize that amid all the loss and confusion associated with developments such as these, there arise a host of new possibilities for living in and relating to our local environment. Many contemporary thinkers—including the Spanish sociologist Manuel Castells, the American geographer Edward Soja, the Peruvian economist Hernando de Soto, and the Martinican novelist and cultural theorist Edouard Glissant—view the contemporary era of flux and change as a moment of opportunity as well as risk and have invested much energy in the effort to adapt to and push these changes in an egalitarian direction. Theirs is the spirit that guides me in this book, as I examine a number of fictional representations of emergent forms of geo-social organization, asking how these texts react to the changes occurring today and what tools they supply for understanding the options available to us as we seek to orient ourselves and react to them.

This willingness to emphasize the positive does not, of course, mean that we should minimize the very real losses that are being incurred all around us. Modernity has wrought great destruction on many cherished places, both at home and abroad—and often in the name of progress. The causes of these losses include many obvious candidates, like indiscriminate destruction in times of war, the despoliation of cultural heritage sites, and the forcible displacement of populations. They also include what might be thought of as friendly fire incidents: the unthinking demolition of significant architectural landmarks or the widespread reliance on standardized and characterless modes of housing and urban development. It goes without saying that such mistakes and/or crimes should be recognized, condemned as such, and guarded against, so that future mistakes can be avoided. But it would be just as much of an error to condemn all infrastructural disruptions out of some blind adherence to the status quo or to underestimate the sheer vitality of humans and their ability not only to adapt and survive in changing circumstances but also to thrive in and develop affection for the very landscapes that are decried by others. Consider the case of Annie Ricks, the last tenant to leave Chicago's notorious Cabrini-Green public housing projects before their demolition: "I feel sad about having to leave, about having to pack up my stuff and my memories . . . I feel comfortable and safe here" (qtd. in Terry). How does one evaluate this complex gesture of regret when the sense of attachment to one's home, combined with the fear of change, outweighs the very real physical and psychological discomforts of life in substandard, crime-ridden housing?

History shows, again and again, that even those developments that are most loudly deplored by the defenders of existing norms have the potential to become, in time, the new norm. This is true, for example, of the new Paris whose birth Baudelaire witnessed. That Paris, of course, is now *our* Paris. Soon after their construction, Haussmann's new boulevards, uniform residential façades, and monuments like the Garnier opera had become the iconic features of the city, immortalized by the impressionist painters (among many others) and idolized by tourists. This is true, moreover, not only of Haussmann's showcase achievements but also of the less laudable aspects of his plan. It is instructive in this regard to note that even the neighborhoods that were hastily built on the outskirts of Paris to house workers displaced from the city center are now included on lists of "neighborhoods with historical character." Often shoddily constructed and reviled at the time for obvious social reasons, they are now defended by activist groups committed to preserving the historical character of the city. Witness the history of *La Bellevilleuse*, a grassroots movement that successfully used the historical character argument to defend the *Bas Belleville* neighborhood in Paris against an insensitive program of urban renewal that would have replaced the neighborhood's existing housing stock with high-rise towers. (I will be studying a Martinican variant of this case in Chapter 6.) The simple passage of time and history has "naturalized" such places, making them part of the established landscape.

This last point—the "naturalization" of a landscape shaped by controversial political decisions—is of particular importance for understanding the virulence of debates surrounding urban renewal on the scale that Haussmann attempted. Once a given social reality has taken on this material form, becoming literally ensconced in the landscape, it eventually comes to seem natural to many—simply an expression of the order of things. Thus the new social geography of Paris created by Haussmann (upper and middle classes in the center and working classes on the periphery) has, over time, come to be accepted by many as simply the way things are, rather than as the outcome of a contested (and contestable) political process.[10] It is at such moments of rapid infrastructural change that the political stakes are highest. We must use caution, however, before choosing sides. No one can dispute that there was a need for some kind of urban reform to modernize the essentially medieval warren of streets and neighborhoods that made up the central districts of nineteenth-century Paris. The old city that Baudelaire loved—with its streets inaccessible to modern transport and with overcrowded, unsafe dwellings poorly served with water, sanitation, fresh air, open spaces, and the like—*had* to change. Inaction would merely have led to other kinds of crises (of which the 1832 cholera epidemic that killed twenty thousand Parisians gives us an idea). Indeed, Napoléon III's London experience and Saint-Simonism (he was a great admirer of London's parks and sanitation and their social benefits) suggest that his renovation projects were conceived with laudably progressive social principles in mind—even if his plans were implemented in a highly authoritarian manner and had the result of creating new social disparities.[11]

This same set of issues is at the heart of more recent debates over the legacies of other titanic figures in the history of urban planning and design, like Le Corbusier and Robert Moses. It is interesting to note, in this regard, that Marshall Berman, despite his insights into Baudelaire's ambivalence toward Haussmann's Paris and notwithstanding his willingness to embrace the progress made possible by those developments, was not able to take such a sanguine stance toward the development projects that Robert Moses carried out in and around New York City. Although there is no doubt that Moses's highway building projects inflicted mortal damage on many of the neighborhoods they passed through, Berman seems to underestimate the importance of the new urban configurations they made possible as they brought New York fully into the automobile era. In fact, Berman gives a fairly conventional account of Moses that shows a perhaps uncritical allegiance to the work of Jane Jacobs and Robert Caro.[12] But Moses's reputation has undergone a kind of rehabilitation in recent years. Some have begun to argue that the time may have come to move beyond the old recriminations and to frame both Moses's achievements and his mistakes in a new light.[13] How can such an evaluation be made? No one, I think, would dispute the need to modernize in response to new technologies like the automobile (or the Internet), nor the need for rapid expansion of housing stocks in response to the huge urban migrations after World War II. It is clear, moreover, that it is inherently difficult to achieve consensus on social and aesthetic priorities and to reconcile the aspirational focus on quality-of-life issues with the downward pressures of cost containment, time constraints, and the sheer scale of the demographic shifts of the postwar years. Add to this the complexity of what is made possible by new building technologies (reinforced concrete, glass, steel, and the skyscraper) and what is made impossible by unresolved social tensions (e.g., the deplorable state of race relations in postwar America) and the full complexity of the question becomes clear. Indeed, given all this, it is perhaps no surprise that it is autocratic figures like Haussmann and Moses who so often take on such projects, for better *and* for worse. My immediate purpose is not, however, to take a stand for or against Moses or Haussmann or the authoritarian model they represent but simply to recall the necessity of taking into account the larger political and economic framework against which this decision-making process is carried out.[14]

I will have this framework in mind, then, in what follows, although my focus is not on the political decision-making process but rather on the places themselves, as seen through the experience of those who, whether by choice or necessity, inhabit them. Whether these places are shaped in a relatively sudden, planned way (as in the case of the Haussmann and Moses projects) or through a more evolutionary process (of which the rise of squatter cities on the outskirts of urban centers provides a powerful example), I am interested in the struggle of communities that, in response to the changing social, political, and economic conditions around them, seek to assert control over their spatial existences and identities *from within*.

The central arguments of this book share the basic premise that our world is in constant evolution and that the loss of one kind of place and of certain ways of relating to place is part of a process that also leads to new possibilities. Much may be lost, but there may also be much to gain. Any attempt to come to grips with the new must overcome a perhaps understandable resistance to change as well as a sense of trepidation or even repulsion that often accompanies exposure to the unfamiliar. As mentioned earlier, there seems to be something about the human relationship with place that brings out the conservative, change-resistant side of even the most progressive, forward-thinking people. But many of the harshest critiques of the modern and postmodern landscape seem to be based, at least in part, on a kind of perspectival illusion—a forgetting that we live in a world where being and becoming are two sides of the same coin.

Needless to say, the existence of interstitial or emergent place forms is not in itself new. Border lands, *faux bourgs*, and other kinds of transitional places have always existed. And every era is, in its own way, a transitional era. Still, ours is characterized by an uncommonly rapid pace of cultural and technological evolution. Demographic upheaval, migratory circulation, economic liberalization, technological innovation, environmental change, and all the other motors of geo-cultural flux have disrupted many of the practices and institutions that have traditionally given us a sense of belonging to a place or community, and they have done so in a spectacularly short period of time. These transformative processes have necessarily generated new modes of spatial organization, new kinds of habitats, and new ways of living together, some of which are destined to become an enduring part of the physical and cultural landscape even if they are not yet fully under-stood or accepted. In this sense, we could say that the *entre-deux* is a kind of master trope for our era. What enables some but not other interstitial sites or communities to become full-fledged places with their own distinct identities, internal dynamics, and productive potentials? In order to answer such a question, we will need to understand not only the conditions that gave rise to the new formations but also what is innovative and productive about their responses to those conditions or, in other words, what enables them to provide solutions that are well suited to the challenges of their time and place.

Literature and criticism, I believe, have a vital role to play in this process. Great works of literature are drawn to the emergent, the interstitial, and the difficult to understand. At their best, they combine the ethnographer's detached attentiveness to cultural practices with the intimate familiarity of the insider, deconstructing obsolete or inadequate explanatory mod-els while also providing a kind of laboratory for the development of new representational practices and identifying new objects of study. For this reason, they can significantly enrich the work on place being carried out by philosophers, geographers, and social scientists as well as by those work-ing in disciplines like architecture, environmental studies, and urban plan-ning. The Canadian geographer Marc Brosseau, for example, has noted that literature provides a "precious resource" for geographers because of its ability to document in the most intimate, innovative, and detailed ways the "personality" of a place (Brosseau 29). The Australian philosopher Jeff Malpas uses a related argument about literature's ability to document the subjective experience of place to suggest that philosophers should take such representations "very seriously indeed" (Malpas 6–7). But I would go further. Because literary texts operate, for the most part, within the hypo-thetical, metaphorical register of fiction and poetry, they may contribute to our understanding of the problems posed by emergent places in ways that extend far beyond the documentary demand for representational accuracy. When successful, they can change the ways their readers view the world around them, making possible new ways of understanding what is actually there and catalyzing new ideas about what might be. In this sense, great works of literature have a performative dimension that may rival in importance the kinds of authority attributed to philosophical or scientific discourse. To the extent that they are successful in this task, we can say that these texts do not just reflect attitudes toward existing places; they help to make possible the emergence and establishment of new kinds of places. In this context, the task of the critic is to help mediate between these two registers—to bring the hypothetical situations and metaphorical language of literature into contact with the more literal, falsifiable assertions to which scientific discourse gives rise—in order to test, expand, and amend received wisdom and common knowledge, improving the quality of public discourse on these issues and contributing to the search for new solutions and better understanding.

To this end, I have organized the central chapters of my study into three parts, each of which brings together literary and theoretical discourses about place in a way that highlights points of resonance between them. Each part explores the question of place at a different level in order to give a more complete understanding of place in its various modalities. Thus part one focuses on the phenomenological experience of place; part two emphasizes the social level of place-bound identities defined in terms of the neighborhood and the nation; and part three looks at place in the larger geopolitical context of postcolonial studies.

Chapters 1, 3, and 5 are largely theoretical in orientation. They lay the conceptual groundwork for the literary analyses to follow. Chapter 1 explores the humanistic approach to the study of place, which tends to emphasize the phenomenology of individual experience, while Chapter 3 emphasizes the postmodern, poststructuralist challenge to the human-ist tradition. In juxtaposing these apparently antithetical approaches to the study of human space and place, I highlight zones of overlap between them, seeking to show how their respective insights can in fact give rise to a more complete and powerful understanding of place than either of them taken in isolation. This is a goal that has often fallen victim to the notori-ous inability of the two sides to see eye to eye, or even to speak the same theoretical language.[15] But one of the central ambitions of my project is to bring these two modes of spatial analysis into contact in order to under-stand how they can complement each other and enrich our understanding of place. In a similar spirit, my account of postcolonial theory in Chapters 5 and 6 contests the implicitly hierarchical division between postcolonial and metropolitan literatures, emphasizing the connections and points of overlap between them.

Chapters 2, 4, and 6 are primarily literary in orientation, focusing on the representation of newly emergent, interstitial places and emphasizing the ways in which the texts studied have contributed to the establish-ment of their identities and recognition of their importance. These chap-ters are devoted primarily to developments in French and Francophone literature and focus on the contemporary period (roughly 1968–present). Following the three-part structure of the book, each of these chapters focuses on a different level of place. Chapter 2 explores the phenomeno-logical dimension of place in Samuel Beckett's writings; Chapter 4 looks at the construction of geographical identities in France's immigrant sub-urbs; and Chapter 6 traces the emergence and evolution of postcolonial place identities in the Caribbean islands of Martinique and Guadeloupe. What all these texts have in common is an ability to identify and explain the unforeseen forms of creative energy germinating within the places in question, a forward-looking rather than nostalgic or reactionary desire to strengthen the bonds that link people to the places they inhabit, and a willingness to stretch the norms of representational language in order to do so. A couple of clarifications may be necessary at this point. Although my analyses lead me to give a fair amount of background information on the real-world places alluded to in the literary texts, this book is not about the places themselves but rather about *representations* of place and, even more so, the poetics that govern those representations. This outlook leads me to focus less on the history and geography of the actual places than on the *kind* of place they exemplify—and less on the kind of place they exemplify than on the role that the literary representations play in establishing the profiles of those place types. Furthermore, my study is not about representation as a passive or imitative depiction of such places, judged in terms of accuracy and conformity to the original, but about representation as a creative, performative act, part of the process that brings places into being *as* places. This is a book, in other words, that seeks to understand how fiction contributes to the way we understand the places we encounter and focuses its attention on a number of places considered to occupy strategic sites in the contemporary landscape—sites in need of new representational strategies. Central to the ambitions of this book is my attempt to show what these literary explorations of the *entre-deux* can contribute to a more general theory of place in a world characterized by postmodern epistemological instability and space-time compression.

My concluding chapter sets the conservative emphasis on rootedness and stability (associated with the Heideggerian concept of dwelling) against the radical refusal to stay put (associated with Deleuzian deterritorialization and nomadism) and attempts to bring together these apparently opposed poles without simply seeking a middle-of-the-road compromise solution. What I seek has more in common with what Jean Paulhan has called the extreme in-between (*l'extrême milieu*), which Paulhan used in opposition to the more familiar term, happy medium (*juste milieu*), in order to suggest the possibility of developing a radical thought of the middle ground.[16] Paulhan sought to avoid the extreme Left-Right polarities of the political discourse of his era (e.g., fascism/communism) without falling into the platitudes of a compromise-at-all-costs liberalism, just as I seek to overcome the humanist/poststructuralist dichotomy, the metropolitan/postcolonial polarity, and the postmodern successor to the fascism/communism polarity, which has taken the form of an opposition between neoliberal market fundamentalism and neo-Marxist conceptions of social justice. Rather than celebrating interstitiality as a virtue in its own right, then, I present the theory of interstitiality as a way to understand the various processes through which emergent spaces are transformed into full-fledged places, becoming established in their turn, and then providing the basis for future developments.

What Is Place?

Before continuing on to the main body of my argument, it will be important to make some preliminary remarks about the concept of place. Despite the apparent obviousness and intuitiveness of the term, it is surprisingly slippery as an analytic concept. Like time in Saint Augustine's dictum, place is something that I seem to understand well enough, provided that nobody asks me to define it.[17] It is also a highly contested concept, which is perhaps a sign of its importance as a category of human experience. What, then, is place? A few theses on place will help us to sketch out, in a preliminary way, some of the boundaries of the concept. Place is

- space enriched with human experience and understanding; an organized world of meaning (Tuan, *Space and Place* 179);
- a spatial predicate—that is, a space plus the attribution of a property or relation (Berque, "Place," in Lévy and Lussault 556);

- a social construct, like space and time (Harvey, *Justice* 293);
- a particular constellation of social relations (Massey, 154);

- the locus of desire (Lippard 4);
- a setting to which individuals are emotionally and culturally attached (Altman and Low 5);

- a locale whose form, function, and meaning are self-contained within the boundaries of physical contiguity (Castells, *The Rise of the Network Society* 453);
- a space in which distance is not pertinent (Lévy, "Lieu," in Lévy and Lussault 560).

As this somewhat discordant and yet far from exhaustive list of claims makes clear, the concept of place is multifarious. It is a shifting term that can take different definitions depending on our needs, which might induce us to put the emphasis on, variously, its ability to generate *meaning* (Tuan and Berque), its *socially constructed* aspect (Harvey and Massey), its *affective importance* (Lippard, Altman and Low), or its ability to reconfigure our experience of *physical space* (Lévy, Castells). As an object of study, then, it is inherently multidimensional. Because it cannot be understood without some sense of its various dimensions, be they spatial, material, psychological, social, political, or metaphysical, it calls for an interdisciplinary approach.

Most of us would agree that the term "place" can apply to locations of vastly different scales: from the cupboards, dressers, and well-worn nooks and hiding spots that are so dear to Gaston Bachelard (and central to the concept of home that most of us carry within us); to the intermediate level of the neighborhood, city, or region (which can be taken in at a glance from the proper vantage point and physically traversed in a manageable period of time); to the macroscopic scale of nation, planet, and beyond—a level at which the totality cannot be directly perceived (at least not in normal conditions) but can still be conceived as a cohesive place with a unitary identity. Moreover, just about any kind of site (urban, wilderness, holy, historic, loved, loathed, etc.) can be usefully thought of in terms of place, depending on the context, although in some cases we may find ourselves contesting the legitimacy or satisfactoriness of a given category of place, as Marc Augé does in his analysis of what he calls nonplaces (Augé). Context matters, in other words. Our approach to considering any given site in terms of place will vary according to the discursive setting in which we find ourselves.

As with all such concepts, there is a temptation to restrict its range in order to suit one's immediate needs. Such restrictions are certainly legitimate and useful, so long as we recognize that they do not cover the whole range of possibilities. Roberto Dainotto, for example, in his *Place and Literature*, has equated the literary emphasis on place with the question of regionalism, arguing on these grounds that the concept of place is inherently linked to xenophobic nationalism and ultimately to fascism (2–5, 163–73). Clearly though, whatever we might think about the merits of Dainotto's argument as a critique of regionalism, it does not cover the entire realm of place.

Place, then, will be understood here, at the most general level, to designate any geographical site (of any size, scale, or type) that is meaningful to someone, for whatever reason. This definition has the obvious disadvantage of vagueness (perhaps necessarily so, for such an encompassing subject), but we can mitigate its apparent vacuity by highlighting two of its salient features. First, place is a *human* relation. There is no set of immanent ontological features adhering to a given site that would allow us to define it as a place. A site does not become a place until a person comes along and enters into a meaning-generating relationship with it. Second, this relation is a variable one: a given site can be thought of in terms of place *to the extent that* someone sees it that way. The same site will be thought of as a place in some situations but not in others.[18]

It is equally important to recognize the contestatory or dialogical dimension of place. Postcolonial critics have been especially sensitive to the ways in which a physical site can be transformed, through representation, into an ideological weapon. Edward Said, for example, emphasizes "how geography can be manipulated, invented, characterized quite apart from a site's merely physical reality."[19] Although highly critical of the many illegitimate ways such representations can be manipulated for political or economic gain, he also recognizes that this imposition of meaning is not in itself improper. It is simply what we do with sites that have value to us. Every geographical location has its own set of unique physical characteristics and its own history, but the identity and significance of each site may have more to do with the discursive meanings projected upon it than on its actual physical and historical constitution. Wherever there are multiple subjects, there are multiple meanings that will be in conflict with each other to a greater or lesser extent depending on circumstances. Any given site is going to be subject to a dialogical struggle over the meaning of that site.

This Rorschach-like ability of place to mean different things to different people and in different contexts makes it useful as a kind of ideological lens—a way to bring into focus and illuminate both the unspoken assumptions and the ideological objectives that bring people to the place. Often, what is most interesting from an analytic point of view is not so much the fact that a given site is designated as a place (although that will likely be a critical issue for the immediately concerned parties) as the reasons for that designation—the elements of the site that are considered salient to its designation as a place. This focalizing function of place is at the heart of my project, which seeks to uncover the metaphysical assumptions, ideological parti pris, intuitive beliefs, and ingrained habits that govern our attitudes toward the environment around us, leaving us with marked affinities for some places (or kinds of place) while others seem valueless, troublesome, or monstrous or simply remain invisible to us, not perceived as places at all.

As a way to navigate the infinitely variegated range of theoretical approaches to the study of place that have been put forth, I have limited myself to the exploration of three broad types: phenomenological, poststructuralist, and postcolonial. And since the *experiential* dimension of place is so crucial to our understanding of its significance, I will begin my inquiry by exploring the phenomenological level of place.

Part I

Phenomenological Place

I

Place, Subjectivity, and the Humanist Tradition

Phenomenology and Humanistic Geography

The modern discipline of geography has straddled the physical and social sciences, with phenomenological questions involving personal experience often entering into conflict with the positivistic quest to amass and analyze objective data. The positivistic trend reached its apogee in the years after World War II with the "quantitative revolution," a development that tended to marginalize cultural considerations and humanistic methods.[1] The concept of place was considered to be too nebulous and subjective to merit serious consideration. Beginning, in the late 1970s, with the work of Yi-Fu Tuan and Edward Relph, however, the proponents of humanistic geography reacted against this state of affairs, sending out a call for a "return to place," with particular emphasis on the individual experience of place.[2] To some extent, they revived the tradition of earlier humanistically inclined modes of geography, like the regional geography of Paul Vidal de la Blache and the cultural geography of Carl O. Sauer, which were committed to the description of identifiable places and the exploration of the ways of life associated with them. The new generation of humanistic geographers, however, has been less concerned with documenting specific regions and explaining differences between them than with exploring the subjective experience of place as an object of study in its own right, with place typically understood to be a "universal and transhistorical part of the human condition" (Cresswell, 20). Their project seems to be more existential than anthropological. This approach to the study of place has recently begun to attract attention in philosophical quarters, notably in the work of Edward Casey and Jeff Malpas, who will be discussed in more detail later. It has also begun to have influence in related fields like architecture and environmental planning.[3] Phenomenology, as the science of human experience, seems particularly well suited to the study of a concept like place, which has a strong experiential component. It also serves to lend methodological heft to a mode of inquiry that is inherently vulnerable to accusations of impressionism and a lack of scientific rigor.

To the extent that humanistic geography has a unifying idea binding together its various strands, it is that the concept of place is central to the study of geography and that human experience is at the heart of any viable definition of place. A place is not simply a location or landscape but, to borrow Tuan's formulation, "an organized world of meaning" constituted in its relation to human subjects (*Space and Place*, 179). If humanistic geographers have felt the need to remind us of the centrality of human experience in place and of the importance of place as a locus of meaning, it is because they worry that the forces of modernity threaten the bonds of affection and identity that link individuals to their habitats. Moreover, they believe that the field of geography has itself contributed to this threat. By embracing a mode of scientific rationality that privileges the search for objectively verifiable facts over subjectively experienced phenomena—one that assumes the superiority of quantitative analysis over qualitative evaluation and defines itself in terms of a "nomothetic" (rule generating) search for generalizable laws—mainstream geography has, according to them, contributed to the scientific neglect of the subjective dimension of human spatial experience and created the need for the (scientifically respectable) return to place that they promote.

Nicholas Entrikin and the Betweenness of Place

The geographer J. Nicholas Entrikin is clearly sympathetic to the humanist approach and, perhaps more importantly, has committed to finding a way to reconcile the study of place with the standards of scientific geography. Significantly for my purposes, Entrikin's outlook leads him to characterize the concept of place in terms of interstitiality ("place is best viewed from points in between") and to suggest that narrative provides a crucial epistemological bridge between the scientific and subjective approaches to the study of place. As the title of his book *The Betweenness of Place* suggests, place occupies a strategic position between two important camps within the field of geography: that of cultural and regional geography on the one hand and that of scientific geography on the other.

Entrikin argues forcefully against those mainstream geographers for whom the inherently subjective nature of place disqualifies it from consideration as a legitimate focus of geographical inquiry. He recognizes the difficulty of establishing any kind of authoritative, scientific discourse about something so elusive as "experience" (a difficulty that is endemic to all phenomenological endeavors) but argues nonetheless that it must remain central. For Entrikin, it is precisely the subjective dimension of place that makes it so important: If geography, as a field, is to contribute something of value to the debate about modernity's effects on human spatial experience and is to make good on its traditional aims of developing a better understanding of "the richness of human experience and . . . human action" (Entrikin 40), then it must find a way to reconcile its scientific emphasis on the measurable, the quantifiable, and the nomothetic with the humanistic emphasis on the subjective, experiential dimension of place. Entrikin frames this disciplinary problem of place with respect to the broader problem of subjectivism in scientific inquiry: "[Mainstream, scientific] geographers present culture as epiphenomenal, connect culture in an ad hoc fashion to an existing theory, or seek to represent it as a naïve fact of the world. Humanist geographers [on the other hand] have had difficulty in stepping back from the subject to gain a more objective view" (59). It is precisely this divide between the all-too-subjective nature of humanist geography and the inability of scientific geographers to get at the cultural significance of place that Entrikin seeks to address in his book, focusing his attention on what he sees as the inherent dualism of place.

A place can be represented in one of two ways: from a depersonalized "outside" perspective as, for example, a point or shape on a map; and from a subject-centered "inside" perspective, as a kind of environing milieu within which we move. Entrikin seeks to overcome the dichotomy between these two positions—the subject-centered and decentered perspectives—by finding a mode of discourse able to encompass both points of view. As he puts it, "To understand place requires that we have access to both an objective and subjective reality. From the decentered vantage point of the theoretical scientist, place becomes either location or a set of generic relations and thereby loses much of its significance for human action. From the centered viewpoint of the subject, place has meaning only in relation to an individual's or a group's goals and concerns (5)." This leads Entrikin to conclude that "place is best viewed from points in between" these two apparently antithetical positions (5). And his goal in *The Betweenness of Place* is to find a way to rethink the concept of place in a way that bridges the gap.

How, then, can we bridge this gap? For Entrikin, only the paralogical procedures that he groups under the heading of narrative can do this.

> This divide between the existential and naturalistic conceptions of place appears to be an unbridgeable one, and one that is only made wider in adopting a decentered view. The closest that we can come to addressing both

sides of this divide is from a point in between, *a point that leads us into the vast realm of narrative forms*. From this position we gain a view from both sides of the divide. We gain a sense both of being "in a place" and "at a location," of being at the center and being at a point in a centerless world. To ignore either aspect of this dualism is to misunderstand the modern experience of place. (134, emphasis added)

The closing chapters of *The Betweenness of Place* are devoted to showing how a judicious use of narrative might form the basis of a legitimate mode of geographical inquiry into place that would satisfy the nomothetic demands of scientific geography without neglecting the experiential dimension of place emphasized by humanistic geographers. Although sketched out rather quickly and in a way that remains too general to shed much light on the specifically literary applications of this insight, his discussion of narrative as a tool for geographical inquiry makes some important points about the epistemological status of narrative.

Following Paul Ricoeur, Entrikin argues that although narrative is a paralogical mode of exposition that can never attain the authority of scientific discourse, it can achieve what Entrikin calls "singular causal explanations." Because they trace a single path through a unique situation, narratives can't establish universally applicable laws on their own in any definitive, falsifiable way. Nonetheless, the chains of cause and effect out of which narrative structures are created can convince us that given a certain set of conditions, the series of events that make up a narrative are related to each other in a way that is logical or necessary and that they are, in this sense, authoritative, exemplifying the local manifestations of more general laws (119). Entrikin refers us to Paul Veyne's theory of historical narrative to explain this distinction between singular causal explanations and universal laws. For Veyne, "History is interested in individualized events . . . but it is not interested in their individuality; it seeks to understand them—that is, to find among them a kind of generality or, more precisely, of specificity" (Veyne 32, qtd. in Entrikin 124). The idea here is that the historian seeks to draw out of a specific sequence of events the elements that are transferable to other situations. To the extent that the causal logic governing the relationship between events is valid, historians are justified in their attempts to interpret individual events as exemplifying general laws, even though no individual narrative chain can be taken on its own to prove the universal validity of the proposed law.

To develop the geographical implications of this insight, Entrikin notes an important link between the function of plot in history and that of place in geography. This is the notion of perspective. Both plots and places are, by their very definitions, "presented from a point of view"

(Entrikin 24). Just as the historian must select from a potentially infinite amount of information the series of events that will form his narrative and lend meaning to them by organizing them into narrative chains of cause and effect, the geographer of place takes a complex set of environmental features and defines them as a single place, transforming them into a coherent whole by virtue of a (perhaps unspoken) principle of selection. In this way, Entrikin argues, accounts of place, like narrative progressions, provide structures through which the chaotic profusion of raw data can give rise to meaningful patterns. Although the individual's principles of selection and organizational logic cannot be considered definitive or exclude other possible configurations, they can be tested for coherence, rigor, explanatory power, and pertinence. And to the extent that they can be applied successfully to other situations, they can be formulated in general, falsifiable terms that might eventually lead to nomothetic declarations taken to have universal validity.

In this sense, both the historian and the geographer of place can contribute to the formulation of universalizable principles. But history as a discipline has a level of institutional respect within both the social sciences and humanities that geographers of place have struggled to earn. Entrikin's intention in using historical narrative as his model for research into place seems, in this regard, to involve using the prestige of history as a way to buttress the reputation of humanistic geography. But beyond this analogy between narrative and place, how does narrative theory enter into Entrikin's approach to the study of place? What does the art of telling stories, stricto sensu, contribute to the theory of place? Entrikin does suggest that first-person accounts of place have an important role within the field of geography. But he seems more interested in the idea that the analysis of a place, like a narrative, is a "configurational act" that is ultimately neither spatial nor temporal but logical. Entrikin borrows the term "configurational act" from Ricoeur, who emphasizes that the syntax of narrative is not chronological (simply one thing after another) but logical (one event "*because of* another"). It is, for both Ricoeur and Entrikin, this logical "grasping together" of the various elements that generates meaning (Entrikin 127). In descriptions of place, as in narrative, there is a potentially infinite amount of information from which a selection must be made. Entrikin argues that it is only by "grasping together" the salient elements of that place and organizing them into a meaningful whole that the subject transforms a (mere) site or space into a (meaningful) place. And that, Entrikin believes, is the fundamental task of the geographer of place.

Entrikin's project is, ultimately, scientific in orientation. He makes it clear that he values the scientific objectives of geography above all ("I have no doubts ... about the power and value of a relatively objective, theoretical viewpoint" [132]) and simply seeks to find a way to extend that scientific rigor to the study of place. By presenting the concept of place and the logic of narrative as a way to overcome the specific problem of geographical dualism (i.e., between the objectivist and subjectivist branches of the discipline), Entrikin's project is of great interest for those of us who study the contributions that the fictive imagination can make to our understanding of the relationship between individuals and their environment. That said, his explorations of the subject-object problem leave several sizable stones unturned, and it is to a more complete exploration of that question that I now turn.

Edward Casey, Place, and Dualism

For Edward Casey, as for the humanist geographers, the sense that modernity poses a threat to the bonds between humans and the places they inhabit has become a major preoccupation. In *The Fate of Place* (1997), Casey traces what he sees as the modern philosophical neglect of place back to the epistemological and scientific revolutions associated with Descartes and Newton. He emphasizes the extent to which this tradition, and its institutionalization during the Enlightenment, has impoverished the philosophical and scientific understanding of place. This is an argument he had already made in more schematic form in his first book on the subject, *Getting Back Into Place* (1993):

> In the past three centuries in the West—the period of "modernity"—place has come to be not only neglected but actively suppressed. Owing to the triumph of the natural and social sciences in this same period, any serious talk of place has been regarded as regressive or trivial. A discourse has emerged whose exclusive cosmological foci are Time and Space . . . For an entire epoch, place has been regarded as an impoverished second cousin of Time and Space, those two colossal cosmic partners that tower over modernity. (Casey, *Getting Back* xiv)

The Fate of Place is, in this sense, an attempt to flesh out the philosophical history of place in order to better understand what went wrong and how the theme of place can be reestablished as a legitimate field of philosophical inquiry. Casey begins with extended accounts of Plato's *Timaeus* and Aristotle's *Physics* (which get generally favorable reviews) and moves through to the postmodern, poststructuralist present. The outline of his historical argument is manifest in the structure of the book, which, after the chapters on Plato and Aristotle, moves on to an account of a long, slow decline of place in Hellenistic, Medieval, and Renaissance thought. This section is titled, tellingly, "From Place to Space" and leads into a chapter titled "The

Supremacy of Space," which gives an account of the period running from the rise of rationalism in the seventeenth and eighteenth centuries to the long nineteenth century.

Throughout this period, Casey sees the experiential richness of place being sacrificed for the abstract (but quantifiable and therefore powerful) uniformity of space. (Michel Foucault, as we shall see in Chapter 3, tells the story in much the same way, except that for him the move from place to space is an unequivocally positive development.) The crucial turning point for Casey comes with Descartes and Newton, who entirely abandon the middle ground of place in favor of, on the one hand, the internalized space of the Cartesian *Cogito* (with the attendant risk of solipsism) and, on the other, the mathematical, objectivist universe of Newton, which subordinates the human perspective to a decentralized, mechanistic view of the universe. The seventeenth century left us, in other words, with the problem of dualism and gave rise to the two opposed epistemological stances that continue to permeate discussions of truth and reality today: subject-oriented idealism and the object-oriented "absolutism" of scientific realism. For Casey, the subject-object split is not only related to the decline of place as a philosophical theme but is itself a result of it:

> Hannah Arendt . . . speaks of a "twofold flight from the earth into the universe and from the world into the self." Nonetheless, rather than emphasize the two extremes of infinite space and infinitesimal self—as if these two directions were merely equal but opposite directions—I would put it another way. *The decreasing availability of place as a personal and philosophical, architectural and physical Archimedean point that anchors much of experience and thought induced Descartes to seek the self-certifying certainty of the cogito and Newton to seek the world-certified certainty of a mathematically specified cosmic space and time.* One absolutely, entirely internal, rejoined the other absolute, wholly external, making common cause for certainty in the face of the abyss of no-place. (*Fate* 186, emphasis added)

It is, in other words, the decline of the concept of place that led to the philosophical problem of dualism—not the other way around. In this sense, Casey's quest for a return to place is understood as a vital part of any attempt to overcome the problem of subject-object dualism.

Immanuel Kant, as the initiator of phenomenological epistemology, marks an important turning point in the history of dualism. For Casey, this also gives him a central role in the history of place. On the one hand, Casey believes, Kant "delivers the final blow to place" by redefining space in "the subjectivity of the human mind" (i.e., as an a priori intuition). But on the other hand, Casey proposes, "Kant also suggests a way to resurrect the importance of place on different grounds" (*Fate* 187). This "different grounds" turns out to be the body, the notion of consciousness as embodied, which seems to Casey to provide the most promising way out of the dualist impasse. And indeed, it is phenomenological thinkers in the Kantian tradition that Casey sees as leading the way back into place as Casey's history moves into the twentieth century. Part four of *The Fate of Place* is titled, consequently, *The Reappearance of Place* and begins with a chapter devoted primarily to phenomenologically oriented thinkers: Kant, Husserl, and Merleau-Ponty, with a section on Whitehead's process philosophy. Casey then devotes the bulk of a chapter to Heidegger's last period—the period of the "turn" in Heidegger's thinking, which is marked notably by a shift away from the prioritization of time in *Being and Time* and toward a growing interest in place, a shift expressed in such texts as "Building, Dwelling, Thinking" (an essay to which I will be turning repeatedly over the course of this study).

Pursuing the thesis of a twentieth-century renaissance of place philosophy, Casey closes out his volume with a chapter titled "Place in the Present" that discusses Bachelard's *Poetics of Space* and also, less obviously, the poststructuralist thinkers Foucault, Deleuze and Guattari, Derrida, and Irigaray, whom he presents as the exponents of a new place-oriented philosophy. Although there is a strong argument to be made for the importance of the body in relation to place in late Foucault, Deleuze and Guattari, and Irigaray (and also Derrida and Kristeva, via, for example, their interest in Plato's gendered use of the notion of the *chora*[4]), the case for place that Casey is trying to make does not seem to mesh well with the larger objectives of the poststructuralists, which tend to lead away from place. One warning sign that Casey is on difficult terrain here is the fact that the poststructuralists show a marked preference for the term "space" (*espace*) over "place" (*lieu*), often going so far as to explicitly denounce the concept of place, as Michel de Certeau does. Of course the terminological difference cannot in itself be considered decisive, but this impression is amply confirmed by the generally antihumanist outlook of the poststructuralists and their emphasis on delocalized power networks and abstract discursive structures. The death of man postulated by Foucault in *The Order of Things* is closely connected to a more general poststructuralist preference for the language of space over place. (These questions will be pursued at greater length in Chapter 3.)

There has indeed been a renewed philosophical interest in place in recent years, but it seems to have come from those who, in the tradition of Merleau-Ponty, have sought to extend phenomenological philosophy into the realm of cognitive science and evolutionary biology. Indeed, if, as Casey argues, the problem of place gives rise to the epistemological problem of dualism, then the phenomenological approach seems to offer some of the most promising avenues of exploration. By rejecting this dichotomy between subject and object, the phenomenological, embodied concept of place sketched out by Casey emerges as a way to bridge this gap. Human subjectivity, in this view, arises not in opposition to material reality but as an expression of material reality, and place is, in this sense, the point at which the consciousness-environment nexus takes shape and can be best understood. This is, roughly speaking, the position taken by Jeff Malpas in *Place and Experience: A Philosophical Topography*, which uses the Heideggerian conception of *Dasein* as the starting point for one of the most compelling phenomenological accounts of place so far.

Jeff Malpas and the *Da* in *Dasein*

Malpas's position overlaps significantly with Casey's, particularly in the influence of Heidegger. But whereas Casey's *The Fate of Place* is, above all, a contribution to the history of philosophy and *Getting Back into Place* a quasi-autobiographical meditation on the experience of place that mixes personal history with philosophical argument, Malpas's *Place and Experience* is conceived as a synchronic exfoliation of the concept of place. Malpas calls his approach topographical—in part because the historical evolution of the concept of place is of little interest to him. Rather, Malpas's goal is to map out the logical contours of this analysis-resistant concept, breaking it into its constituent parts in a way that shows how they fit together and form a heterogeneous but nonetheless coherent conceptual whole.

In order to provide a solid ground for his analyses, Malpas brings in the work of philosophers in the Anglo-American analytic tradition to test and refine the view of place developed under the aegis of his primary influence, Heidegger. He constructs his definition of place in a way that bridges the gap between the phenomenological and analytic traditions, borrowing elements from both and identifying the areas in which they can be brought into alignment.[5] This leads him to consider the phenomenological approach to place exemplified by Heidegger and Merleau-Ponty in relation to the work of analytic philosophers whose approach has led them in very different directions. These notably include Peter Strawson and Gareth Evans's inquiries into the referential relationship between mind and world and the "externalist" arguments of Tyler Burge, Hilary Putnam, and Donald Davidson. Malpas reads both of these tendencies as supporting his emphasis on the inseparability of people and their environment in place (11–13). As for the French theorists of space like Foucault, Lefebvre, and Certeau, whose work whose work I will consider later, he shows some concern for the ways in which his work meets up with theirs (in remarks relegated almost entirely to footnotes), but he demonstrates very little interest in pursuing their respective approaches. His inquiry remains tightly focused on the zones of overlap between the analytic and phenomenological schools.

As was the case for Entrikin, Malpas's examination of place begins with the recognition that it is a concept that has both a subjective (experiential) dimension and an objective (material and spatial) dimension and that amputating place of either of these dimensions would gravely undermine the analytic power of the concept, depriving it of its specificity and value. But whereas Entrikin left this duality in place, simply positing narrative as a bridge between the two, Malpas seeks, in phenomenological fashion, to overcome the problem of dualism itself. For Malpas, the experience of place is a unitary whole, and our habitual, commonsense divisions of experience into such categories as objective and subjective are artificial constructs.

Malpas equates place with the Heideggerian concept of *Dasein*, telling us that "something like the Heideggerian thinking of *Dasein as* place is what motivates the inquiry in this book" (33). For Malpas, place is neither subjective nor objective—nor some combination of the two—but something that precedes that very opposition. Place is something *out of which* emanate both apparently objective facts, like location, and apparently subjective facts, like sense of place. Both are founded in human-being and human-being has its ground in *Dasein*, conceived by Malpas as essentially a synonym of place: "I . . . want to establish the idea of place in such a way that it can begin to be seen, neither in terms merely of some narrow sense of spatio-temporal location, nor as some sort of subjective construct, but rather as that wherein the sort of being that is characteristically human has its ground" (33). Malpas emphasizes what he considers to be the foundational nature of place: place is not an object of thought so much as that which makes thinking possible.

But what does it mean to equate place with *Dasein*? Does it add a new richness to our understanding of the concept? Or might it actually be a way of subtly changing the subject—of conflating two sets of meanings that may overlap to some extent without being identical? Malpas's equation of place with *Dasein* does, as I will try to show, enrich in a number of ways our understanding of what is at stake in the concept of place, but that enrichment comes at a price. For one thing, his definition of place is so expansive that it becomes difficult to know how we should distinguish it from related but more general terms like "environment" or "milieu." Malpas's definitions of place tend to lose their grip on the geographical specificity of the term (i.e., that places are *singular*, in the sense that they are unique and can be located on a map). Before getting to such issues, however, we need to have a better understanding of how Malpas relates place to *Dasein*.

Dasein is a quintessentially phenomenological concept—a term that emphasizes the extent to which human existence is intertwined with and inseparable from the world in which we find ourselves. Although identified specifically with Heidegger, the concept is derived from Husserl and Brentano's celebrated insight into human consciousness as intentional. Being (*Sein*) is always being *there* (*Dasein*) for much the same reason that consciousness is always "consciousness-of" something: human subjectivity cannot exist in isolation from the world around it. Accordingly, Malpas emphasizes that, for Heidegger, "*Dasein* is properly understood as already inclusive of the world" and quotes Merleau-Ponty's dictum: "the world is wholly inside and I am wholly outside myself" (6). Or, as Wittgenstein emphasized, whatever we may believe about the existence of foundational egos or noumenal objects in themselves, such entities cannot be found *in our experience*. All that we can know are those hybrid mixes of consciousness and world known as phenomena.

One of the most important early moves that Malpas makes is to emphasize the multiplicity and complexity of place. Rather than treating it as a single monolithic entity, trying to define it univocally—in a single breath, as it were—he prefers to think of place as a conceptual "region" or framework defined by the intersection of the many different sets of concerns that impinge on our experience of place. Place is conceived not as a unitary concept but as a complex network of overlapping elements out of which a coherent image or idea or sense of what place means can be formed. This antiessentialist move builds on the insight that many things that had been thought to be unitary (like intelligence, consciousness, and subjectivity) are better understood as modular entities, made up of many different subcomponents or subroutines that can be analyzed in isolation. Thus as Malpas puts it, "rather than understanding place as a notion that provides a single principle in terms of which everything else is understood," we must think of place as "a model within which the various elements at stake can be distinguished and assembled so as to allow the construction of a single complex structure" (18). This means that place "cannot be reduced to any one of the elements situated within its compass" but must instead be understood as "a structure comprising spatiality and temporality, subjectivity and objectivity, self and other." Indeed, for Malpas, these apparently independently existing elements can only be "established in relation to each other and so only within the topographical structure of place" (163). These various dimensions of place create a complex system of interlocking relationships that can for the purposes of analysis be broken down into its constituent parts, but that is perceived as a unitary, holistic experience. It is, for Malpas, this complex but unitary experience that we mean when we use the term "place."

Keeping in mind this caveat—that subdividing the different levels of the experience of place into discrete levels is an artificial, analytic, exercise—we can nonetheless identify the salient features of Malpas's definition, many of which will be useful in the literary analyses in the chapters to come. These elements can be grouped into two clusters: one emphasizing the spatial dimension of place and the other emphasizing its experiential dimension. Taken together, these two clusters constitute not so much a definition of the concept of place as a survey of the field designated by that term.

For Malpas, place in its spatial dimension is
1. a bounded yet open space,
2. a spatio-temporal entity,
3. nested.

Place in its experiential dimension is
4. perspectival,
5. subject inducing,
6. linked to agency,
7. intersubjective.

Some exfoliation of these elements is in order here.

To say that a place is *a bounded yet open space* is to emphasize that the sense of place arises when a space is grasped from within, as a unity, by an observer. To be perceived as a unity, it must be perceived as having boundaries—limits of some kind—although they need not be of a physical nature. The boundaries provide a way to define the unity and coherence of any given place. Those boundaries may, on the other hand, be *porous*, in the sense that they do not exclude an awareness that there is an environing world that interacts with and impinges on the locally defined place in various ways. Malpas refers us to the Greek etymon *plateia* to explain what he means. The term *plateia* (Latin: *platea*), which gives us the modern words place, platz, plaza, piazza, could be translated as "broad way" or "open space" and is close to the idea of the town square (Malpas 22). Just as the structures surrounding the *plateia* define an easily perceptible exterior limit, a place is defined, in Malpas's sense, by external boundaries. But just as there are necessarily pathways in and out of the town square, the boundedness of place does not preclude permeability to the rest of the world.

It is equally important to note the *spatio-temporal* nature of place. This is to say that the spatiality of place is not of an abstract, geometrical, or static kind. A place cannot be defined in isolation from its temporal dimension any more than it can be isolated from its qualitative aspects like color, texture, and so forth. If we think of how we come to know a place, the importance of this caveat becomes clear. Just as the geographer or surveyor must move through space in time as he seeks to map out a region, place requires both time and space in order to make its coherence felt to an observer.

It is equally important to note that places are always *nested* within each other. There is not, as some have argued, any definitive scale for place, be it on the level of the individual home, neighborhood, viewable landscape, city, or region. On the contrary, every conceivable place contains, at least in principle, smaller places and is itself contained within larger places. A child's favorite cupboard, nook, or hiding spot is a place that is contained within a house that is contained within a neighborhood, and so on. This nested quality of place should not, of course, be taken to imply a single center around which everything else is organized. Any given place looks out upon other places and may overlap with or transition into other places. Just as I can look out through the window of my house and see other houses or travel to another neighborhood that may overlap to some extent with mine, my "place universe" exists alongside and intermingles with those of others in a variety of complex ways.

A further corollary of this insight into the nested nature of place is that any conceivable place is defined by isolating it from a larger network that has no definite limits. To clarify this point, let us return to the image of the *plateia*. Just as the streets leading in and out of the town square hook up with other streets that in turn connect with highways and other circuits of travel whose reach is potentially global, the place of immediate experience is connected to a global network of potential relations. This makes it possible, conversely, for even the most distant agents to have an influence, however indirect, on what is going on in this place. Any conceivable place, however well-defined and apparently self-contained, remains open to these influences and resonates, so to speak, in response to them. As A. N. Whitehead puts it, "You are in a certain place perceiving things . . . But this functioning of the body in one place, exhibits for your cognizance an aspect of the distant environment, fading away into the general knowledge that there are things beyond." In a sense, then, "everything is everywhere at all times. For every location involves an aspect of itself in every other location" (Quoted in Casey, *Fate* 213).[6]

Each of the preceding points implies that place is *perspectival*—that is, it requires the presence of an experiencing subject to be activated as a place. Place is not an objective, material fact there to be discovered but rather an interaction between a physical environment and an active, experiencing agent who both shapes and is shaped by that environment. Such considerations lead Malpas into a careful consideration of the domain of subjectivity. But as Malpas (ever the conscientious phenomenologist) is careful to argue, we need not understand subjectivity here in the Cartesian or Romantic manner as something private or radically opposed to the materiality of the physical world. Rather, Malpas considers the human subject as a function of place. Indeed, For Malpas, place is not the product of a subject but something that is itself subject inducing. For these reasons, and to avoid some of the baggage that the term subject carries with it, Malpas often prefers to use the more neutral term "agent."

In keeping with Malpas's phenomenological orientation, places are not constituted by preexisting subjectivities but arise in conjunction with them. It is in this sense that we can say that place is *subject inducing*.[7] Indeed, for Malpas, there can be no such thing as consciousness or subjectivity without place: "the very structure of the mind is intrinsically tied to locality and spatiality" (10). Or again: it is not that place is "something only encountered 'in' experience, but rather that place *is integral to the very structure and possibility of experience*" (32, emphasis in original).[8] Malpas's theory of place builds on the theory of embodied mind—that is, all cognition of whatever kind is embodied in the sensorimotor systems of the body, which have themselves arisen in conjunction with the surrounding environment. In fact, Malpas goes so far as to consider the possibility that the idea of "cognitive mapping" is more than a metaphor. If consciousness arises in relation to place, then it must necessarily correlate at some level with the structures of that place.[9]

For Malpas, the human subject is defined not in opposition to its animal or material corporeality (i.e., as an autonomous mind, soul, or spirit) but through its ability to navigate within its environment. Of course, the decisions of such an agent may be unpredictable and idiosyncratic (Malpas is not a determinist), but they are not different in any essential way from the kinds of decisions made by nonhuman animals. What differentiates humans from their animal brethren is their highly developed ability to create densely ramified, abstract representations of their environment and to communicate them successfully to others. In this sense, the humanity of the human subject is linked to its representational capacities—its ability to form, use, and communicate complex symbolic representations.

A human subject, in Malpas's sense, is necessarily a self-interested subject, whose perceptions of the world are organized in view of its needs and wants and the actions it must take to achieve them. In this sense, place is *linked to agency*. Our awareness of the world around us, including our strategies for organizing that world into meaningful structures, is conditioned by the need to move within and act upon our environment in ways that favor our interests, beginning with the skills necessary for survival (the ability to find food, shelter, protection, mates, etc.). Reversing the Cartesian presumption of subjectivity as dependent on a foundational ego, Malpas sees the ego as arising from this kind of activity: "That which does the unifying [of both the subject and its relation to a place] . . . is . . . nothing over and above activity itself, and is not grounded in the prior existence of an agent . . . Action and agency provide the necessary *foci* around which thought and experience are unified" (107–8). Human subjectivity is defined in terms of agency and representation and as a product of environmentally constrained activity. The demands of this struggle motivate the agent to create ever-better representations of its environment, and this representational groundwork contributes in turn to the further development of the agent's sensorimotor and cognitive abilities, enabling him to gain better control over his environment. This creates a kind of virtuous cycle or positive feedback loop through which what we refer to as human subjectivity grows out of more primitive forms of animal agency. In all of this, Malpas seems to be following the basic tenets of embodied cognition theory, which will be explored further in the next chapter.

Place is *intersubjective*. Although Malpas devotes almost all of his attention to individual consciousness in *Place and Experience*, he does not deny that place has a social dimension involving interactions between individuals that have political implications. Here again, he refers us to the Greek term *plateia*, emphasizing the social function of the public square. Recalling that the *plateia* played a central role in Greek civic life, he notes that the public square is a place where individuals encounter and interact with others. This aspect of place, however, remains a peripheral one for him. Despite devoting a full chapter to the theme of intersubjectivity, the social dimension of place remains on the horizon of his concerns, rarely becoming a central focus of attention. He repeatedly reminds us that his relative silence on this subject should not be construed as denying its importance, but he refers us to a host of other thinkers (including many of those who will be considered in Chapter 3) for those interested in further investigation of the social dimension of place.

It would be unfair to the spirit of Malpas's inquiry to call this lack of interest in the social dimension of place a *limitation* (there is nothing that would prevent us from expanding the inquiry into this domain), but it does mark a clear *limit* of his inquiry—a frontier zone that is dimly perceived at the outer boundaries of his topography of place. There are two other limits that should be mentioned before moving on.

The Locational Limits of Malpasian Topography

As mentioned earlier, one of the potential problems with Malpas's approach is that he seems to lose touch with the specifically geographical dimension of place. The salient feature of Malpas's concept of place is simply to be the environment in which the subject in question finds itself. He loses the sense of place as a *locatable* site and turns it into something closer to the "immediate environment" or "world" of the observer. As he says, "There are obvious affinities between this idea [of place] and the idea of 'the world' that Merleau-Ponty articulates in the *Phenomenology of Perception* . . . The very idea of the world as Merleau-Ponty employs it is, in fact, the idea of just such a topographical structure (a field or region) as that which I have set out here" (36fn44). For this reason, Malpas's definition of place is more useful for someone who wants to think about the interplay between human consciousness and environment than for someone who seeks to understand the ways in which humans interact with specific geographical sites and differentiate between them. This is already perhaps apparent in his equation of place and *Dasein*. It is the phenomenological question of being-in-the-world that interests Malpas—not the specificity of places themselves, which is central to my inquiry. As Edward Relph puts it, "Place [for Malpas] loses any sense of located entities and comes to mean 'that open, cleared yet bounded region in which we find ourselves' . . . A place is where being happens" (Relph, "Disclosing," 5–8).

The choice to set aside the locational specificity of individual places has several important consequences for his argument. It seems to imply either a sedentary subject (one who knows only one place or one kind of place) or such a vast and vague understanding of place that it would equate to something like the sum total of places we have ever known, as if the succession of places through which an individual moves over the course of her life could be merged into a single general conception of place. This becomes clear in a passage on Simon Schama's *Landscape and Memory*. For Malpas (and Schama):

> The very character of subjectivity, in the general and the particular, and the very content of our thoughts and feelings, is necessarily dependent on the place and places within which we live and act . . . the landscape that is in us, that we find in 'myth and memory', as Schama says . . . is the same landscape that we find around us and that provides the stuff of our dreams, thoughts and feelings; for that landscape is not only formed, to a greater or lesser extent, through our activity within it, but is itself constitutive of our character and identity—the landscape in which we find ourselves, and through which we are defined, is thus as much a part of what we are, of

our minds, our actions and our selves, as is the food we eat and the air we breathe. (Malpas 189; see also Schama 578)

Although this passage begins with a tacit acknowledgment that we may "live and act" in different places throughout our lives, it quickly settles on the singular form of the word "landscape," as if only one landscape could be truly formative. This formative influence might be pastoral, as in the landscape paintings examined by Schama, or urban, as in the "knowledge" of London taxi cab drivers (which Malpas evokes later in the same passage), but it seems to assume a fairly circumscribed range of experience. This raises a number of important questions that Malpas begs: in particular, how the increased range of experiences available to us in the era of television, the Internet, and jet travel has changed the modern experience of place and to what extent it might even contradict the relatively stable place-based subjectivity that Malpas seems to assume.[10]

Malpas's treatment of evolutionary considerations also raises a number of questions. As we have seen, Malpas emphasizes that subjectivity is: intentional (there is no consciousness without something to be conscious of), embodied (in our sensorimotor capacities), and action-oriented (driven by the need and ability to act). He also emphasizes that all of these factors assume that subjectivity is environmentally constrained. It is through an individual's interactions with his or her environments that both subjectivity and place arise. Subjectivity cannot be conceived apart from the subject's sensorimotor capacities, which cannot be isolated from the surrounding environment that shapes them. These factors imply a related area of inquiry: the question of *how* the perceptual and cognitive capacities that allow the interface between subject and world developed as they did, which leads into evolutionary theory. But this is not a question that interests Malpas, who, in keeping with his synchronic orientation on place, assumes the existence of a human protosubject who already has the capacity to interact with his or her environment. We could say that Malpas's outlook is ontogenetic (pertaining to the developmental history of an organism within its own lifetime) rather than phylogenetic (pertaining to the evolution of a species or population).

There is nothing wrong with emphasizing the ontogenetic over the phylogenetic, of course, but curiously he brusquely dismisses the possibility that there might be an evolutionary component to his understanding of place and subjectivity. One would think that he would be interested in how the principles of adaptation and natural selection support and extend his contention that human perceptual and cognitive faculties arise in relation to environmental constraints. But Malpas refuses to allow evolutionary concerns into the picture. On the contrary, he explicitly condemns this approach as mistaken, associating evolution with mere contingency:

> Of course, the significance of such a sense of place may be seen, and sometimes is seen, as largely a consequence of biological or evolutionary factors. The considerations set forth here, and in earlier chapters, should indicate that I take such approaches to be essentially mistaken—the significance of place should not be construed as just a contingent feature of human psychology or biology, but instead as rooted in the very structure that makes possible experience or thought of the sort that is exemplified in the human (though this is not ruled out by the possibility that certain particular features of our response to place may be contingently based). (188)

This objection to "biological or evolutionary factors" seems strange in the context of an argument built in large part on the principle of embodied cognition, and it may be based on a misunderstanding. Malpas's use of the term contingency is linked to evolution in a way that seems to imply inconsequentiality, as if any evolutionarily determined components of our involvement with place were simply epiphenomenal by-products of the struggle for survival.[11] But the principle of natural selection implies, on the contrary, that the relationship between individual organisms and their local environment plays a determining (although not necessarily deterministic) role in the evolution of populations, including whatever spatial abilities and preferences they might show. Thus any widespread predilection for a certain kind of place (grassy clearings vs. dark caves; densely populated or sparsely populated regions; icy tundra, temperate forest, or desert; etc.) might be explained, at least in part, as the result of a certain evolutionary history—the product of a long series of positive or negative survival and reproductive outcomes involving these kinds of places. The relationship between evolution and the human response to place, in other words, would seem to be the *opposite* of contingent.

What, then, does Malpas mean when he opposes "experience or thought of the sort that is exemplified in the human" to the mere contingency of "psychology or biology"? Is he trying to define human consciousness as a kind of cultural superstructure that can be detached from our biological infrastructure? Or is he trying to shift the debate onto the terrain of metaphysics, situating the relationship between humans and place at a level that is somehow more fundamental than the biological makeup of our bodies? Either way, he would seem to be ignoring the implications of his own theory of embodied cognition, which is reliant on the (evolutionarily shaped) configuration of the body and its sensorimotor apparatus for its very existence. By opposing "human identity" to (mere) "biology" and "psychology" he seems to be arguing against himself. Indeed, this opposition seems to surreptitiously reintroduce Cartesian dualism into his account at a critical juncture, with the human opposed to the biological and the rational opposed to the psychological (as in Descartes's treatment of the passions). Ironically, this is precisely the juncture at which it would become possible to explain why certain sites are more likely than others to generate a "topophilic" response (to borrow Tuan's term) and also, to a lesser but still significant extent, to explain why different people will react differently to the same site or type of site. Evolutionary considerations, of course, are not the be-all and end-all of environmental aesthetics—far from it. But by dismissing as merely contingent the evolutionary basis of the sensorimotor apparatus that makes embodied cognition possible, Malpas would seem to undermine a key implication of his own project, which flows from the premise of the consubtiantiality of the material-spatial and psycho-spiritual dimensions of human subjectivity. If, as Malpas argues, human subjectivity is inconceivable without a place on which to found that subjectivity, then we have a compelling interest in understanding the historical interactions that led to the particular forms of subjectivity that fall into the domain of the human.

This is not, of course, to say that Malpas should have written that history himself but instead that he errs in discounting the relevance of such an account to the considerations that do interest him. In fact, an evolutionary approach to the epistemological problems that interest Malpas could offer a number of tools useful for thinking through the relations between consciousness and place and to resolve some of the questions he leaves unanswered. Central among these is the classic epistemological problem of "Cartesian anxiety," which concerns the distance between belief and knowledge.[12] How do we know that our beliefs correspond to facts in the outside world? And even more fundamentally, how can we pose such questions about our knowledge of the outside world in ways that don't already presume a dualist outlook? (The very opposition between "our" beliefs and "outside world" shows how difficult it is to avoid presuming precisely what is in dispute: the dualist distinction between the "inside" of subjectivity and the "outside" of the world of objects in space.) Malpas's synchronic approach to the study of *Dasein* provides some important clues (building on the Kantian and externalist arguments of Strawson, Evans, Burge, Putnam, and Davidson) but stops short of a complete account, which cannot, I believe, be done without some understanding of the ongoing evolutionary history that has shaped the varieties of human subjectivity.

The advantages of an evolutionary approach to the problems of dualism, Cartesian anxiety, and place will be considered in the next chapter, in relation to Samuel Beckett's well-known "subject-object crisis." Before turning to that argument, I will simply emphasize that we have reached three of the limits or outer boundaries of Malpas's thinking on place: (1) the *social* or intersubjective dimension of place, which gets left aside in his phenomenologically inflected focus on individual experience; (2) the *locational* dimension of place (understood in terms of specific places that can be situated on a map and differentiated from each other); and (3) the *evolutionary* dimension of place consciousness, which, despite his emphasis on the embodied nature of cognition, gets dismissed by Malpas as implying a merely "contingent" view of place. The first two of these limits will be explored in chapters three through six; the third will be addressed in the next chapter.

2

Samuel Beckett and the Postmodern Loss of Place

First the body. No. First the place. No. First both.

—Beckett, *Worstward Ho*

There is no getting around place. We do not live in suspension in an indefinite space.

—Edouard Glissant, *Tout-monde*

It might seem odd to enter into the study of literary representations of place with a chapter on Beckett, since so many of his most memorable fictions are set in almost abstract, unlocalizable spaces. Studies like Eoin O'Brien's pictorial *The Beckett Country* (1996) or Mary Junker's *Beckett: The Irish Dimension* (1995) discern a hidden referential dimension in Beckett's landscape descriptions but do little to dispel our doubts about how relevant such links might be for getting at the deeper significance of his works.[1] The meaning of Beckett's mature works depends to such an enormous degree on the preservation of ambiguity and the resistance to specificity of any kind that the search for a geographical or cultural "key" to the places in Beckett's fictions would seem to be a kind of curatorial pastime. There are exceptions to the rule (e.g., *All That Fall*), but most readers would have no trouble agreeing with Jean-Paul Riquelme's assertion that Beckett's mature style becomes increasingly "anti-locative" (Riquelme 543). To the extent that Beckett's work does address questions of place, it seems closer to the kind of poststructuralist deconstruction of place that will be studied in Chapter 3 than to the phenomenological approach studied in the previous chapter. This does not mean, however, that Beckett lost interest in place as a category of human experience. On the contrary, his increasingly daring deconstructions of place are motivated by a growing recognition of its tenacity as a category of human experience.

What is most striking about Beckett's explorations of the spatial dimension of human experience is their identification with the interstitial space or *entre-deux* of consciousness, conceived, in phenomenological terms, as a space between the two inaccessible realms of subject and object. This is the psychological and conceptual territory that he spent his entire career exploring, with greater determination and insight than just about anyone else. Indeed, it is because of Beckett's lifelong rejection of all facile conceptions of place—combined with his insistence on the need to consider ourselves as inhabiting an indeterminate zone without access to any foundational certainties—that his work provides such an instructive test case for the literary representation of space and place. Because Beckett's protagonists are so studiously situated outside of any recognizable place world, the insights they have to offer (and those they fail to offer) provide us with important clues about the centrality of place in the constitution of personal identity and worldly knowledge. On the most obvious level, the sheer extent of their alienation already provides us with an idea of what the utter disorientation of living in a placeless world would feel like. By systematically eliminating the markers that shape and define place, Beckett's works may provide a kind of *e contrario* proof of the importance of place awareness as a foundation for developing other kinds of know-how. On the other hand, the fact that Beckett's narrators are never fully able, despite their best efforts, to extract themselves from some kind of localizable situation provides precious clues for understanding why place might be considered an ineliminable component of human experience.

Did Beckett, despite the antilocative tendencies of his mature writing, begin to think of place as a source of possible solutions to the aporias he encountered in his work? I believe so. Having pushed the antilocative style to its limits in the trilogy's progression from *Molloy* to *Malone Dies* to *The Unnamable*, he soon began to realize the costs associated with this progressive elimination of place—costs that are powerfully evoked in the *Stories and Texts for Nothing*. He then set out again, almost immediately, to search for a way back into place. This push back toward place that slowly took shape in his later work parallels, in interesting ways, work being done in fields like cognitive science and the philosophy of mind. Indeed, the works of this period might be best understood as thought experiments designed to help think through the relationship between individuals and the world around them and to question deeply ingrained assumptions about the nature of the relationship between human subjectivity and its environing milieu. In so doing, these works illustrate the extent to which embeddedness in place is a central feature of human experience, conditioning not only one's sense of the world but also one's sense of self.

We have already seen the importance that Casey and Malpas attribute to the relationship between self and place. In this chapter, I will be pushing that analysis one step further, invoking the work of the neurophenomenologist Francisco Varela to approach this understudied side of Beckett's work and use it as a way to rethink what it was that Beckett was up to in the second half of his career. The works of this period are often considered minor, but they are, I would argue, crucially important—not only for appreciating the full arc of Beckett's career but also for getting a sense of the light that Beckett's unique (and uniquely rigorous) treatment of place sheds on the relationship between mind and world.

Understanding the Impasse

Chroniclers of Beckett's career usually divide it into three roughly defined periods: the early years, comprising all his texts written in English through *Watt* and the end of World War II; the "heroic" phase or siege-in-the-room period that lasted from the end of World War II until the mid-1950s; and the increasingly minimalist third period, which is like a long fade to silence. There is, however, a continuity between the first two of these phases that makes it equally useful to think of Beckett's career as divided into two somewhat longer phases of about equal length. The first phase is characterized by Beckett's narrators' progressive loss of contact with the outside world. It stretches from his very first novel, *Dream of Fair to Middling Women* (written in 1932 but published in 1992), through to *The Unnamable* (1953).[2] The second phase depicts the struggle to find a way back out into the world, which is explicitly and consistently conceived in spatial terms. This theme is first voiced toward the end of *The Unnamable*, comes to the fore in the *Stories and Texts for Nothing* (1954), provides a central focus of Beckett's prose and the television dramas beginning in the 1960s, and continues to preoccupy Beckett until the end of his life in 1989.

How might we explain the progressive loss of place that characterizes the first period? The trajectory of Beckett's career was determined in large part by his early infatuation with Cartesian skepticism and Kantian idealism, which led him to pursue the path of an increasingly radical form of subjectivism, according to which all presumed knowledge of the material world is subjected to extreme doubt and uncertainty. The consequent waning of interest in the outside world can be seen clearly in the passage from the third-person narratives of his first two English novels to the internal monologues of the trilogy. Although the *protagonists* of his first novels already displayed marked solipsistic tendencies, pushed by some to the point of madness, the *narrators* of these novels went through a profound evolution, becoming increasingly self-centered and progressively merging with the voices of their characters.

This shift is reflected in the landscapes of these novels. From the still-recognizable (and sometimes named) places of Ireland and London in *Murphy* to the vaguely Irish landscapes of *Watt* and *Molloy*, and from the closed chamber of *Malone Dies* to the almost purely abstract space of *The Unnamable*, we watch as the outside world becomes increasingly distant and inaccessible, while the "here" of the narrator becomes increasingly abstract, alien, and mutable, bearing so little resemblance to the world we live in that it is hard to know what to make of it. As for his narrators, they are so thwarted in all their attempts to gain verifiable knowledge of the outside world that they begin to forget what it's like. Their attention turns inward, to the exploration of the inner world of consciousness, which appears to be the only realm still available to them. Having quite literally lost their place in the outside world, they try to compensate by seeking self-knowledge. But as their exploration of this inner world progresses, they begin to realize that knowledge of the self is just as elusive as knowledge of the outside world.

This second loss, the loss of self, which profoundly marks all of Beckett's characters, leaves them in a kind of no-man's-land between an unknowable outside world and an unlocatable self. With no foundation on which to ground their beliefs, whether in the outside world of objects or the inside world of the self, Beckett's characters find themselves in a position of extreme epistemological weakness. It is no doubt Beckett's depiction of this interstitial zone of uncertainty between subject and object that is his most enduring contribution to world literature. But it also leads Beckett into what he considered to be a dead-end: the famous "impasse" that he complained of after completing *The Unnamable*.

He would spend the rest of his career trying to escape from that impasse. Indeed, the impasse—the sudden sense that there was no way out of the existential and epistemological corner into which he had painted himself—is one of the two central events of his career, as important in its own way as the creative breakthrough that transformed the still-hesitant author of the early English novels into the burning voice of the trilogy. The second phase of his career lasts about as long as the first (approximately 30 years, from the impasse of the mid-1950s until the end of his life in 1989) and is, by some measures, the most prolific and productive period of his career—provided, that is, that we count titles and not words, since his late texts are characterized by their extreme brevity and cryptic minimalism. To be sure, this phase is not marked by the kind of creative breakthrough that enabled him to create such memorable characters as Molloy, Malone, Worm, Didi and Gogo, and Hamm and Clov, but his attempts to break out of the impasse led to a deepening of the Beckettian voice—a radical-ization of the procedures that made it possible to explore potentialities that could only be alluded to from a distance in the earlier works. This is the voice that critics like Riquelme, Barry, and Abbott have called the "middle voice," which is perhaps most eloquently figured in the image of the tympanum or vibrating membrane that occurs toward the end of *The Unnamable*: "I'm in the middle, I'm the partition, I've two surfaces and no thickness, perhaps that's what I feel, myself vibrating, I'm the tympanum, on the one hand the mind, on the other the world, I don't belong to either" (*Three Novels* 383).[3]

My goal in what follows is to show how Beckett's attempts to find a way out of the impasse lead him into a profound exploration of place as a constituent element of human consciousness. Indeed, one of the most distinctive things about the second phase of Beckett's career is his tendency to spatialize being, whether by imagining punishing landscapes through which to wander or by constructing elaborately minimalist refuges to inhabit. Much of what I have to say, then, will be intended to show how Beckett's unique approach to place provides a way to rethink the nature of human subjectivity in terms of a three-way interplay between mind, body, and environment. Close attention to the role that place plays in these texts suggests that in his later work, he may have found (or at least pointed the way toward) a viable path out of the onto-epistemological impasse that had foreclosed the subjectivist line of attack he had adopted in the first half of his career.

For Beckett, I hasten to add, this problem is not an abstract philosoph-ical problem. Beckett refused to be, as Porter Abbott has emphasized, a philosopher (see Abbott, "I Am Not a Philosopher"). Although the episte-mological crisis that shaped his work is a philosophical one, his attempts to deal with it have a pragmatic, experiential focus. His work, we could say, depicts, from the inside, the kinds of phenomena that philosophers talk about from a certain distance.

Beckett, Dualism, and the *Entre-Deux*

In order to understand how Beckett's treatment of place is linked to the impasse, it will be important to understand the role that subject-object dualism played in shaping his existential outlook. As early as his 1937 letter to Alex Kaun, he referred to the phenomenal "veil that must be torn apart in order to get at the things (or Nothingness) behind it" (Beckett, *Disjecta* 171). This preoccupation with what he would later call the "subject-object crisis" (*Disjecta* 146) in Western philosophy became a major theme in his writing on the arts, as documented throughout the critical writings collected in *Disjecta*. More importantly, he grappled with the epistemological problem of dualism in his creative work, and continued to do so up until the very end of his career. One particularly telling allusion to his ongoing struggle with dualism occurs in a latish prose piece, *neither* (first published in 1976):

> TO AND FRO in shadow from inner to outershadow
> from impenetrable self to impenetrable unself by way of neither
> as between two lit refuges whose doors once neared gently close,
> once turned away from gently part again. (Beckett, *CSP* 258)

Both self (subject) and unself (object) remain inaccessible to the narrating consciousness, which sees only the shelters in which they reside—not the reality of the things themselves. This leaves it wandering back and forth between subject and object in that epistemological no-man's-land of the *entre-deux*. This dual inaccessibility sets into motion a kind of oscillation, which, significantly for our purposes, is represented in spatial terms—as an interminable voyage back and forth along a path between two equally inviting but ultimately inaccessible refuges. If it were possible to open up the doors of one of these two refuges, it would then be possible to break out of this to-and-fro oscillation.

J. P. Riquelme sees Beckett as responding to the inaccessibility of the two refuges by redefining the very notion of home. No longer would being "at home" be conceived in terms of the embrace of a sheltering enclosure but as, instead, a kind of austere stoicism: a heroic readiness to face exposure to the elements, a willingness to take up residence in the existential wilderness of the *entre-deux*. In fact, Riquelme sees this resolute embrace of the interstitial condition as one of Beckett's major achievements. My sense, however, is that Beckett, although willing to face up to this kind of deprivation (as all of his characters, without exception, do), is actually striving to transcend the opposition between subject and object in a way that would make it possible to revive the lost Eden of epistemological and existential plenitude. Like the searchers in *The Lost Ones*, he has not given up on the goal of finding his lost other or of finding "a way out." Like them, he continues to search—against all odds. Some of Beckett's works (*The Unnamable* and *Company*) attempt a subjectivist solution to the problem, tending toward solipsism; others (*The Lost Ones*) emphasize the objectivist side of the equation. But ultimately, both of these unipolar approaches fail. By opting for one or the other, they simply mark moments in the dualist oscillation described earlier. The ideal for Beckett would be to unlock the doors of self and nonself, allowing the inside and the outside to flow back into the middle ground, making it possible for both self and world to become fully available (present) to phenomenological consciousness.

Jacques Derrida spent much of his career showing how this kind of desire for full unmediated presence of any kind is a metaphysical one— that is, one that cannot be fulfilled.[4] But one doesn't need to be a Derridean to understand that direct contact between knower and known is, by definition, an impossibility. As humans, we perceive the world through the mediation of our senses, and even something as apparently immediate as consciousness is subject to all kinds of doubts. This does not mean, however, that the desire for such contact can be wished away or that there are no ways to achieve various kinds of meaningful "presence effects." Indeed, I believe that it is this more moderate goal—the creation of presence *effects*—that shapes the work of phase-two Beckett. In this sense, his later works can be construed as trying to establish the conditions under which momentary flashes of relative plenitude might still be achieved in a postlapsarian world. We could say that the *mistake* (if it can be called that) of phase-one Beckett was the all-or-nothing approach. He was swinging for the fences, demanding nothing less than a triumphant reentry into the realm of full presence, where one would finally be able to "see the beauties of the skies, and see the stars again" (*CSP* 103) and to "Say I" (and mean it). The ambitions of phase-two Beckett are more moderate. But by scaling back his goals, he actually succeeds in ways that the first Beckett could not—despite his continued reliance on the rhetoric of failure.

What is significant for my purpose is the central role that depictions of places play in this scaled-back search for a way out of the in-between world of mediation. Where the phase-one works thought it better to dispense progressively with any sense of a concrete setting, the phase-two works focus obsessively on detailed descriptions of carefully defined places, albeit highly contrived and artificial ones. Why might this be? What is it about these settings that would make of them such an important focus of attention in this revised project? Part of the answer may simply be that Beckett had pursued his previous abstractive path as far as it would go. He had initially conceived of the elimination of place as a way of eliminating distractions, making it possible to focus attention on the speaking subject—to "seize" him by isolating him from all extraneous considerations. But this, he eventually decided, is what led him into the impasse. In this context, the renewed focus on physical descriptions of place seems to have provided a welcome new outlet, another possible avenue out of the dualist impasse. Of course this approach didn't magically solve his problem, but it did point him in the direction of a solution to the dualist dilemma—a solution whose existence he was able to intuit without ever being able to articulate clearly.

The Three Modes of Beckettian Spatiality

In order to push this argument further, we need to get a better sense of the different modes of spatiality that Beckett works with. There is not one unified approach to place in Beckett's works but rather three: the open spaces of wandering; the closed spaces of shelter; and the abstract spaces he sometimes called the void.

In an important early article on Beckett and place, Ludovic Janvier notes that the vast majority of Beckett's writing is organized around an opposition between shelter and wandering (Janvier, "Place of Narration," also published in French as "Lieu dire"). The dialectic of wandering and shelter is established in Beckett's earliest fictions. Belacqua, for example, from *More Pricks Than Kicks*, is an inveterate wanderer who prefers the road to the resting points between journeys; Murphy, on the other hand, seeks respite from the outside world by locking himself in his room and "going womb-tomb"; and *Watt* depicts the eponymous hero's progress along a road leading from shelter to shelter. Molloy, Moran, and Malone also fit into this pattern. By the time we get to *The Unnamable*, however, the narrator/protagonist has become an almost (but not quite) disembodied voice situated in an indeterminate space. For him, the only kind of wandering possible is discursive. Having lost contact with the two refuges of self and unself, he finds himself in a different kind of wilderness, which is both a form of imprisonment and exile. The *Texts for Nothing* emphasize the self-imposed, paradoxical, even insane nature of this sense of entrapment or exile but insist nonetheless on its reality. "If I said, There's a way out there, there's a way out somewhere, the rest would come. What am I waiting for then, to say it? To believe it?" (*CSP* 136). This indeterminate space of the *entre-deux* will, henceforth, be the space of all Beckett's narrators. Given its importance as the *nec plus ultra* of the Beckettian reduction, it seems logical to begin our account of Beckettian spatiality with this paradoxically abstract space, which is very precisely a nonplace.

It is, as we've seen, *The Unnamable* that initiates the deployment of abstract narrative spaces. Later examples include *Company* (which features a voice that "comes to one in the dark"), *Not I* (which features a speaking mouth isolated on a bare, dark stage, accompanied only by a shrouded listener), and *Cascando* (which is dominated by the voice of an Opener who speaks from an indeterminate space we cannot identify). With little to no perceptible décor, these works focus our attention on the vagaries of the discourse we hear, which seems to be that of a consciousness focused inwardly upon itself. The lack of visual stimuli leaves little to focus on except for the voice. It is, consequently, the sense of hearing that predominates in the abstract space works.

Generically speaking, this kind of abstract space is associated with the interior monologue feel of *The Unnamable*. The radio medium is also particularly well suited to the presentation of voices in a void—like that of the Opener in *Cascando*. The theater, on the other hand, is an inherently visual medium and seems less well suited to this kind of abstract space. Nonetheless, many of Beckett's staged plays push in this direction, situating the actors on a bare, almost featureless, and often darkened stage. As for the film and television plays, the inherent concreteness of the televisual medium makes it the least suited to abstraction.

Existentially, the characters in the abstract-space works find themselves subject to extreme disorientation. The absence of spatial definition is tied to an absence of material to work with (in both the concrete and creative senses of this term). Unsurprisingly, perhaps, these works invariably end in failure and negation. The second-person protagonist of *Company* ends up not in good company but "alone." Like the speaker in *Not I*, who refuses to identify herself with the subject of her monologue ("No! Not I! She!"), he refuses, or is unable, to accept the stories he hears as his own. Similarly, the Opener of *Cascando* feels that he is on the verge of success in his version of the quest for presence ("Come on, come on, almost there"), but he can only stand by, impotently, and listen. He has no control over the performances that come to him from some unspecified elsewhere. Thus if the works emphasizing abstract space take up the legacy of *The Unnamable*, it must be said that they have a tendency to demonstrate the futility of that legacy. They serve, as a group, to remind us of the persistence of the post-*Unnamable* impasse. They work *with* it—in the sense of turning that failure into a source of creative activity—but they are unable to work their way *out of* it.

In so doing, however, they already help to sharpen our understanding of the problem. What the failure of these texts suggests is that contact with an environing milieu is not something secondary or extraneous (a mere distraction) but something necessary—something ineliminable that may in fact be the key to all the rest. *Company*, notably, marks some important advances in this regard. For example, the narrator of *Company* considers introducing a few derisory environmental specifics into the scene (e.g., a fly and a dead rat). He ultimately decides that such specifics do not contribute to his project and so banishes them from the scene. But there is one element that he cannot banish: pressure to the hindquarters. This apparently trivial tactile sensation will, as we shall see, have an important role to play in Beckett's struggle with radical doubt, because it suggests the ineliminability of the body and, through the body, the world. This, we could say, is the corporeal corollary to the Cartesian cogito: Where there is pressure, there is something to feel that pressure and also something to exert that pressure. This first hint of a reengagement with the environing milieu brings us to the theme of wandering.

Wandering, the second mode of Beckettian spatiality, was already an important theme in the first phase of his career, but it begins to play a somewhat different role in the second phase.[5] Beckett's phase-two wandering texts include *How It Is, From an Abandoned Work, Enough,* most of the *Fizzles,* and *Worstward Ho.* (We might also include in this list Voice's narrative in *Cascando,* which is distinct from the abstract space of the Opener.) Like *Watt* and *Molloy* before them, these works tend to emphasize the progress of bodies in motion through an open, often moor-like landscape. Curiously though, despite the openness of the landscape, these are stories of constraint—not freedom. They emphasize the constraining forces of the natural and social environment, which weighs on the protagonists, determining their actions. Epistemologically speaking, these texts lean toward the objectivist end of the subject-object oscillation: It is the environment that determines the states of mind and actions of the characters.

The wandering stories also tend to draw our attention to the body, emphasizing the kinetic sense of movement through a landscape and the tactile sensations of the protagonists (the shock when resistance is encountered, the pain of a beating, the aches and fatigue of an aging body, and so on). They tend to feature an active protagonist—in that he likes to walk (or crawl or creep when necessary)—but one without much in the way of individual agency. In purest form, as in *Fizzle 1* (which will be discussed shortly), these stories tend to conceive of the relationship between subject and environment in the minimalist terms of a stimulus-response model: rather than volition, the protagonists' actions express primarily the urge to avoid pain and injury and (to a lesser extent) seek pleasure and sustenance.

In Beckett's earlier preimpasse wandering stories—from the Belacqua stories of *More Pricks Than Kicks* to *First Love*—the environmental considerations were relatively complex, involving familial, social, and cultural considerations and even the stray reference to politics: "Union ... brothers ... Marx ... capital ... bread and butter ... love. It was all Greek to me" (*The End, CSP* 94–95). Nonetheless, like the later texts, which are less environmentally complex and more single-minded, these stories already seem to imply an environmental response to the problems of individual identity and agency. All of Beckett's wandering stories operate within the constraints of a harsh social, physical, and cultural environment, showing us the ways it has shaped a physically and epistemologically weak, passive protagonist. From the outset, Beckett seems to have been seeking a way to explain the comically alienated attitudes of his characters, all of whom seem to have been born into dysfunctional families, raised in bleak landscapes surrounded by unsympathetic neighbors, disciplined by unforgiving authorities and institutions, and then "expelled" into the world, where they have to learn to fend for themselves. Given all this, it is perhaps not surprising that they show little aptitude for self-preservation and only the mildest inclination to take care of themselves. What they excel at is enduring the many indignities they are forced to suffer with a kind of stoic equanimity and dissecting, with comedic insight, the absurdities of the situations in which they find themselves. This they do from the bemused ironic distance of someone who has become detached from the physical world, to the point that they are able to make reports like the following: "my body [is] doing its best without me" (*From an Abandoned Work*, *CSP*164).

Fizzle 1 (*CSP* 224–28) pushes this behaviorist tendency about as far as it can go. We are presented with an almost deterministic image of a protagonist who must negotiate a narrow, hilly path. The path is bounded on both sides by stone walls, which are brought into play by its many twists and turns. The protagonist's decision making process is reduced to a question of stimulus and response, aggravated by the fact that he seems practically devoid of foresight and willpower. Unwilling or unable to take precautions, his progress requires him to go, quite literally, bouncing off the walls:

> Spite of the dark he does not grope his way, arms outstretched, hands agape and the feet held back just before the ground. With the result he must often, namely at every turn, strike against the walls that hem his path . . . (224)

It's as if he had been parachuted into an alien landscape that he is not equipped to deal with and so must go through a period of harsh training or reeducation. Theoretically, one supposes, he has some ability to control the situation. He could decide to stop, for example, or to turn around and abandon the journey. But this is a possibility that the story explicitly considers and rejects. He will continue to move forward, we're told, until he reaches the end of the road. At that point, he will turn and "return to the other terminus" (yet another image of oscillation).

As always with Beckett, the apparent absurdity of this situation invites allegorical interpretation: Is it an existential commentary on abjection? A self-referential statement on the artist's creative process? A philosophical parable of free will and determinism? Whatever level one chooses to emphasize, it is clear that this is a story about *constraints*—about making progress along a path where almost all options are foreclosed by the obstacles and boundaries encountered in the landscape.

It is also possible, of course (and this option can never be excluded in Beckett), that this character is simply deluded about his apparent lack of options. Is he on the right road? "That he is," we're told with initial confidence, "for there are not others." But then doubt creeps back in: "unless he has let them slip by unnoticed, one after another" (226). In other words, even if we accept the aptness of this quasi-deterministic image of constrained choices, we cannot rule out the possibility that this character has determined his own fate by not seizing or even noticing alternatives when they present themselves. This suggests reading the text as a kind of epistemological parable, perhaps as a rejoinder to Plato's cave allegory that seeks to emphasize the ways in which our preconceived expectations and stubbornness cause us to misread the signs we encounter as we move through the world.[6]

If texts like *Fizzle 1* work through the physicalist metaphor of a landscape able to tightly constrain our choices, *How It Is* reintroduces an important social element to the landscape. Alain Badiou, Leo Bersani, Ludovic Janvier, and others have identified this text as a crucial turning point in Beckett's career—in part because it is one of the rare texts of Beckett's second phase to incorporate an account of social interactions, however tortured (see Badiou; Bersani and Dutoit; and Janvier). In this novel, Beckett's narrator describes the world "down below." Once again, he does so in almost behaviorist terms, emphasizing the terrible discipline that reigns on this narrow path in the mud that is followed by Pim, Bom, and the others. Janvier calls it "a route within prison," which is a remark that could be made about most of Beckett's outdoor, wandering pieces, whether they put the emphasis on the physical landscape or the social landscape.

There are, to be sure, some stories that give more freedom to the wanderers, allowing them to range across the countryside. But even this kind of apparently unconstrained wandering is revealed to be subject to strict constraints: first, the gravitational force of the focal point of the wanderer (home, refuge, grave, body, etc.), which establishes a maximum range and a trajectory (usually a centripetal spiral); and second, the force of habit, which leads the wanderers to choose the same paths over and over again, often to the point that they wear grooves or channels into the ground. Freedom, in this context, is a very relative kind of freedom. When it is not environmental constraints determining the movement of Beckett's protagonists, it is some equally implacable force that they carry within themselves.

The wandering theme will persist until the end of Beckett's career, playing, notably, an important role in *Worstward Ho*, one of Beckett's very last and most austere texts. By establishing the importance of the body and its interactions with the environment as a central concern, these texts make an important contribution to Beckett's ongoing effort to overcome the inside-outside dichotomy, suggesting a model, however primitive, for understanding the relationship between individuals and their environments. As Ulrika Maude, following Steven Connor, writes of the trilogy, these texts "could, in fact, paradoxically be read as a reaffirmation of the body; a body which refuses to be refused throughout Beckett's writing" (Maude, "On Beckett's Landscapes" 69). For Maude, this perhaps unintended reaffirmation of the body suggests a corollary reaffirmation of "nature and the outer world," which must now be seen not just as a space within which the body is situated or as a force that acts upon the body but "as a *continuation* of the alienated body, a displacement, a sign that appears incomprehensible to the shattered first person narrators in their attempt to decipher their mental processes" (Maude 70, emphasis added). This idea of the landscape as a continuation of the body is a point I will be pursuing at great length in the next section.

We saw earlier how the abstract space narratives emphasize the subjectivist principle, tending toward solipsism in their elimination of all distractions from the outside world. We also saw how *Company* grudgingly allows the body back into the picture via the theme of pressure on the hind quarters. The wandering narratives work the same question but from the objectivist end of the spectrum, beginning with the body and seeking a zone of subjectivity. Neither of these two modes of narrative fully succeeds in bridging the gap between consciousness, body, and world, but both provide important pieces of the puzzle.

If few critics have been able to capitalize fully on the scattered insights into the nature of place that these texts provide, it may be, in part, because the bizarre, enigmatic remoteness of these scenarios causes them to flip over into allegory, which tends to stifle the exploratory thought experiment dimension. It is also in part because Beckett has not yet fully transcended the dualist ontology of subject and object. It is in his third mode of spatial representation—the shelter or "closed place" narratives—that Beckett comes the closest to succeeding in that endeavor. But in order to understand what is significant and new about this third mode of Beckettian spatial writing, it will be useful to turn away from Beckett momentarily in order to think more carefully about the dualist dilemma from a philosophical and scientific perspective. It is particularly interesting to see how the questions raised by Beckett have been addressed in the field of cognitive science, which attempts to bridge the gap between the philosophy of mind and the biology of the brain.

Beckett and Varela: From Cartesian Anxiety to the Embodied Mind

We saw in Chapter 1 how the phenomenologically inspired philosophy of place exemplified by Casey and Malpas has helped to put place at the center of a postdualist understanding of the relations between mind and world. I would now like to extend that inquiry by reference to the work of Francisco Varela, which I have found to be a particularly useful guide in understanding both what Beckett was trying to accomplish and why he found the dualist dilemma to be so intractable. Varela's work is particularly pertinent for a study of place in Beckett, because Varela was engaged in a project that, although couched in the language of philosophy and scientific research, overlaps in suggestive ways with Beckett's literary search. Varela, an evolutionary biologist and founder of a hybrid discipline he called neurophenomenology, sought to reconcile the externalist, objectifying methodology of scientific inquiries into the mind with a more properly phenomenological emphasis on understanding human consciousness from the inside. By juxtaposing Beckett's work with that of cognitive scientists, I hope to highlight the experimental dimension of Beckett's work, showing how it not only fits in with but also contributes to the ongoing scientific and philosophical exploration of the mind-world interface. My guide in this effort will be *The Embodied Mind* (1991), written by Varela in conjunction with Evan Thompson and Eleanor Rosch. The book is organized around an account of what they call, following Richard Bernstein, Cartesian anxiety. And although they make no mention of Beckett, their book reads at times like a commentary on his work.

A word of warning about *The Embodied Mind*: It is in some respects a quirky and atypical representative of the field of cognitive science. (It seeks, among other things, to present Mahayana Buddhism as a kind of scientific project that could serve as a corrective model for the western scientific tradition.) It is also a book that goes too far in some respects, overshooting its mark in a way that has made it somewhat controversial within the cognitive science community. Nonetheless, it remains extremely useful as a companion to Beckett's work, because its "enactivist" response to the problem of mind-body dualism provides some interesting insights into what Beckett was trying to accomplish through his literary experiments.

The account of Cartesian anxiety given in *The Embodied Mind* fits Beckett to a tee: "Cartesian anxiety requires not only that we believe in a self that we know cannot be found but also that we believe in a world to which we have no access" (Varela, Thompson, and Rosch 143). And their description of the absolutist demands of radical doubt—be it in its classical (Cartesian) or contemporary (postmodern) variants—evokes very precisely the existential disarray of Beckett's characters as they butt up against the blind wall of his epistemological impasse: "Either we have a fixed and stable foundation for knowledge, a point where knowledge starts, is grounded, and rests, or we cannot escape some sort of darkness, chaos and confusion. Either there is an absolute ground or foundation, or everything falls apart" (140). For the authors of *The Embodied Mind*, the problem is not only the demand for a stable foundation but also the fact that the demand tends to be framed within the terms provided by the dualist tradition that goes back to Descartes. For them, the history of subject-object dualism has left us with what amounts to a series of false choices between the subjective principle and the objective principle: mind or matter, body or soul, realism or idealism. The aporias of subjectivism lead to objectivist rebuttals that eventually fall short, leading to further subjectivist counterattacks and so on. All of this results in a back-and-forth movement between two inaccessible poles that, once again, is strongly reminiscent of Beckett: "By treating mind and world as opposed subjective and objective poles, the Cartesian anxiety oscillates endlessly between the two in search of a ground" (141).

As with Beckett, this oscillation is not for the authors of *The Embodied Mind* just an abstract philosophical issue; it is something that calls into question our ability to gain any kinds of certainties about the world around us. In the current postmodern era, they argue, the effects of Cartesian anxiety have become more debilitating than ever, leading ultimately to nihilism:

> As we set out in search of other ways of thinking, the Cartesian anxiety arises to dog us at every step. Yet our contemporary situation is also unique, for we have become increasingly skeptical about the possibility of discerning any ultimate ground. Thus when the anxiety arises today, we seem unable to avoid the turn toward nihilism, for we have not learned to let go of the forms of thinking, behavior and experience that lead us to desire a ground. (141)

They are no doubt thinking here of developments like Jean Baudrillard's embrace of the simulacrum and his self-declared affinity for nihilism, but to the extent that Cartesian anxiety is at the heart of postmodern skepticism, Beckett's work could also be considered emblematic of the postmodern movement as a whole. And indeed, Beckett's work has been interpreted in this way—as, for example, Lukács does.[7] But as I have already suggested and will continue to argue in what follows, Beckett's outlook is diametrically opposed to that of a Baudrillardian ironist. Despite the utter disarray of his protagonists as they fall into the oscillating rhythms of Cartesian anxiety, Beckett strongly resists the temptations of nihilism and the cool comforts of postmodern irony, insisting instead on the imperative to carry on in the search for that missing ground for knowledge that is so strikingly formulated in the famous "I can't go on I must go on I'll go on" of *The Unnamable* (*Three Novels* 414). Is there, then, a way out of Beckett's impasse? Was he able to find it? And can Varela help us to see what it might be? To these questions, I would respond, respectively, "yes," "no," and "yes."

The core thesis of *The Embodied Mind*'s argument is implied in its title: It is through full recognition of the embodied nature of human consciousness that Cartesian anxiety can be overcome. The fact that the mind is rooted in what the authors call the "sensorimotor apparatus" of the body is what enables them to put an end to the dualist oscillation. "Our intention," they declare, "is to bypass entirely this logical geography of inner versus outer by studying cognition not as recovery [of a pregiven, objective, world] or projection [of a subjective consciousness] but as embodied action" (172). What do they mean by embodied action? That the body's input (perception) and output (motor processes) mechanisms are inextricably intertwined; that the body is itself inextricably intertwined with its environing milieu; and that thinking is a form of physical activity in the sense that cognition is necessarily, from an evolutionary standpoint, action oriented:

> By using the term *embodied* we mean to highlight two points: first, that cognition depends upon the kinds of experience that come from having a body with various sensorimotor capacities, and second, that these individual sensorimotor capacities are themselves embedded in a more encompassing biological, psychological, and cultural context. By using the term *action* we mean to emphasize once again that sensory and motor processes, perception and action, are fundamentally inseparable in lived cognition. (Varela, Thompson, and Rosch 172–73)

Prescientific theories of subjectivity identified the self with an incorporeal soul, as many naïve or folk theories of identity continue to do. Modern scientific theories of subjectivity have tended to equate it with the mind, which is itself localized in the brain. Cognitive scientists have tended to push the modern view one step further by emphasizing that the brain is connected to and inseparable from the larger nervous system that runs throughout the body, culminating in the body's various sensory organs and motor systems. What Varela and the enactivist school contribute to this view of cognition is an emphasis on the extent to which the individual's sensorimotor systems are themselves *productive of* the subject's world. Having evolved to enable the individual to interact successfully with other elements of the environment, they argue, the mind is not only a product of that environment but also a *member* of it, in the strongest (i.e., anatomical) sense of that word: the mind interacts with the world like an organ in the body or a part in a machine—not like a mirror that can be opposed to it or a visitor that has been parachuted into an alien world. (The parachutist metaphor is one of their favorite ways to discredit accounts of the mind that do not sufficiently recognize its evolutionary history.)

It is on this point that the thinking of Varela, Thompson, and Rosch meets up with the philosophy of place as conceived by thinkers like Casey and Malpas. And it is on this point that their work has the most to offer for our understanding of Beckett's closed place narratives. But the authors of *The Embodied Mind* take their argument one highly controversial step further. Before returning to our discussion of Beckett's refuge narratives, then, I would like to offer a few words about what they consider to be their most far-reaching contribution to cognitive science. Although few cognitive scientists would be willing to follow them this far, their proposal does have interesting implications for Beckett's work on place, since it involves the role of the imagination.

It is clear that for the authors of *The Embodied Mind*, cognitive science provides the best available model for furthering our understanding of human consciousness. They are, nonetheless, critical of what they see as cognitive science's lack of attention to the concerns of continental philosophy and, in particular, to the phenomenological tradition of exploring subjective experience from the inside—through the analysis of one's own mental states. In fact, their commitment to the phenomenological approach is so strong that it leads them to contest one of the bedrock principles of the scientific tradition: its presumption of the existence of a world "out there" that exists independently of our awareness of it. "The challenge posed to cognitive science" by their approach, they say, "is to question one of the more entrenched assumptions of our scientific heritage—that the world is independent of the knower" (Varela, Thompson, and Rosch 150). They develop a whole array of concepts designed to further this argument, proposing that the relationship between mind and world can only be understood in terms of the "mutual specification and dependent coorigination" of mind and world (150), which they also term "structural coupling" (151) and "coevolution" (203). Their argument, in a nutshell, is that if consciousness is so fully intricated into the fabric of the world as to be inseparable from it, then the world is as much a product of the mind as the mind is a product of the world: "We are claiming that organism and environment are mutually enfolded in multiple ways, and so what constitutes the world of a given organism is enacted by that organism's history of structural coupling [with its environment]" (202).

Any modification in the state of mind of an individual is also a modification of the world. That much is unobjectionable. (If the mind is a part of the world, then a modification to that mind is a modification to the world.) Where they seem to err is in giving too much weight to individual consciousness. While individual organisms certainly do have an impact on their environment—and perhaps even in exceptional cases a major one (the proverbial butterfly flapping its wings)—it is still possible to talk about the environment as, for all practical purposes, stable with respect to the consciousness of individuals. It is not difficult to accept that the mind-world relationship is a "mutually specifying" one, but it seems obvious that this relationship is so lopsided in favor of the world that in almost any conceivable situation, the influence of any individual's mental states can be factored out. As Daniel Dennett puts it in his review of *The Embodied Mind*, "it [the world] can be safely treated as a constant (an 'external', 'pregiven' condition), because its changes in response to local organismic activity are usually insignificant as variables in interaction with the variables under scrutiny" (Dennett 126).

It seems safe to conclude, then, that this farthest-reaching argument of *The Embodied Mind* is guilty of overreaching—at least insofar as it is meant to change the way scientists approach their research into the material world. But there is a special category of "organismic activity" in which the logic of mutual specification and dependent coorigination of mind and world manifests itself in full force, a category that includes dreams, fantasies, memories, wishes, thought experiments, language games, working hypotheses, counterfactual arguments, theories of all kinds, and, of course, works of art and literature. This is, in short, the virtual realm of the imagination and memory.

The coorigination hypothesis of Varela, Thompson, and Rosch has special pertinence in the realm of the imagination and memory, because although these faculties are necessarily formed by the same evolutionary forces that shaped the rest of the organism, their output is of a particular kind: representational. If we were to limit our conception of the mind to being nothing more than the helmsman of a sensorimotor system—a behavioristic input-output mechanism—their argument would necessarily fail. But to the extent that we emphasize the representational capacities of the brain—its ability to form states of mind that correlate with (are about) something—the coorigination argument may succeed.[8] Imagination is the ability to recognize that there is more than one possible state of the world and, by extension, more than one possible course of action available. And memory requires the ability to represent past states of the world as nonactual but real. The representational moment and, in particular, the imaginative moment, is of crucial importance, because it implies the possibility of a pause—a respite from the behavioristic cycle of input and output that gives rise eventually to the more specifically human ability to imagine alternative worlds—and the possibility that things could be (imagination) and have been (memory) otherwise. Rather than assuming that the mind is an organ that is able only to react, behavioristically, to stimuli in the present tense, representational thinking implies the ability to work from the past toward the future and vice-versa.

This kind of thinking—the ability to recognize virtualities—in combination with the communicative and social faculties of the mind, helps us to understand how the individual's states of mind can indeed have as much of an impact on the world as the world has on the individual. Wishing (or remembering) that the world was different does not make it so, of course. But if that wish gives rise to some sort of systematic change in behavior—the implementation of a new code of conduct, for example, or of a new explanatory concept or some kind of technological innovation—then that imaginative state begins to have a more significant impact on the world. And to the extent that idea is communicated to and acted upon by others, its effects are amplified and might eventually even have profoundly transformative effects on a global scale. From this, although it is not clearly stated in *The Embodied Mind*, we could say that their rebuttal to Dennett's otherwise entirely reasonable objections is that he underestimates the importance of the social implications of the enactivist model.

This detour into the question of imagination and memory within the larger theory of the embodied mind has special significance for Beckett and his closed place narratives—not just because he is, himself, an imaginative artist, but because the interplay between perception, imagination, and memory is at the thematic heart of these pieces. What Beckett *gives* us in these works is the image of a body in an environing milieu, which interacts in mysterious ways with an imagining/remembering consciousness that may or may not be related to the body. What he seems to be *pursuing* in these pieces is the idea that for the sufferer of Cartesian anxiety it might, paradoxically, be imagination and memory—not perception—that provide the best solutions to the aporias of radical doubt. There are reasons to believe that Beckett succeeds (at least partially) in this endeavor. And his use of décor in these pieces provides major clues as to what he is trying to accomplish. These considerations, then, will serve to bring us to the third mode of Beckettian spatiality: the shelter or closed place or refuge narratives.

Embodiment, Place, and Beckett's Refuges

What is new and interesting about Beckett's closed place narratives is the way they depict the relationship between the body and its immediate environment. All of these places contain bodies—that is their primary function—and these bodies are firmly ensconced in the décor, as if they had been secreted by it. We no longer have the first-person flood of discourse that had characterized the trilogy but rather a third-person narrative voice that describes the scene from the outside. This new attitude toward the relationship between the narrative discourse and the image of the body has its origins in the short sketch-like texts of the early 1960s, as Stan Gontarski has noted in his editorial introduction to the *Complete*

Short Prose: "If the *Texts for Nothing* suggest the dispersal of character and the subsequent writing beyond the body, *All Strange Away* signaled a refiguration, the body's return, its textualization, the body as voiceless, static object, or the object of text, unnamed except for a series of geometric signifiers, being as mathematical formulae" (*CSP* xv). Curiously, Gontarski's essay doesn't pay much attention to the sudden prominence accorded to the places in which the characters are located. But this, I will be arguing, is the critical factor for understanding what Beckett was striving to achieve in these texts. The places are quite literally inseparable from the bodies that inhabit them—and vice versa—as if, following Varela's principle of mutual specification, it is neither the place nor the body but the relationship between the two that generates meaning in these texts. And it is on the basis of this sudden promotion of the environing milieu—which can no longer be thought of as mere setting or décor but as an active participant in the drama—that a more general analysis of the significance of Beckettian place can be mounted.

Indeed, one of the most remarkable features of the closed place or refuge narratives is that they tend to be as much about the places as about the beings found in them. *All Strange Away, Imagination Dead Imagine, Ping, Lessness, The Lost Ones, The Cliff, Ghost Trio, . . . but the clouds . . .* , and *Ill Seen Ill Said*: all of these works treat their human figures as a function of the place in which they are located, as if it were the place that made the body possible. It is also important to note that these places are highly contrived, artificial enclosures that could never be confused with places we might encounter in the real world. Every element of the décor has a clear function—but only within the context of a thought structure. Is there a loo? Such questions are simply beside the point. Even *Endgame* still had a kitchen, but these late-period places are no longer places for *living*; they are, rather, places for dwelling, in the Heideggerian sense of the term, except that they have been *thought up* by an imagining consciousness (who is always present and active in the text) and have very explicitly been designed to *elicit* certain kinds of thought—to *push thought* in certain directions.

Unlike the wandering stories discussed earlier, which presume an inhuman environment that constrains the actions of the characters (following the objectivist principle), the refuge stories begin from the subjectivist principle, with an environment that is controlled by a narrating consciousness. The presumption is that the narrator can do whatever he wants with the environment so long as he obeys certain rules—rules that he has set up for himself. The main rules seem to be as follows:

a. "There is nothing but what is said" (*Fizzle 5, CSP* 236).
b. "Imagine what needed, no more" (*All Strange Away, CSP* 170).

   c. The purpose of the refuge is to have "done the image" (*The Image*, *CSP* 168).

In other words: (a) This is not one room in some larger world but a *microcosm*, a world unto itself; (b) it is a *simplified* version of the world, with all the richness but also distractions of the real world eliminated; and (c) it has been designed with a single purpose, which is to help the narrator "do" an image, which means to create an image that is able to induce the inhabitant of the room to fully see it, in the sense of acknowledging it and appropriating it for himself. It is this last function that is hardest to understand. What does it take to *do* an image? What makes this so difficult to do? And why is this so vital?[9] In my reading of these texts, the image is that which makes it possible to bridge the gap between inside and outside; in other words, to introduce an element of the outside world—the real world—into this chamber, which offers only an impoverished, phenomenal version of the real world. The image, then, is what makes it possible to overcome, however briefly and however partially, the barriers that keep Beckett's protagonists locked in the *entre-deux*, and to do so in a way that the reductive tendencies of the abstract space narratives and the wandering narratives could not.

We should note in this regard that the refuge narratives emphasize the sheltering, protective functions associated with home but also the restrictive constraints of entrapment and imprisonment. There is "no way in, none out," as we read in *All Strange Away* (*CSP* 169). These enclosed spaces might, then, be thought of as both homes and prisons. As microcosms, simplified versions of the cosmos, they are homes; but as impoverished versions of the world, they are prisons, like Plato's cave, offering no direct access to the noumenal realities of self and nature in all their fullness. They represent, in other words, what some have called the prison house of the mind. This is no doubt why they are so often compared to skulls and are sometimes said to be composed of a bone-like substance. In this sense, they must be considered stand-ins for the *entre-deux* of phenomenal reality, establishing the impoverished aspect of the phenomenal world as the only accessible level of reality.

The fact that there is little to no room for movement in these skull-like enclosures is significant. Although these places are presented quite explicitly as *imagined* places, they are just as constraining in their way as the hard realities of the stone corridor that determined the path of the wanderer in *Fizzle 1*. Custom designed by Beckett's narrators, their function is to stimulate certain kinds of thinking, which they do, in part, by molding the body inside into certain postures. Indeed, in some of these texts, the shape of the refuges is highly malleable and evolves significantly over the course of the piece, as if the narrator were experimenting, trying to find a configuration that would elicit the desired response.

In *All Strange Away*, for example, the cubical shape of the refuge is transformed, halfway through, into a domed rotunda, and the dimensions of the rotunda are progressively reduced. Although it is not initially clear why this happens, we gradually become aware that the narrator is homing in on the shape that will eventually generate the image he seeks. (A series of "Aha!"s in the text enables us to track his progress.) The central turning point in the drama—the climactic moment of recognition—comes with the narrator's realization that the rotunda is only half full. This is significant because it leads to the realization that there is room for two in the rotunda—a realization that leads, in the final "diagram" section of the text, to the revelation that the piece involves a kind of elegy or lament about a "faint memory of a lying side by side and fancy murmured dead" (*CSP* 181). The abstractness of the main refuge image is progressively intercut with this memory image and with cryptic evocations of the sense of nostalgia and loss that accompanies the image. Somehow, the scene before us—the refuge image—*induces* this memory image, perhaps because the newly rounded configuration of the enclosure forces the body inside into a kind of spooning position consistent with that evoked in the memory image. If so, then we could interpret this piece as a kind of nostalgic testament to past happiness. What has been lost? The most obvious answer is a loved one (or the love of that loved one). But also lost is the ability to ever have such a powerful experience again, for it is only in the world outside that such direct, unmediated experiences are to be had.

In a sense, the narrators of these pieces are playing God, but it is a God who has been cursed with creatures who have free will. The narrators have the ability to shape and reshape at will the milieus they control, but they cannot directly control the thoughts of the inhabitants. The only tools available to them for controlling the inhabitants are their manipulations of the environment.

Although the narrators of these texts are obsessed with the images to be produced, we do not learn much about the images themselves. We get few details about each image and no contextual information that would enable us to narrativize it. Indeed, rather than telling us about the image itself, the narrators tend to focus their attention on the process of doing what is necessary to generate a successful image. For this reason, it is possible to say that—despite the ambiguity of the images, the lack of narrative context, and the emphasis on description (which would seem to lead in the direction of stasis)—these are still eminently *narrative* texts: What we get is the narrative of the process of generating an image. These texts are, in this sense, metaphors for the imaginative process itself.

Most of the short prose refuge pieces play out like laboratory experiments, with small adjustments made to the enclosure in order to observe their effects on the bodies within. Other works, however, emphasize a different process for generating the image—a process that involves the activities of the resident. This is true of many of the dramatic works—especially media plays like *Words and Music*, *Ghost Trio*, and *. . . but the clouds . . .* In these works, the refuge is more like a temple than a laboratory. They present the refuge as a place of worship—a place where one goes to conjure the image—that requires something akin to a ceremony. In *. . . but the clouds . . .* and *Ghost Trio*, for example, we find a figure in a chamber who goes through a series of ritualized movements meant to result in the appearance of the desired image. In *. . . but the clouds . . .*, the figure is successful—the desired image fleetingly appears—but in *Ghost Trio*, two repetitions of the ritual fail to achieve the desired result. (Only a boy, reminiscent of Godot's message boy, makes an appearance at the door of the chamber, giving a negative shake of the head, which we take to mean that "she"—the desired female presence—will not appear.) We find a similar setup in two earlier radio plays, with similarly mixed results. In *Words and Music*, the combination of music and text orchestrated by the central figure (named Croak) succeeds in bringing forth the desired image, but a parallel alliance of music and speech is inconclusive in *Cascando*.[10]

Why is there success in some cases but not in others? To some extent, it seems, it is a matter of sheer luck and perseverance. (We are told in *. . . but the clouds . . .* that the success rate is on the order of one in a thousand.) But success also seems to have something to do with the relationship between the protagonist and his environing milieu. It is, in other words, at least in part, a matter of place. And the question is: why this might be? One thing is clear: the fact of *having* a concrete environing milieu greatly increases the chances of success. Indeed, if the protagonist-narrators of works like *Company*, *The Unnamable*, and *Cascando* fail, whereas those of *Words and Music* and *. . . but the clouds . . . .* succeed, it is because the latter are fully engaged in the wandering/shelter dynamic (wandering the backroads by day, seeking the image by night), while the former have become isolated in the featureless void discussed earlier. The very abstractness of the void (associated with solipsism) is the problem. What Beckett gradually came to realize in *The Unnamable*, and put to the test in texts like *Cascando* and *Company*, is that the "Beckettian reduction" the elimination of allegedly extraneous detail, was part of the problem—not the solution.

The reductive strategy having failed, Beckett begins, in phase two, looking for ways to reintroduce the world into the impoverished phenomenal reality of the interstitial chambers his characters now inhabit. It is a sign of Beckett's integrity—his commitment to the conditions of the epistemological framework he had accepted as inviolable—that he did not simply revert to a more or less realist mode of representation. Instead, he tried to work his way back toward a solid epistemological ground while maintaining the constraints imposed by his epistemological framework. These are not gratuitous or formalistic exercises but rather an attempt to solve a problem experimentally, making Beckett a kind of empiricist of the imagination.

The closed chambers, by virtue of their relative clarity and simplicity, may be more amenable to "the Cartesian mind" than the complexity of the outside world, as Elizabeth Barry has suggested (Barry 123). But their *purpose* is to enable access to images that will make it possible for the messy complexity of body, face, and subjecthood to come flooding into the chamber. They provide a place where the subjective and objective can meet, given the right confluence of circumstances. They are designed to focus our attention on the transition from one to the other, in a process that is not always successful but sometimes—perhaps surprisingly, given Beckett's insistent rhetoric of failure—does succeed. The detailed descriptions of a highly contrived environment, like the ritualized movements of the inhabitants of these chambers, seems meant as a way for the narrator to build up momentum—to edge closer and closer to the desired image until reaching an epiphanic breakthrough. But as Beckett wrote in *The Unnamable*, "it is easier to raise a shrine than bring the deity down to haunt it" (*Three Novels* 343). And so the rituals mostly fail.

These failures are due to an inability to bridge the gap between subject and object despite the fact that the narrator knows that it must be possible to do so and so feels obligated to continue trying. What Beckett's narrators seem to need, and what Beckett himself seems to be seeking, then, is a theory for understanding how this gap can be bridged in a more than haphazard, semiaccidental way. If his characters could find a way to systematically bridge that gap between subject and object, they might be able to find a way out of the impasse. But what, they need to know, is the key to making the image appear?

Recognition and the Rhetoric of Success

Given Beckett's insistent emphasis on the rhetoric of failure, it might seem surprising, but many of Beckett's phase-two texts end with strong, albeit ambiguous (and potentially ironic), gestures of satisfaction and success. Some examples:

- "Now it's done I've done the image" (*The Image*);

- "Aha!" (a refrain in *All Strange Away* that marks significant moments of progress in achieving the image);
- "Enough my old breasts feel his old hand" (*Enough*);
- "Know happiness" (the last words of *Ill Seen Ill Said*); and
- "Enough. Sudden enough . . . Said nohow on" (the last words of *Worstward Ho*).

What permits these narrators to declare victory in this way? How do they know when they've got it right? And conversely, how do the others know when they've failed, as in *Ping* (which ends with its figure "perhaps not alone" but still "imploring" [*CSP* 196]) or the bitter gesture of good riddance that brings *Imagination Dead Imagine* to a close: "Leave them there, sweating and icy, there is better elsewhere. No, life ends and no, there is nothing elsewhere, and no question now of ever finding again that white speck lost in whiteness, to see if they still lie still in the stress of that storm" (*CSP* 185). What, in other words, goes right in the former texts that does not in the latter?

In *Worstward Ho*, the event that makes it possible to bring the text to an end is the narrator's success in propelling the father-son couple off into the distance. This development enables him to say, "Enough. Sudden enough. Sudden all far. No move and sudden all far . . . Vasts apart. At bounds of boundless void . . . Nohow on. Said nohow on" (*Worstward Ho*, in *Nohow On* 116). The word "Enough" confirms the move toward successful closure, which is made possible by the "sudden" realization that "all [is] far," a realization that in its suddenness seems to have surprised even the narrator. This is, in other words, a moment of recognition. By pushing these figures as far away from himself as possible, to what he calls the "bounds of boundless void" (an aporetic distance that is only possible in imagination), he has somehow been able to achieve his goal—to say "nohow on." But why is it that this terrible distance is what makes success possible? Part of it seems to be simply that he has rid his landscape of any clearly discernible human presence (an ongoing ambition of Beckett's narrators): The two human figures have become an indistinct blur at the outer limits of the field of vision; they are no longer recognizably human—at least not to the eye. Another factor is that at this distance, the father-son couple appears to have merged into a single figure: "the as one plodding twain" (98). This is a kind of fusional epiphany: The two have been united as one. But there is an almost tragic irony at work here: The strategy that succeeds in uniting these two figures is to exile them to the outer limits of this landscape—to the bounds of a boundless void. Proximity between the two characters is possible but only at the cost of maximal distance between the narrator and his characters. Their gain is his loss. If we consider the potential autobiographical resonance of this image—as, for example, a gesture of mourning for the long-dead father with whom the young Sam would go on extended rambles—the painful irony of this success becomes clear.[11] This is one of many moments in which Beckett's efforts to "worsen" reveal hidden emotional depth that is all the more powerful for the many layers of resistance that had to be fought through in order to arrive there.

Ill Seen Ill Said culminates in a related moment of closure—but one that depends on an effect of ultimate proximity rather than distance: seeing the beloved face of the dead mother figure in extreme close-up, looking into her eyes as she expires, as if the narrator were literally and figuratively "seeing the image to death." This resolution might seem to be diametrically opposed to the dénouement by distantiation of *Worstward Ho*, but actually, the function of ultimate proximity and ultimate distance is much the same. Both have the effect of achieving the image by pushing it to one of its limits (proximity/distance) and both result in an unexpected moment of recognition—a realization. And once we notice that the last words of *Ill Seen Ill Said* incorporate a terrible pun (the final words, "know happiness" could also be read as "no happiness"), the poignancy of this image of looking into someone's eyes as they lose the ability to look back resonates all the more strongly. It is as if the narrator were only able to establish contact with the mother figure at the moment of losing her. It is this kind of painful realization that makes it possible to say "I've done the image," thereby generating the brief flash of emotion that pierces a small and quickly repaired hole in the barrier that separates the inside of the closed place from the outside of the real world.

This rule could be applied, I believe, to all cases of success in phase-two Beckett. But what exactly does it have to do with recognition? Here, a couple of negative examples can help us. In *The Unnamable*, the narrator finds that he is unable to say "that is mine." That is to say, he is able to relate a number of stories he has heard—and those stories concern people, places, things, and events that would seem to belong to his past history—but he is unable to acknowledge them as his own. We find a similar problem in *Company*, in which a voice comes to a body in the dark, telling stories of someone's past. If the body could say "yes, I remember," recognizing these stories as his own, the quest for companionship would be complete. But once again, this is something he apparently cannot do. The kind of recognition that concerns us here, in other words, involves a moment of *convergence* between present self and past self, speaker and listener, voice and body, subject and object. Some gesture of assent is required from the listener for the narrator to know that the required level of recognition has been achieved. Both *Company* and *The Unnamable* fail in this respect: No convergence takes place in either of these texts. But we do get this convergence, momentarily, in the successful examples mentioned earlier.

This is where things start to get interesting for our theory of Beckettian place, because there are two main elements that have the ability to bring the outside of the real world into the impoverished inside of phenomenal reality: the body and memory. And they are related to each other through place.

Ineliminability

What has made such attempts to move back outwards possible? I believe that it may be an insight akin to the one that Varela promotes: that the groundlessness of the *entre-deux*—that of the middle voice and phenomenal experience—is not the problem but the solution. Far from being something that needs to be treated with the existential dread of radical doubt, it can be embraced as the starting point for a new kind of nonfoundational (pragmatic) thought that is robust enough to overcome even the most demanding forms of Cartesian or postmodern doubt. The advance here is that these places are constructed from elements that Beckett, despite his best (worst?) efforts to reduce all to nothing, has found to be ineliminable. What Beckett discovers through the process of elimination that defined the first part of his career is that there are elements of reality (in the strong sense of pieces of "the world out there") which, although not directly accessible, are nonetheless able to impose themselves with such force that they overcome all attempts to apply the principle of radical doubt to them. For Beckett, there are exactly four such elements: voices, images, bodily sensations, and certain kinds of memories. What all of these elements have in common is an ability to impose themselves with the force and clarity of Descartes's cogito. A few words about these four ineliminable truths are in order here.

Voices and images. We have already spent quite a bit of time exploring the presence of voices and images. These are the two elemental building blocks of the Beckettian universe. In a sense, they are unproblematic. Just as Descartes could not doubt the existence of his own thoughts, Beckett's characters cannot doubt the existence of the voices they hear. The *problem* is that they cannot be sure of the provenance of the voices. They hear them in their heads but are unable to verify that they originate there or are about them. For similar reasons, the reality of the visual images is incontrovertible. But it is not clear where they come from and whom they concern. What these characters *need* (in order to reestablish contact with the world outside) is some kind of proof of a link between the voices/images and the world they purport to represent. This is where the body and memory come into the picture.

The body. Try as even his most skeptical narrators might, bodily sensations like pain and the shock of impact overcome any doubts they might have about their reality. This point was already being made in the wandering narratives examined earlier. There, even the rather obtuse, disoriented protagonists of *How It Is* and *Fizzle 1* cannot deny that their environing milieu is pushing them in certain directions. They have the bruises to prove it. This is something like Dr. Johnson's kick-the-stone refutation of Bishop Berkeley's argument for solipsism: Although our perceptions may not tell us everything we want to know about the "true nature" of the rock (if there even is such a thing as "the truth" of a rock), they do tell us everything we need to know about the brut fact of its existence. In Beckett's later closed place narratives, the behavioristic brutality of *How It Is* and *Fizzle 1* is transformed into something gentler but just as persuasive. The reality of the body and its imbrication in its milieu is guaranteed by sensations as simple as the pressure of the ground on one's hindquarters or the curved walls that force one to bend the knees and round the back. Moreover, it is well known that such sensations have an impact on the direction of one's thoughts, whether unconscious (as in the Proustian madeleine or the evocative bodily configurations of *All Strange Away*) or conscious (as in certain meditative practices that encourage focusing on bodily sensations as a calming and awareness-heightening technique).

Memory. There is a special class of memories that, like physical pain and other bodily sensations, has the ability to overcome the doubts of even the most skeptical of attitudes. This is the class of memories that have such a powerful affective charge that they cannot be set aside. This class includes traumatic memories of all kinds—but also other particularly intense kinds of memories: memories of love and extreme joy, for example. Like the body, such memories link a subject to the outside world, making solipsism untenable: they have a *persistence* and an *affective force* that defies the transitory nature of consciousness in the present tense. There is a wonderful illustration of this in an important passage from *Ill Seen Ill Said*:

> If only she could be pure figment. Unalloyed. This old so dying woman. So dead. In the madhouse of the skull and nowhere else. Where no more precautions to be taken. No precautions possible . . . How simple all then. If only all could be pure figment. Neither be nor been nor by any shift to be. Gently gently. On. Careful. (*Ill Seen Ill Said, Nohow On* 58)

Because this memory involves the loss of a beloved woman, it is easy to understand why it would be preferable for such a memory to be "pure figment." Imaginary loss is less painful than actual loss. But it so happens that it is *impossible* to evacuate the affective power of this memory image. Because of the sharp pang of mourning that accompanies it, there is no way to deny the fact that this memory "belongs" to the narrator. In no case can this be construed as a mere creation of the imagination or as something overheard. The shock of recognition that the narrator feels here suggests that he is, in a very real sense, suffering the (past) loss of this woman in the present tense. (This is part of the specificity of trauma and mourning: The past invades the present and cannot be dismissed.) The sense of loss is so great that the suffering strikes with the force of a direct perception. This, it seems, is what determines the difference between the outcomes of *Ill Seen Ill Said* and *Company*. *Company* had made use of a similar play with memory images but avoided exploration of the affective charge of those memories. What *Ill Seen Ill Said* shows is that it is the *unbearable* memory that succeeds in breaking down the barriers of radical doubt— the kind of memory that one would gladly dispense with, if only that were possible.[12]

The narrator goes on to draw the necessary epistemological conclusion from this observation: If this pain is real, then the rest (or at least some of the rest) must be real, too. This is implied in the movement from "If only she could be pure figment" to "If only *all* could be pure figment." This realization complicates things enormously for him. If he were able to somehow eliminate the affect associated with this image, he could remain in the comfortable prison of his solipsism; he would be able to take a certain philosophical distance from this image of loss. But his inability to dismiss the image proves that it is his own loss that is at issue. In this sense, traumatic memories are like pressure on the buttocks: they are the ineliminable remainders of the outside world that unequivocally demolish solipsism and make the ironic distance of nihilism impossible. Indeed, a large part of the affective power of this passage comes from the realization that the narrator would be willing to sacrifice everything—the entire world—to his solipsism in order to avoid this pain. That is love.

It should also be noted that memory images can do something that tactile impressions cannot: provide a link between the figure in the refuge and the world outside the refuge. If such memories exist, and if they involve other places and other times, then the universe extends beyond the immediately perceptible place and the present moment. Bodily sensation had already guaranteed the link between the experimental subject and the immediate world of sensations, but ineliminable memory images such as these are required to extend that world temporally and spatially into the past and beyond the immediately perceptible environing milieu.

Such considerations highlight the epistemological insights afforded by the memory images that become such a central preoccupation of the late Beckett. The characters of the early Beckett had tended to be focused on the present moment, self-pursuit, and the future. But the late Beckett is much more focused on the recovery of memory images—to the point that they become his central theme, largely displacing the monomaniacal pursuit of self that dominated his work through *The Unnamable* and *Texts for Nothing*. The search for a way back out replaces the search for self. *Krapp's Last Tape* provides an interesting—and, very likely, autobiographical—account of the period of transition between these two phases, as Krapp is riven by nostalgia for the path not chosen. (Like Beckett, he chose the literary life and self-pursuit over more placid contentments and must now live with the solitary consequences of that choice, even as he has lost faith in the quest as he originally conceived it.)

"How it is, in my home"

This acceptance of the image as one's own through the power of memory makes it possible to build a momentary bridge between the middle voice of consciousness and the world "out there." Instead of trying to say *who I am*, which was the goal in *The Unnamable*, or to prove that the narrated body and the narrating consciousness are one and the same, as in *Company*, the narrators of *Ill Seen Ill Said* and *Worstward Ho* give up trying to define human subjectivity as something that would be *extractable* from its milieu. Instead, they explore the interactions of a consciousness and a milieu. They seek to say *"comment c'est chez moi"* or "how it is, in my home" (*Three Novels* 399).[13] This is a more humble but achievable—and therefore more powerful—strategy. What is the advantage of this new approach? By emphasizing the interrelations between each of the elements in the representation (body, voice, milieu; subject, object, context), rather than trying to pin down the precise location of the borders between them, Beckett is able to defer the ontological questions that had so stymied him before. Gone is the need to try to say "what is mine" and what is not, as the *Unnamable* had sought to do. Saying "how it is" rather than "what is mine" makes it possible to focus on the empirical task of describing a situation without making any unwarranted assumptions about the "true nature" of things (i.e., what belongs to whom). The new goal is to present the relationship between place, body, voice, and memory as a whole, emphasizing the mutually specifying, as Varela would say, nature of the relations between them. This approach enables his narrators to limit themselves to empirical questions, questions that require careful observation rather than making assertions reliant on *a priori* categories like subject and object. The various elements compose a single "thought system," and the question of what belongs to whom is deferred. Even with the limitations of phenomenal consciousness, this is an achievable task.

Jacques Lacan famously suggested replacing the Cartesian "I think" with the more ambiguous "there is thought" (*ça pense*, which might also be translated as "*id* thinks"). Similarly, Beckett's protagonists begin to realize that even if they cannot determine the source of the voices they hear, the fact that there is thought "in the system" and that they can describe the system is enough to get them where they need to go. There is no longer any need to posit the existence of some foundational principle—like an isolatable metaphysical ego or an outside world that exists independently of the observing subject.

Given all this, we might think of Beckett as an empiricist of the imagination. To be sure, the images that we get are not empirical in the sense that can be directly observed in nature. They are imaginary constructions, but they belong to the scene of the narrator, whose job henceforth is emphatically not to allot certain elements to the world in here and others to the world out there but, rather, to report on the circulation of meaning within the system that he is able to observe, which is located on the interstitial stage of place, conceived in phenomenological terms, at the intersection between a mind, a body, and a milieu.

Beckett, Distributed Consciousness, and Situational Knowledge

The way Beckett's bodies interact with their environments and the narrative consciousness that controls them both meshes with Varela's insistence on the distributed nature of consciousness, whose reach extends out from the brain, through the sensorimotor apparatus, and into the environing milieu via the mutually specifying interactions that its evolutionary history has made possible. It seems unlikely that Beckett thought of his work in anything resembling these terms, but if my previous analyses hold true, it seems entirely plausible that Beckett was in fact moving in this direction. Phase-two Beckett progressively abandons the rationalist, Cartesian insistence on foundational knowledge and gradually embraces—via the grudging recognition of the body and memory (especially pain and trauma) as ineliminable—what *The Embodied Mind* authors call situational knowledge. I would like to conclude, then, with a brief word about some of the implications of this shift—in particular, the change that this represents in terms of what counts as knowledge.

When it comes to the question of radical doubt, most of us make the pragmatic decision to avoid getting too preoccupied with its antinomies. Common sense, received wisdom, and custom seem to serve us pretty well in our day-to-day lives, making such questions moot. From a philosophical or scientific standpoint, however, it would be unethical to simply sweep such doubts under the rug—especially since so many scientific findings run contrary to subjective experience (i.e., that the Earth revolves around the sun). Intellectual integrity demands that we find a grounding principle for our beliefs. Without such a ground, or so it seems, we have no way to test the veracity of our beliefs and the wisdom of our practices. But if neither objectivist nor subjectivist accounts of reality have sufficed to overcome our doubts, where are we to look for such a ground?

The authors of *The Embodied Mind* respond to this question by rejecting its premises. They propose that we abandon altogether the demand for a universally valid ontological foundation of the subject-or-object variety. Indeed, they make of groundlessness and the epistemological *entre-deux* a kind of virtue. The only grounding authority they invoke—far from relying on the existence of some timeless ontological substance or some unvarying principle of truth—is historical, context-dependent, contingent, and highly variable. This is the principle of natural selection. As for most contemporary cognitive scientists, the principle of natural selection has become for the authors of *The Embodied Mind* the foundation on which rest all arguments about our ability to form reliable beliefs about the world and act appropriately. As Steven Pinker explains, "Causal and inferential roles tend to be in sync because natural selection designed both our perceptual systems and our inference modules to work accurately, most of the time, in this world" (81).

Of course, the kinds of mental traits and cognitive skills that are perpetuated via natural selection need only be good enough for survival; they do not need to be perfect. In other words, natural selection does not provide some kind of absolute guarantee against mistaken beliefs of the kind that philosophers have traditionally sought. This may help to understand why the philosophical demand for foundational principles and absolute certainty has led to the many paradoxes and antinomies that give rise to Cartesian anxiety in the first place. There is a tendency for radical doubters to jump from the observation that we are mistaken about many things to the conclusion that we can't be sure of anything. But the evolutionary principle of natural selection can reassure us on this point, reminding us that situational knowledge (knowing how to find food, get out of a scrape, attract a mate) is more important, evolutionarily speaking, than the kinds of absolute certainty, logical rigor, and clear and simple ideas to which philosophy has traditionally aspired. This emphasis on situational knowledge, which Pinker, following John Tooby and Leda Cosmides, calls "ecological rationality," is subject specific and context dependent. Ecological rationality does not have to satisfy the philosophical demand for universal validity, because "our brains were shaped for fitness, not for truth. Sometimes the truth is adaptive, but sometimes it is not" (Pinker, 304–5). Indeed, it may be that the kinds of thinking that philosophers like to do is somewhat of an aberration—an inessential by-product of natural selection or, to borrow Stephen Jay Gould's widely cited metaphor, a spandrel. As Pinker puts it, with characteristic irreverence, "Natural selection . . . did not shape us to earn good grades in science class or to publish in refereed journals. It shaped us to master the local environment" (302).

This does not mean that the philosophical search for truth, rigor, and certainty is somehow misguided but, rather, that the search for first principles and foundational certainties will always come up short and that the demand for absolute certainty will always result in aporias of one kind or another. If the best guarantee of our ability to understand the world around us is evolutionary, and evolutionary know-how is situational, context dependent, and distributed, then any search for context-independent (i.e., universal) truths will eventually lead to an impasse of the kind that Beckett found himself in. What Beckett seems to have intuited in the second half of his career is that this kind of situational knowledge was, in fact, the missing link in his search for a way out of the dualist impasse. And this, I believe, is what explains his fascination with the refuges and shelters of his late period. By providing him with an image of the distributed nature of consciousness—consciousness as engaged in a symbiotic relationship with the environment in which it finds itself—these refuges helped him to start thinking of place as a key for resolving the paradoxes of the dualist dilemma.

Conclusion: Beckett's Place in the Postfoundational Pantheon

What does Beckett's work contribute to the overarching argument of this book, which emphasizes the contributions of literature to the emergence of new places and place types that fall between established categories? The answer to this question is not immediately obvious. Beckett shows little concern for specific places, preferring instead to construct artificial abodes or wander through minimally realized landscapes. His contribution is on a different level: it participates in the more general rehabilitation of place carried out by the humanist geographers and philosophers of place studied in Chapter 1. It is, then, his perhaps belated but hard-earned return to place, motivated by his arduous struggle with the aporias of dualism, that makes his work significant for the study of geographical emergence. Well before Casey, Malpas, Varela, and the humanist geographers, Beckett's work helped make clear to those who doubted it that the messiness of the world is not a distraction from the search for "the shape of being" but a necessary part of it.

Beckett's struggle with place would perhaps not have been necessary were it not for the radical contestation of the humanist tradition that was being carried out by French thinkers in the years following World War II. Beckett shares with thinkers like Blanchot, Derrida, Lacan, Baudrillard, and Deleuze a belief in the importance of learning how to think without relying on the *a priori* epistemological principles of the humanist and rationalist traditions. Ultimately, however, Beckett rejects the flight into formalism and antihumanism that came to characterize so much of the Parisian avant-gardist literature of the postwar decades, as the still largely phenomenological outlook that characterized the *nouveau roman* in the 1950s evolved into the textualism of the *Tel Quel* group in the 1970s and ultimately self-destructed in the early 1980s. What enabled Beckett to escape from this formalist implosion was his refusal to accept the nihilistic conclusions that thinkers like Baudrillard and Jean Ricardou were drawing from the apparent inaccessibility of any foundational truths. Even though Beckett accepted many of the premises on which the postmodern deconstructions of presence, subjectivity, and knowability were based, and even though his literary works provide some of the most vivid and moving illustrations of those themes, Beckett always maintained the imperative to keep searching for meaning, with all available tools. This is the ethical imperative of Beckett's work, and it is this ethical imperative that guarantees the lasting importance of his *oeuvre* and differentiates it from the formalist noodling of so many of his contemporaries in the Parisian postwar avant-gardes.

Beckett's struggle to come to grips with place makes it clear that he never accepted the linguistic fundamentalism and antihumanism that were so fashionable at the time. This does not mean, however, that Beckett simply sought to find a way back toward the comforting foundational truths of humanism in the Enlightenment tradition. What he sought, rather, was a way to learn how to think without relying on *a priori* foundations. In that sense, Beckett's work meshes with the poststructuralist revolution of the 1960s and 1970s. And for that reason, Beckett's work can help us to understand what is worth retaining from that revolution. Of course, the postmodern, poststructuralist branch of French thought was never reducible to textualism, formalism, or antihumanism, despite its willingness to take seriously such ideas. In the following chapter, then, I will be using my study of place in Beckett as a springboard for understanding the contribution that the thinkers grouped under the poststructuralist heading have made to our understanding of place. This will entail a shift from the psychological, phenomenological emphasis of the two preceding chapters to the social level of power and discourse. Maurice Blanchot's essay, "The Conquest of Space," will help us to make this shift.

Part II

The Social Production of Place

Poststructuralism and the Resistance to Place

The Continental Divide: Space, Place, and the Poststructuralist Countersciences

The second major strand in contemporary thinking on place that we will be considering comes out of the French poststructuralist movement, which has its origins in the structural anthropology of Lévi-Strauss and the linguistics of Saussure and is also heavily influenced by the psychoanalytic emphasis on the unconscious determinants of conscious behavior and the Marxist theory of mediation. Of particular interest for my purposes are the spatial analyses of Michel Foucault and Michel de Certeau and of two of their most important fellow travelers, Maurice Blanchot and Henri Lefebvre. As spatial thinkers, they all share an interest in what has, in the wake of Henri Lefebvre's work, come to be called "the social production of space" (Soja, *Postmodern Geographies* 16 and passim). That is to say, they are less interested in phenomenological issues involving the subjective experience of place (often dismissed as epiphenomenal) than in the ways that our spatial practices are simultaneously constitutive of and conditioned by the network of social forces that structure individual existences. They tend to emphasize the usually unperceived power structures and discursive networks that shape our understanding of the world around us and to examine them in terms of ideology, political economy, language, and other social institutions. Science itself is subject to their social critique—a critique that emphasizes the social norms and expectations that govern scientific research and shape the formulation of its laws, making them much more unstable than we are usually led to believe. They are less interested in nature (even human nature) than in discursive power as a kind of second nature or supernature, the source of behavioral determinants that come to us so deeply embedded within the institutions into which we are born that they seem entirely natural to us—even, and perhaps especially, when they are oppressive.

To present the poststructuralists as thinkers of place and to consider them alongside the phenomenologically oriented, geographically minded thinkers studied so far might seem counterintuitive—even wrongheaded. For one thing, all of these thinkers have tended either to avoid or denigrate the term place (*lieu*) itself, preferring instead to conduct their analyses in terms of space (*espace*). This is true of many of the most important thinkers of this generation, despite the fact that they often make Aristotle's term for place (*topos*) a centerpiece of their arguments, as in Foucault's concept of "heterotopia" or Bachelard's emphasis on *topophilia* and *topanalyse*. Place, for them, is at best a secondary term, either left unmarked and untheorized or used (as in Certeau's essays on "spatial practices") as a term of opprobrium, the name for a mode of spatial organization that must be overcome. Even Bachelard, whose work is closest in spirit to the phenomenological orientation of the thinkers studied in Chapter 1, decided to title his work *The Poetics of Space* (*Poétique de l'espace*) and avoid using the term *lieu* in any theoretical sense.

This difference is clearly more than just a terminological quibble, then. It has important consequences for their approach to the subject of this book and may, in some ways, pose a threat to it, calling into question the very legitimacy of the concept of place. But before dealing with that question, we need to understand how to explain the poststructuralist preference for space over place.

What the radical critique of the poststructuralists has in common with the phenomenological/humanist discourse on place is the experience of radical doubt. For the humanists, the central problem is the problem of Cartesian anxiety, with the imperfect mediations of the body, perception, and cognitive abilities as the primary focus of interest. (Can we trust our senses? How can we test and verify our beliefs? What is the material infrastructure on which consciousness is founded?) For the poststructuralists, on the other hand, the central problems are social in nature and involve problems of discursive doubt and ideological uncertainty. (Can we believe what we've been told? Who controls the discursive networks within which we operate? On what level of our media-saturated society is the real to be situated?) And if phenomenology as a discipline is committed to overcoming the problem of radical doubt by "bracketing" or withholding judgment on the actual ontological status of our beliefs, the poststructuralist emphasis on social determinations implies a symmetrically related move, treating our beliefs as the result of the play of signs within a system. As Entrikin, himself a phenomenologically inclined geographer, says of the poststructuralist "retheorization of spatiality":

> Such a retheorization raises questions similar to those found in previous attempts to theorize the relations of humans to the natural world. Questions of necessity and contingency, objectivity and subjectivity remain, but they are no longer phrased in terms of the natural production of places and natural law. Rather, the present concern is with the social production of space and place, which has been theorized in terms of a mix of structural forces of political economy and human agency. (Entrikin 45)

This emphasis on structural forces has important implications for the way human subjectivity is understood. On this point Marc Brosseau quotes I. G. Cook, who aptly summarizes the central consequence of this shift in the individual-society relationship: "Both approaches are of course concerned with the interactions between the individual and society, but humanist geographers consider consciousness to be the result of the individual's interpretation of the world, flowing outward to society, while radical geographers consider it to be the result of the individual's position in society, flowing inward to the individual" (Cook qtd. in Brosseau, *Des romans géographes* 43, my translation).

Tellingly, the French poststructuralist critique of place takes place at roughly the same time as the humanist geographers' reassertion of the importance of place. Lefebvre published his *La production de l'espace* in 1974, the same year as Tuan's first humanistic interventions; one year later, Foucault published his celebrated analyses of classical spatial practice in *Surveiller et punir* (1975); and Certeau published his *L'invention du quotidien* four years later, in 1980, just as the humanist geography movement was shifting into high gear.[1] In other words, at the same time that a group of American geographers was contesting the scientist assumptions of their field and reintroducing the importance of intimate experience by way of a turn toward "continental philosophy" (equated with phenomenology), French theory was moving away from phenomenology and toward a new science: a metascience or counterscience whose goal was to subject all authoritative discursive structures—including (and especially) scientific ones—to a deconstructive analysis. Although moving in opposite directions, both movements were reacting against the same thing: technological modernity, with what they saw as its exaggerated faith in science and scientific progress. The consequences of this difference in direction, however, are far-reaching.

The poststructuralist preference for space over place flows directly from this difference in direction. One non-negligible feature of the term "space" is its scientific pedigree, which, as we've seen, was definitively assured by Descartes and Newton and implies a de-centering of the human perspective. (Thomas Nagel famously called this scientific objectifying impulse the "view from nowhere.") The poststructuralists, of course, like the humanist geographers, were highly skeptical of the putative neutrality or objectivity of scientific discourse. But rather than trying to achieve some kind of equilibrium between objectivity and subjectivity (as we saw Entrikin do in Chapter 1), the poststructuralists decided to up the ante: They saw themselves as participating in a kind of Copernican revolution that would show the putatively objective perspectives of scientific discourse to be themselves localized, parochial points of view in need of relativization. Rather than critiquing the sciences for their excessive distance from the human experience of place, then, they criticized them for their excessive reliance on humanist notions of the self, which were considered to be a mythical construct of the Enlightenment tradition.[2]

The concept of space, as opposed to place, comes to play a significant role in this critique of the western humanistic tradition. As Jan Baetens has written, à propos of Marie-Claire Ropars-Wuilleumier's *Ecrire l'espace*:

> Space, which admittedly must be thought of at first in terms of place, should in no way be conceived as simply a property or expansion of the concept of place. *Space is on the contrary that which (to put it roughly) "deconstructs" place.* Space is a task, a relation, a kind of (why not?) montage, having the effect of revealing that which cannot be captured by place and showing, as a pure negativity, that no place can coincide with itself, neither in itself nor through the perspective of an observer. (Baetens, emphasis added)

So what precisely is it that lends this deconstructive edge to the concept of space? Or, at least, why was space taken by the poststructuralists to have this edge? A perhaps minor but nonetheless telling essay by Maurice Blanchot offers us a useful point of entry into this question.

Maurice Blanchot's Conquest of Space

Maurice Blanchot's 1961 essay, "The Conquest of Space," was occasioned by Yuri Gagarin's first flight into space and is first of all a celebration of that achievement. But in typical Blanchotian fashion, the essay quickly morphs into something more ambitious, giving rise to an implicit critique of the Heideggerian theory of dwelling that flows into the broader theoretical arguments outlined in his magnum opus, *L'espace littéraire* (literary space). The article begins thus: "Man does not want to leave his own place. He says that technology is dangerous, that it detracts from our relationship with the world, that true civilizations are those of a stable nature, that the nomad is incapable of acquisition. Who is this man?"[3] To this question, those in the know might be tempted to answer: Heidegger. With its insistence on place, rootedness, and the critique of technology, this text seems to be engaging in a thinly veiled polemic with Heidegger's 1951 essay, "Building, Dwelling, Thinking." But if Blanchot takes up the same key terms as Heidegger, his use of those terms moves him in a different direction. Although the sedentary, place-bound, technophobic man described in this passage resembles Heidegger's, and although he is identified with "each one of us," Blanchot adds the immediate qualification that it is each one of us "at the times we give in to lethargy" (269). The sedentary place dweller is considered to embody a universal element of human nature—but a negative one. The rest of the essay builds on this point—the attachment to place as a sign of weakness—arguing for the need to wean ourselves off of the atavistic reliance on being rooted in a given place and to embrace "the abstract distance of pure science," associated with "a space which has no being or nature but is the pure and simple reality of a measurable (almost) void" (268).

This abstractive ideal, needless to say, is antithetical to the phenomenological view, as exemplified by Heideggerian dwelling, and also calls into question, for related reasons, both Casey's injunction to get back into place and Malpas's claim that place is that which makes thought (and pretty much everything else) possible. For Blanchot, the man defined by his attachment to place is associated with a whole series of negative, archaic characteristics, including superstition ("the man who . . . is eternally seduced by paganism") and territorial avidity ("the possessive man who wants to have land and who has land, who knows how to take possession and how to cling on") and even, perhaps, colonial rapaciousness ("who desires above all . . . to take over the earth"). This archaic side of the human personality, "eternally encrusted in his tradition, in his truth, in his history," is profoundly territorial: he "does not want the sacred seats of his beautiful landscape and great past to be attacked" (269–70).

For Blanchot, Gagarin's voyage is important precisely because it literalizes the struggle to free oneself of all such place-bound illusions. It foreshadows "the breaking down of all sense of belonging and the questioning of place, in all places" (270). Blanchot's description of Gagarin's escape from the place world prefigures contemporary debates over the geocultural significance of globalization, linking it to the technology of travel (space flight) and telecommunications. Contrary to Heidegger and the critics of globalizing modernity, however, Blanchot sees this break with place as a good and desirable thing. The five closing words of the essay assert "that the truth is nomadic" (271), foreshadowing an important Deleuzian theme and emphasizing the extent to which Blanchot believes that the attachment to place is something that must be overcome.

Noting the patriotic atavism of Khrushchev's welcome-home speech (which emphasizes that Gagarin has returned to his "homeland"), Blanchot realizes that the threat to our traditional sense of place represented by Gagarin's mission was not appreciated—that it was used, instead, in a way that simply "gave grounds to the Russians to inhabit Russian land even more staunchly." Indeed, Blanchot suspects that this attempt to cling to traditional territorial discourse may be too firmly entrenched in us to be overcome: "the superstition about place cannot be eradicated in us except by a momentary abandonment to some utopia of non-place" (270). The only alternative to place (as territory or as homeland) is nonplace, which is something that is utopian in every sense of the word. It is no doubt for this reason that Blanchot is so interested in Khrushchev's apparently ramblingly incoherent and symptomatically nationalistic welcome-home speech, which Blanchot reads as an emblem of the human condition:

> Something disturbs us and dismays us in that rambling: it does not stop, it must never stop; the slightest break in the noise would already mean the everlasting void; any gap or interruption introduces something which is much more than death, which is the nothingness outside entered into discourse. (270)

Devotees of Blanchot will recognize in this gloss on Khrushchev's speech an iteration of one of Blanchot's pet themes: that of the "murmur" or "*entretien infini*"—that discursive middle ground or no-man's-land between what it is possible to say and what must be said, which constitutes for him *l'espace littéraire*, the (true) space of literature.[4] Curiously though, Blanchot is criticizing Khrushchev's speech in the same terms he has used to *praise* Kafka, Beckett, and other modern masters. Or, more accurately, he is using Khrushchev's speech to highlight what has become the modern predicament: the loss of assurance in our traditional beliefs (those *common places* on which our arguments have traditionally been founded), which leaves us wandering in a metaphysical wilderness. Paradoxically, the rise of rationalism and the scientific progress that has accompanied it has entailed a loss of assurance—a loss of the common ground on which we have traditionally stood. And Blanchot's point is that we must learn to embrace this condition, to live with it, and to push it to its logical conclusion. It is in this sense that Blanchot's work can be considered postmodern.

This new focus on the significance of Khrushchev's speech marks a major shift in the tone and subject matter of the article. He soon leaves behind any consideration of space in its literal sense (i.e., as the "outer space" explored by Gagarin) and moves into the domain of discursive space, *l'espace littéraire*. But this, as Hélène Frichot has remarked, "is no space at all," since discursive space bears a strictly metaphorical relation to physical space 172). Suddenly, it seems, the occasional event for this essay—Gagarin's flight—and the reflection on the attachment to place to which it gave rise have been left behind. They have become metaphors for a very different kind of argument about modern (or postmodern) discourse as a nonfoundational or ungrounded discourse. The broader perspective of the spaceman—whose ability to take in the entirety of the planet Earth in one glance makes the old-fashioned attachment to a homeland seem quaint— has become a metaphor for the broader perspective of modern or postmodern discursive strategies.

It is here that Blanchot's work meets up with that of the poststructuralist thinkers who wrote in his wake. Like him, they believe in the necessity of developing a mode of discourse able to radically relativize our commonplace assumptions about the world. Indeed, the loss of place symbolized by Gagarin, with the gain in perspective that is symbolized by the move to a deep space or deeply spatial perspective is not far from the kinds of perspectives made possible by the "death of man" prophesied by Michel Foucault. In a sense, the place that is lost to man in Blanchot's text is precisely the place *of* man in Foucault. Bruno Bosteels has described this link between man and space in terms of Marc Augé's concept of the "nonplace":

> For the author of *The Order of Things: An Archaeology of the Human Sciences*, first published in 1966, the nonplace is first and foremost the vacancy or blank left gaping at the heart of modern anthropologism with the announced "death of man." Both his archaeological and his genealogical work are written from the impossible point of view of such a void or empty center in the midst of the well-entrenched fields of the human sciences. In the absence of a stable universal subject, capable of taking its own speaking, living, and exchanging as its very object of reflection, the humanities are literally left without a ground to stand on. Foucault's strength in other words derives from his capacity to reveal the extent to which a truly an-archic stance, one that is ungrounded or nonfoundational, emerges as the logical outcome of the trajectory of modern humanism itself. (Bosteels 117)

This "ungrounded or nonfoundational" stance is that of Blanchot's astronaut, who literally has no ground under his feet and who is no longer bound by the singular but atavistic attachment to place. As his perspective broadens to the point of encompassing the whole Earth in a glance, the influence of its social and psychological laws, like that of gravity, has been reduced to the vanishing point. The astronaut (cosmonaut) is freed from these constraints but is also subject to the terror of having no fixed orientation points.

These, then, are the key points to retain from Blanchot's analysis of the space/place relation. First, the affective bonds that have traditionally been taken to tie people to the places they inhabit must be held in suspicion; such affections actually express an archaic, superstitious bond that must be superseded if humankind is to be able to transcend its atavistic territorial urges. Second, this severing of the bond between people and place will make possible a new spatial science—one that will reframe the old ways of understanding human spatial existence as local subsets of universal laws that had not been fully understood. (This is the Copernican dimension of the revolution in question.) Third, this new outlook will require a fundamental change in the way we understand humanity itself; it will require a shift to a posthumanist or antihumanist point of view that radically relativizes the phenomenological perspective of individuals—perhaps revealing them as epiphenomenal—and makes necessary a new nomadic science that attempts to understand human subjectivity from the outside, as a confluence of impersonal forces.

This is a powerful set of conclusions, the consequences of which I will be attempting to work through in the following sections of this chapter. Before proceeding with that analysis, however, it is important to note that, from the point of view of my study, which puts the emphasis on place (and space) as a *geographical* category, something troubling happens in Blanchot's essay. It is not the privileging of space over place that is troubling (on the contrary, it provides a quite invigorating way to test the concept of place and put it in perspective) but rather the unannounced rhetorical sleight of hand that enables Blanchot to shift from the domain of *actual* space and place (i.e., outer space and the question of the homeland) to the *metaphorical* domain of discursive space (i.e., "the nothingness outside entered into discourse"). Having begun with an argument about geographical identity and its limits, Blanchot veers suddenly, but surreptitiously, toward a much more abstract epistemological and metaphysical question concerning the nature of truth and meaning. The initial opposition between place and space involved quite literal concerns about territoriality and the attachment to place, but this shift to discursive space seems to pull us far away from any such concerns.

This is, in many ways, a typical move in poststructuralist studies of spatiality. Foucault, as we will see momentarily, does this regularly. So do literary critics, like Joseph Frank, who were influenced by structuralist thinking.[5] And perhaps, indeed, we all do. But for the purposes of this book, it is important to try to keep the focus on space in its geographical sense and to treat the recurrent tendency to slide from literal space to metaphorical space as a problem that needs to be examined. At the very least, we need to remain aware of this tendency so that we can guard against confusion between physical space and its metaphorical extensions.[6] But we also need to consider the implications of this tendency: What exactly is the relationship between spatial configurations of the literal varieties studied by geographers and geometers and the metaphorical spaces designated by such terms as cognitive mapping, rhetorical topoï, discursive spaces, and structuralist grids? Michel Foucault's essay "Of Other Spaces" carries out this kind of shift in a very deliberate and significant way, and a brief consideration of that essay will help us to build upon Blanchot's essay by showing what is at stake in the poststructuralist tendency to extend spatial concepts beyond their literal confines.

Michel Foucault, Heterotopia, and Spatialized Power

"Of Other Spaces" is no doubt best known as the piece in which Foucault made the oft quoted assertion that "the present epoch will perhaps be above all the epoch of space" (22)—an assertion that has launched a thousand spatial theories. The essay also provides a provocative, albeit schematic, history of western conceptions of space. "Space itself has a history in the Western experience" (22), he tells us, and he goes on to give us that history in an abbreviated ("rough," as he writes) form. Significantly, as for Blanchot, this history entails a progression from place to space, in which place serves as the devalued term (that which has been superseded) and space serves as the favored term. But Foucault goes one step further than Blanchot, adding a third stage in the evolution away from place. This stage is probably best characterized as a (post)structuralist "beyond" of space itself, and its significance has not always been sufficiently recognized by those who seek to use Foucault's essay as a contribution to spatial theory.

Foucault's version of the history of space is divided into three epochs, which can be summed up as a movement from place (*lieu*), to space (*étendue*), to something that he at first calls "the site" before settling on the more explicitly structuralist notion of a "set" or "bundle" of "relations" (*ensemble/faisceau de relations*). In the Middle Ages, he tells us, space was organized into "a hierarchical ensemble of places," with, for example, "sacred places and profane places; protected places and open, exposed places," and so on. He uses the word "place" (*lieu*) no less than thirteen times in this passage (Foucault, "Of Other Spaces" 22). The Middle Ages, then, is the era of "em*place*ment" (emphasis added).[7] The following epoch, which he calls the era of "space" or "extension" (*espace/étendue*) begins in the seventeenth century with Galileo, who enables "the constitution of an infinite, and infinitely open space" (23). This rationalist conception of space is corrosive ("In such a space the place of the Middle Ages turned out to be dissolved, as it were") but is characteristic of rationalist thought and will make possible the scientific progress that came in its wake. This characterization of the rationalist era's foregrounding of abstract space, we should note, corresponds precisely with Casey's account, except that Casey interprets this turn of events negatively (as a loss of place) and Foucault interprets it positively.[8] Foucault refrains from making any explicit value judgments but clearly implies a preference for rationalized space. There is, at any rate, no indication of nostalgia for the loss of place during the Middle Ages. Indeed, Foucault's third stage in the history of space makes it clear that he believes the trend is toward increasing abstraction, an increasing distance from the kinds of medieval places that came preloaded with meaning, and that this is a good thing.

Struggling at first to explain the third era of his informal chronology (the era of "the site"), Foucault tells us, somewhat obscurely, that it is defined by "relations of proximity between points or elements" (23). He then seeks to clarify his meaning by explaining that he means not geographical sites, nor even points in an abstract, geometrical space, but "relations" that can be described in terms of "series, trees, or grids" (23). With this, we have left the realm of the physical world and entered into the realm of information. Indeed, Foucault goes on to mention electronic data storage and, more obscurely, "the identification of marked or coded elements . . . that may be . . . arranged according to single or to multiple classifications" (23). If this sounds a lot like the space of structuralism, it is no accident: "Structuralism, or at least that which is grouped under this slightly too general name, is the effort to establish, between elements that could have been connected on a temporal axis, an ensemble of relations that makes them appear as juxtaposed, set off against one another, implicated by each other—that makes them appear, in short, as a sort of configuration" (22). The kind of space we are talking about here can only be considered so in a virtual (metaphorical) sense. What counts in these networks of information is the "classification" of information. To be sure, the series, trees, and grids that Foucault mentions have a spatial aspect on the page, but that spatiality is incidental: Flow charts, diagrams, and family trees provide a way to visualize relationships that are logical—not spatial—in nature. They are represented spatially for the same reason that time is often represented as a timeline: for the sake of convenience. For Foucault, then, the specificity of the modern attitude toward space is that it is becoming informational in nature. This is a provocative idea—especially given the extent to which the information age has helped to derealize our sense of physical place. And it is this sense of derealized space that leads Foucault into his celebrated discussion of heterotopias. Foucault's heterotopias are actual sites/places, located physically in the real world, but they enable us to enter into a kind of structuralist hyperspace that has less to do with actual spatial relations than with the ability of heterotopias to bring together, in one place, representations of other places and spaces that may be distant geographically but close functionally.

The heterotopia is of particular interest for my purposes, because it is presented as a kind of intermediary or interstitial site, existing in the *entre-deux*, between existing spatial categories. It is an actual place (he uses the word *lieu*) but to which one goes in order to be (virtually) somewhere else. Although places fulfilling the functions that Foucault attributes to the heterotopia have always existed, he is among the first to present the heterotopia as a unique category of place.[9] It might seem ironic that this proponent of spatiality who decries place as a kind of superstition would participate in the theorization of a new (kind of) place, but there can be no doubt that Foucault's analysis helps to conceive of the heterotopia as a kind of place that is comparable in its cultural and social significance to Jeff Malpas's *plateia*, Martin Heidegger's clearing, Jane Jacobs's city street, or Gloria Anzaldúa's borderland.

Most of the examples of the heterotopia that Foucault gives fall under the heading of "spaces of illusion" (theaters, cinemas, oriental gardens, Persian rugs, museums, libraries, fairgrounds, and brothels). Others are what he calls places of crisis, which also tend to be places of transition. Following Van Gennep, he mentions the role, in primitive societies, of retreats for adolescents, menstruating women, pregnant women, and the elderly, and he notes that modern equivalents of these include the honeymoon hotel, the boarding school, and the cemetery. These are all virtual passageways or thresholds—intermediary spaces whose function is to put two distant realities into contact. For this reason, in Foucault's estimation, heterotopias have an inherently critical social function:

> Either their role is to create a space of illusion that exposes every real space, all the sites inside of which human life is partitioned, as still more illusory ... Or else, on the contrary, their role is to create a space that is other, another real space, as perfect, as meticulous, as well arranged as ours is messy, ill constructed, and jumbled. This latter type would be the heterotopia, not of illusion, but of compensation. (27)

This critical role of heterotopias is important, because it makes of them "countersites," zones of resistance and freedom "in which the real sites, all the other real sites that can be found within the culture, are simultaneously represented, contested, and inverted" (24). Foucault notes ominously, however, that the traditional heterotopia of crisis is being replaced in the modern era by heterotopia of deviation: prisons, psychiatric hospitals, and retirement homes.

With these remarks, we arrive at what is no doubt Foucault's central preoccupation: the question of power: how it is distributed throughout society, how it controls us, and how it can be resisted. And Foucault's vision of structuralist space (which is not space in any literal sense but rather a system or network of relations within which power relations can be charted) plays a crucial role in his attempt to map out the spatial distribution of power.

As we've seen, Foucault, like Blanchot, uses the term "space" in a way that leverages its scientific connotations, opposing it, notably, to place, which is considered to be too compromised by "superstition" (Blanchot) or, as Foucault puts it, "not entirely desanctified" (23). This demotion of place is linked to his demotion of historical temporality, which is conceived in terms of narrative. Although trained as a historian, Foucault's approach to the study of history is premised on the conviction that we must overcome the nineteenth-century equation of historical meaning with narrative causality and learn to think instead about how power structures are disseminated throughout the social landscape. Like the historians of the *Annales* school, much of Foucault's work is devoted to describing relatively stable structures of relations rather than "the eruption of events" ordered into dramatic (i.e., narrative) sequences (Sheridan 92). One part of this project involves learning to think of historical temporality in archeological and genealogical terms as discreet epistemes (which are defined as the "epistemological unconscious" of an era) that are layered one upon the other and are related in obscure ways that have more to do with the paradigm shifts described by Thomas Kuhn than with the clearly observable causal chains of historical narrative in the humanist tradition. Foucault's emphasis on spatial analysis provides him with an alternative structuring principle for his investigations. Henceforth, it is the ability to discern the patterns governing discursive networks, and not the ability to organize events into narrative chains of cause and effect, that will serve as the primary test of historical insight.

One of the major objectives of Foucault's work, then, is the study of power structures that are disseminated throughout a society. Although these networks are not, in themselves, spatial, they do have a spatial, geographical dimension or aspect: They are manifested in the landscape through the spatial configurations, architectural styles, and institutional emplacements of a society. Whence, to use the best known example, his analysis of the prison in *Discipline and Punish*, which he reads as a kind of crystallization of the power structures that make up what he calls the carceral system of modernity. Here we see how the literal space or *étendue* that he associates with the Enlightenment in his history of spatiality meets up with the structuralist, relational space of virtual *sites* that he equates with the current epoch. The geographical sites that he studies can be located on a map and visited, but their meaning is to be sought within the network of power structures that made them possible. A prison is, to be sure, a kind of place, but for Foucault, the physical structures (the sites or emplacements themselves) are ontologically unimportant. They are considered to be little more than the tangible manifestations of the power structures that regulate social life. The physical places Foucault describes have been transformed into emblems or metaphors for power structures that pervade every aspect of social existence. And it is the structures that are the real objects of study—not the places. Thus "The scaffold . . . was replaced by [the prison:] a great enclosed, complex and hierarchized structure that was integrated into the very body of the state apparatus. A quite different materiality, a quite different physics of power, a quite different way of investing men's bodies had emerged" (Foucault, *Discipline and Punish* 115–17). Although the prison should, in principle, represent only the punitive side of the state, it becomes, in Foucault's hands, an emblem of the functioning of the state as a whole—the "carceral system" that Foucault identifies with modernity (271): "The practice of placing individuals under 'observation' is a natural extension of a justice imbued with disciplinary methods and examination procedures . . . Is it surprising that prisons resemble factories, schools, barracks, hospitals, which all resemble prisons?" (227–28). This use of the prison as an emblem of *the* carceral system of modernity leads him to move away from the specificity of geographical location (place) and toward the generality of conceptual *topoï*. Real-world places become, in his handling, instantiations of abstract social structures.

If we compare Foucault's use of space to the humanistic geographers' use of place, we see that the vector of the relationship between the individual and the category—the specific and the general—is reversed. Individuals are considered to be incidental players in a game of structures. This is entirely in keeping with Foucault's self-professed antihumanism, most famously asserted in *The Order of Things*, where he writes that "Man . . . is probably no more than a kind of rift in the order of things . . . a recent invention, a figure not yet two centuries old, a new wrinkle in our knowledge" (xxv). Thinking back to his "Of Other Spaces" article, however, we might ask what Foucault is leaving out. A few obvious questions come to mind. First, for all of its defamiliarizing appeal, doesn't his emphasis on impersonal structures risk underplaying the significance of individual experience, much as his (lack of) analysis of the Damiens ordeal underplays the subjective experience of torture in *Discipline and Punish*? It is, after all, the experience of pain that made torture so effective as a method of social control (and that continues to do so, notwithstanding the epistemic shift Foucault posits, which is away from corporal punishment and toward confinement). Second, aren't the social relations of any era—especially an era that has also been described in terms of the rise of bourgeois individualism, sexual liberation, technological innovation, and exploration—too complex to be reduced to such a specific and yet all-encompassing concept as the carceral system? Third, doesn't his structuralist-inspired mode of analysis neglect the routes and spatial configurations that people actually use in their daily lives, failing to bridge the gap between theory and praxis? Finally, by insisting on the deep penetration of micropower and the implacable force and all-encompassing reach of the carceral system, hasn't he underestimated the possibility of effective resistance to such a system and, with it, the possibility of human agency, whether conceived in an individual (humanist) or collective (Marxist) manner?

I am not the first to ask such questions. The first of these objections is raised by Entrikin (and by extension all humanist approaches to place), as we saw in Chapter 1; the second and third objections are raised by Henri Lefebvre in *The Production of Space*; and the fourth is Michel de Certeau's. Although this is by no means an exhaustive list of possible objections to Foucault's methodology, these four are significant for what they have in common: the desire to establish a link between the abstract, nomothetic, and anti- or posthumanist level of analysis typical of Foucault's work in particular (and poststructuralist antihumanism in general), with the messiness, complexity, variability, and opacity of history as it is lived by individuals. Without disputing the validity or usefulness of Foucault's insights into the spatial dimension of power, such questions remind us of the need to bridge the gap between theory and experience that poststructuralism seems to open up. These questions will guide us in the next two sections of this chapter. Henri Lefebvre's work provides what is no doubt the most interesting Marxist response to Foucault's study of spatial relations, while Certeau comes closest to bridging the gap between the humanists and the poststructuralists by placing the emphasis on individual praxis.

Henri Lefebvre, Radical Geography, and Spatial Ambivalence

Henri Lefebvre is, of all the postwar French thinkers discussed in this chapter, the one whose concept of space comes closest to the problematics of place explored in Chapter 1. Unlike Foucault and Blanchot, who, as we saw, tend to derealize space, drifting away from geographical space and into the metaphorical domain of discursive or structural space, and unlike someone like Bachelard, who tends to convert lived space into an abstract psychic space shaped by psychoanalytic archetypes, Lefebvre insists on the importance of keeping space itself—and in particular the ways in which space is produced by historically determined modes of social behavior—at the forefront of his concerns. For this reason, his work provides a useful way to bridge the gap between the antihumanism and social constructivism of the Foucauldians and the humanists' refusal to let go of the individual human subject as the organizing principle of their studies. To be sure, Lefebvre, as a committed Marxist thinker, is allergic to the (bourgeois?) emphasis on place as subjective experience that is so characteristic of humanistic geography. For him, it is the socioeconomic dynamic of collective, class-bound subjects that governs the production of space (and the individual's experience of it). For this reason, he has been more influential among radical geographers like David Harvey, Edward Soja, and Derek Gregory than among humanistic geographers. Be that as it may, his emphasis on the problematics of spatial production and reproduction, which is linked to the question of representation, is of great value for anyone interested in understanding how thoroughly spatial practice is bound up with the problematics of representation.

In keeping with the "scientific bias" toward space that we encountered in Blanchot and Foucault, Lefebvre shies away from the term *place* almost completely. He explains this tendency by saying that he seeks to avoid "a new fragmentation of [the Hegelian concept of] the concrete universal into its original Hegelian moments: the *particular* (in this case descriptions or cross-sections of social space); the *general* (logical and mathematical); and the *singular* (i.e. 'places' considered as natural, in their merely physical or sensory reality)" (Lefebvre 16). For Lefebvre, as for Malpas, a complete understanding of space requires overcoming the ingrained habit of dividing it up into perceptual, conceptual, and existential strata. We must, he argues, relearn to think together these various levels of space as engaged in an ongoing dialectical interaction. Space, in the richer sense that Lefebvre wants to reinstate, cannot be broken down into its constituent parts without denaturing it completely. It is not, then, that Lefebvre contests the importance of what we have been calling place but rather a widespread but reductive use of the term that restricts its meaning to the *singular* (physical and sensorial) dimension of space. Space for Lefebvre is conceived not as opposed to place but as an englobing term that has many of the same attributes humanist geographers associate with place. Edward Soja emphasizes this in his explanation of Lefebvre's avoidance of the term place:

> Lefebvre rarely used the concept of "place" in his writings, largely because its richest meaning is effectively captured in his combined use of "everyday life and "lived space." Many cultural geographers, in particular, have persistently attempted to separate the concepts of place and space and to give place greater concreteness, immediacy, and cultural affect, while space is deemed

to be abstract, distanced, ethereal. As Lefebvre's work demonstrates, this is an unnecessary and misleading separation/distinction that reduces the meaningfulness of both space and place. (Soja, *Thirdspace* 40)

Soja—himself a proponent of the term "space" and, as a radical geographer, resistant to the humanistic approach to spatial studies—uses this occasion to stake out a polemical position against the use of the term "place." But if we recall Malpas's insistence on the multileveled, polyvalent, interlocking, nested nature of place, it becomes clear that both Malpas and Lefebvre are moving in the same direction in their definition of space/place. Lefebvre prioritizes the social-political dimension, while Malpas stresses the phenomenological, experiential dimension, but both share a sense of place/space as a complex entity that both shapes and is shaped by human agency and that is best thought of as a highly complex, ramified but indissociably unitary entity. Having begun at opposite ends of the spectrum (Lefebvre with the political and Malpas with the personal), their definitions of space and place converge.

It is perhaps no surprise, then, that what Lefebvre has to say about the problematics of space in the modern world echoes, and is echoed by, the humanist/phenomenological discourse on place, from Heidegger to Tuan. The *problem* with space, according to Lefebvre, is that we have lost touch with it. For Lefebvre, our ability to maintain authentic (meaningful and productive) relations with the space around us is one of the many things that has been taken away from us in a society characterized by relations of domination, exploitation, and alienation from the fruits of our labor. These artificial social divisions have led to a concomitant (and equally artificial) intellectual partitioning of the world into series of binary oppositions: subject and object, mental and material, imagined and real, and so on. In fact, he suggests, it is such dichotomies that make his focus on understanding the production of space so necessary and yet so hard to grasp: "To speak of 'producing space' sounds bizarre, so great is the sway still held by the idea that empty space is prior to whatever ends up filling it" (Lefebvre 15).

For Lefebvre, as for the phenomenologists, this artificial partitioning of spatial experience makes the problem of representation a central concern. This becomes clear in his well-known—and notoriously obscure—division of space into three interdependent levels, which he sometimes refers to as "the perceived-conceived-lived triad." This "conceptual triad," might be thought of as the three levels or moments of the production of space, none of which is separable from the others and none of which can be entirely liberated from the uncertainty of mediation, be it of the senses, of the dominant social structures, or of the individual consciousness. Before going any further, then, we will need to examine Lefebvre's tripartite division of spatial production.

The perceived-conceived-lived triad is divided into the following levels:

1. spatial practice (= perceived space)
2. representations of space (= conceived space)
3. representational spaces/spaces of representation (= lived space)

Lefebvre's use of these three categories seems somewhat shifty at first and not at all self-evident. On what grounds, for example, does he associate the first level of analysis, "spatial *practice*," with the first term of his triad, "perception"? And in what sense is the third level of analysis, "spaces of representation," more "lived" (*vécu*) than the *practice* of space? He returns over and over to this conceptual triad from different angles, refining it as he goes along, but it will take some close reading to tease out the coherence of his triadic conception.

As a way to get a sense of this order, I have assembled the most important of his definitions by category, with a few words of explanation for each. This will, I think, make it easier to understand what, precisely, he is getting at in his somewhat ungainly presentation of this conceptual triad, which cuts a transversal path across many of our usual ways of speaking of space:

1. "*Spatial practice* . . . embraces production and reproduction, and the particular locations and spatial sets characteristic of each social formation" (33). "The spatial practice of a society secretes that society's space; it propounds and presupposes it, in a dialectical interaction" (38). "This is the realm of the *perceived*" (40).

The category of spatial practice—and its links with the production and reproduction of space—becomes clearer if we think of it in terms of a Rousseauian first man, whose physical and social landscape is shaped by his spatial practices. He first finds himself in an overwhelmingly complex landscape. But as he goes about his daily affairs (seeking food, shelter, companionship, etc.), he falls into regular patterns. His behavior is shaped by the space as he discovers paths of least resistance, shelters, vantage points, and so forth, but his spatial practices begin to shape space itself as he learns how to organize that space around his needs. In this way, the individual and his space are brought into a mutually determining ("dialectical") interaction. Over time, this initial, spontaneous marking of the landscape will be formalized and reproduced, resulting, for example, in networks of paved, named roads, fenced-off plots of private property, cities, nations, international networks of trade, and all the other institutions that are first shaped by and then begin to shape the members of a society.

This, then, is the level of spatial practice. But in what sense is this "the realm of the perceived"? Lefebvre seems to be suggesting that we engage in these activities at a preintellectual, sensorial level of experience. His use of the term "secretion" is significant in this regard. In saying that "a society secretes that society's space," he implies that there is a kind of automatism involved in our spatial practices.[10] The term perception, then, is opposed to the intentionality of rational planning. Our spatial practice is something that we do not fully control. Shaped by our environment in a quasi- (but, as we shall see, not completely) deterministic manner, we obey the signals delivered to us by our senses before we ever get to the stage of planning our environments rationally.

Lefebvre's second level of spatial existence—representations of space—is at the opposite end of the cognitive spectrum: that of abstraction:

> 2. "*Representations of space* ... are tied to the relations of production and to the 'order' which those relations impose, and hence to knowledge, to signs, to codes, and to 'frontal' relations" (33); [this is the level of] "conceptualized space, the space of scientists, planners, urbanists, technocratic subdividers and social engineers, as of a certain type of artist with a scientific bent—all of whom identify what is lived and what is perceived with what is conceived" (38). "Representations of space are certainly abstract, but they also play a part in social and political practice" (41).

This is no doubt the easiest to understand of the three categories. It is also the sole category to be presented in a negative light. For Lefebvre, the level of representations of space is the level of the official order. It is primarily conceptual, abstract in nature, and therefore cut off from spatial practice as something that involves the activities and perceptions of individual bodies. This is a top-down mode of knowledge, closely related to Foucault's conception of space as constructed by state power: It involves the social order's ability to regulate behavior by imposing on us a representational framework that both explains and constrains our daily practices, despite the fact that such conceptual abstractions are by definition inadequate to the bodily practices and perceptions they are meant to regulate.

This inadequacy of (abstract) representation brings us to Lefebvre's third category, spaces of representation:

> 3. "*Spaces of representation* [a.k.a. representational spaces], embod[y] complex symbolisms, sometimes coded, sometimes not, linked to the clandestine or underground side of social life, as also to art." (33); "space as directly *lived*

through its associated images and symbols, and hence the space of 'inhab-itants' and 'users', but also of some artists and perhaps of those, such as a few writers and philosophers, who *describe* and aspire to do no more than describe. This is the dominated—and hence passively experienced—space which the imagination seeks to change and appropriate. It overlays physical space, making symbolic use of its objects" (38); "Bodily *lived* experience, for its part, may be both highly complex and quite peculiar, because 'culture' intervenes here, with its illusory immediacy, via symbolisms . . . The 'heart' as *lived* is strangely different from the heart as *thought* and *perceived*" (40); Representational spaces . . . need obey no rules of consistency or cohesive-ness" (41).

This is the most perplexing level of Lefebvre's conceptual triad and is ill served by the ambiguous name he gives it, spaces of representation, which seems to have been chosen primarily for its symmetry with the label he uses for level two, representations of space. Indeed, at first glance, there seems to be considerable overlap with category two, since both involve sym-bolic representations. Given the emphasis on representational abstraction in level two, it seems odd to associate this third level of space with "*lived* space," as if there could be representation without mediation, until we read the qualification that he makes to that equation: A space of representation is "space as directly lived *through its associated images and symbols*" (38). Thus if level two designates the level of "official," authoritative, top-down knowledge (the *dead* knowledge of the *lieu commun*), the representations of level three are important because they come from the bottom up, from the individual, *in vivo*. These are still representations, but they are "directly lived," in the sense that the actors and eye witnesses themselves provide these representations. They are not considered to be more *perceptually* immediate than other kinds of representations (that was the specificity of level one), but they are developed inductively, through reflections on lived experience, rather than deductively, by way of the institutionalized abstractions of level two. The goal of this third level of representation is to cobble together a representation that will make the individual's experience meaningful *to him or her*—not to provide universally valid explanations or definitions. It is for this reason that Lefebvre associates such representa-tions with the "clandestine or underground" and with modernist experi-mentation in the arts. In this sense, Lefebvre's spaces of representation have a critical role comparable to Foucault's heterotopias: They provide a poten-tial base of resistance against the hegemonic representations imposed on us from above by the representatives of the state and its power.

It is at this point that we can begin to understand Lefebvre's insistence on the artificiality of separating these three levels of spatial production from each other. They are the constantly interacting forces in an ongoing process, a dialectical process of give and take between praxis and theory, with the individual playing a doubly significant role in that dialectic: first, in stage one, as a historical actor who acts in accordance within an almost (but not quite) deterministic framework of material constraints, and then, in stage three, as a historical actor who has developed a sense, however tentative, of the significance of his praxis. Lefebvre has established a role for individual agency that seemed to be denied to the individual in Foucault's system, as well as in the deterministic, teleological economism developed by the doctrinaire Marxism against which Lefebvre defines his own approach.

This third moment in the dialectic (or "trialectic," as Soja somewhat glibly but astutely calls it in his *Thirdspace*) is what I would call the interstitial moment in Lefebvre's theory. It is what enables him to break out of the binary oppositions of Cartesian dualism (subject and object, mind and body, and concrete and abstract) and sketch out a prototheory (which is to say a space of representation) of human subjectivity conceived in a post-Cartesian, quasi-Bergsonian mold: as a messy but plausible passageway between the brute perceptions of a body in space and the abstract conceptions of a universal mind. This happens via the paralogical representations of level three: that of a mind or body reacting to its environment. This emphasis on the spatial and experiential dimensions of abstract thought has the added advantage of creating a space between, on the one hand, historical materialism as a deterministic model of historical change and, on the other, the Romantic (or "bourgeois") model of the autonomous, freewheeling, "heroic" subject. Lefebvre proposes a model of historical change that respects the constraining force of material conditions while also emphasizing the ability of individuals to nudge, however minimally, the system into which they were born in new directions. On this point, he is in full accord with Malpas (and, as we shall see, Certeau).

At the center of his account is the body itself. And Lefebvre shows in his treatment of the relationship between body and consciousness the influence of Merleau-Ponty. This becomes clear in the "Spatial Architectonics" chapter of *The Production of Space*, which gives an account of the body in space that is fully compatible with the kinds of phenomenological/neurological analysis found in Merleau-Ponty. This involves what Lefebvre, following Hermann Weyl (a mathematician), calls a relationship of mutual or reciprocal *inherence*, which recalls Varela's insistence on mutual specification and coorigination of mind and world that we studied in Chapter 1:

> The body with the energies at its disposal, the living body, creates or produces its own space; conversely, the laws of space, which is to say the laws of

discrimination in space, also govern the living body and the deployment of its energies . . . Bodies—deployments of energy—produce space and produce themselves, along with their motions, according to the laws of space . . . Here then we have a route from abstract to concrete which has the great virtue of demonstrating their reciprocal inherence. (Lefebvre 170–71)

This insight leads in turn to one of the crucial elements of Lefebvre's sociopolitical argument: the desire to bridge the gap between theory and praxis by more fully delineating the links between Marxist theory and the physical and biological underpinnings that make Marxism a materialism.

Emphasizing the constraints that material and (by extension) economic conditions place on the individual, but refusing the (at times) rigidly social constructivist outlook of Foucault, Lefebvre proposes reformulating the Marxian conception of social forces in terms of the Darwinian conception of adaptive evolution: "This [biological] thesis is so persuasive that there seems to be little reason for not extending its application—with all due precautions, naturally—to *social* space. This would give us the concept of a specific space produced by forces (i.e. productive forces) deployed within a (social and determined/determining) spatial practice" (Lefebvre 171). We should notice how this attempt to situate social production within the evolutionary paradigm differs from Engels's attempt to explain the natural world in terms of a "dialectic of nature." Although the emphasis on material constraints is nothing new to Marxism, Lefebvre's path to this insight enables him to preserve the centrality of the individual's body in the determination of social space, something that is critical to his larger goal of reinvigorating Marxian thinking by reclaiming social space for individuals conceived not just as social actors but as desiring subjects. For Lefebvre, "the body serves both as point of departure and as destination" for this argument (194).

This emphasis on the body may be one of Lefebvre's most important contributions to the Marxist thinking of his generation, and follows as a consequence of his efforts to incorporate consideration of everyday life into Marxism's traditional focus on labor and the workplace.[11] It certainly helped to make Lefebvre's brand of communism more compatible with the individualist aspirations and youthful rebellion of 1968. Deeply influenced by Marx's analysis of the 1870 Paris Commune, Lefebvre saw the Commune as a preview of socialist self-rule conceived as a carnivalesque utopia. Thus he sees the kinds of "détournements" or "situations" beloved of the Situationists as forerunners of the kind of appropriation he has in mind. He cites with particular approval a student-led occupation of the *Halles Centrales* in 1969–1971, which was "for a brief period . . . transformed into a gathering-place and a scene of permanent festival—in short, into a centre of play rather than of work—for the youth of Paris" (Lefebvre 167–8). It is this emphasis on the revolutionary potential of everyday life, on the reappropriation of public space, and on "the right to the city" that linked his work (however momentarily) with that of the *Situationnistes* and made it so influential among the student activists of May 1968.

Ultimately, though, Lefebvre emphasizes the inadequacy of such impromptu, ephemeral operations as the *détournements*, which can be seen at best as foretastes of a more enduring revolution. "Diversion is in itself merely appropriation, not creation—a reappropriation which can call but a temporary halt to domination" (Lefebvre 168). What is really needed is a more durable imposition of the egalitarian socialist spirit onto the landscape, the development of new forms of spatial and architectural organization that would put into practice the communal ideals of the revolution. Without such a renovation of the landscape, Lefebvre believes, no revolution can be said to have succeeded. "What," he famously asked, "would remain of the Church if there were no churches?" (44). Or, more generally: "What is an ideology without a space to which it refers, a space which it describes, whose vocabulary and kinks it makes use of, and whose code it embodies?" (44). The point is that a mode of production, ideology, or way of life can only be said to have succeeded, to have a practical existence, to the extent that it has shaped or reshaped the landscape in its own image.

What, concretely, might such a success look like? Despite such symbolic successes as the *Halles* occupation or the memory of grand social experiments like the Paris Commune, Lefebvre sees only negative examples around him, including that of the Soviet Union, whose construction priorities Lefebvre reads (uncontroversially enough) as catastrophic, on both an aesthetic and social level. Soviet architecture, for Lefebvre, is a symptom of its larger betrayal of Socialism's promise of freedom from tyranny. Lefebvre's desire for a quasi-anarchical reappropriation of space leads him to be much more favorably disposed to Mao's "Chinese road" to Socialism (see Lefebvre 421) that is premised on the "self management of the masses," which Lefebvre opposes to the top-down socialism of the Soviet system. (In retrospect, of course, the humanitarian toll of the Great Leap Forward and the Cultural Revolution makes clear the risks of such an approach.)

If, then, in both capitalist and socialist societies, we find such deep incompatibilities between the state's management of social space and the needs and desires of the people it is meant to serve, what can be done to resist the grip of the institutional forces that seem to control us and our spatial practices? If, as Lefebvre assumes, the establishment of satisfactory spatial practices requires the complete overhaul of an entire system of production (i.e., the demise of capitalism), then the odds of immediate success are long indeed, and the risk of excesses of the kind associated with the Terror and Mao's Cultural Revolution is very real. Perhaps, in other words, the very same revolutionary aspirations that give Lefebvre's vision its utopian grandeur are part of the problem. If so, it will be more useful to conceive of such activity on a smaller scale, in an evolutionary rather than revolutionary framework. This would, at any rate, seem to be more in keeping with the Darwinian update to the socialist model that Lefebvre flirts with in the passage on the "biological thesis" quoted earlier. It is on this point that the work of Michel de Certeau dovetails most clearly with that of Lefebvre. By emphasizing the importance of small-scale, localized, individual activities over the concerted collective action necessary to achieve the revolutionary ambitions of Lefebvre, Certeau reorients the agency-structure debate between Lefebvre and Foucault in an important new direction. And in so doing, he offers us the closest approach yet to a reconciliation between poststructuralist spatial analysis and humanist geography.

Michel de Certeau: Space, Place, and Interstice

Eschewing both the gloomy institutionalism of Foucault and the anarchic Marxism of Lefebvre, Certeau proposes that we "try another path"—one that accepts many of the premises of Foucault's argument about the pervasiveness of state power while also accepting the liberatory implications of Lefebvre's ideal of spatial praxis but insists on the need to navigate a third path between them, placing the tools for successful spatial practices squarely in the hands of the individual. Thus his influential "Walking in the City" essay features a direct, even strident, challenge to Foucault:

> Rather than remaining within the field of a discourse that upholds its privilege by inverting its content . . . one can try another path: one can analyze the microbe-like, singular and plural practices which an urbanistic system was supposed to administer or suppress, but which have outlived its decay; one can follow the swarming activity of these procedures that, far from being regulated or eliminated by panoptic administration, have reinforced themselves in a proliferating illegitimacy, developed and insinuated themselves into the networks of surveillance, and combined in accord with unreadable but stable tactics to the point of constituting everyday regulations and surreptitious creativities that are merely concealed by the frantic mechanisms and discourses of the observational organization. (Certeau 96)

Although Certeau does not call Foucault out by name, many of the latter's most recognizable keywords are there: fields of discourse, panoptic administration, and networks of surveillance. But Certeau emphasizes the ability of individuals to overcome such barriers to their liberty. This individualism of Certeau seems, then, to move in the direction of the humanistic geographers studied earlier, with his emphasis on individual spatial practices meeting up with their emphasis on the individual experience of place. But as his references to microbes, swarms, and proliferating illegitimacy suggest, Certeau's understanding of individual agency is not a cozily humanistic one.

Indeed, Certeau's work remains, in many respects, squarely within the structuralist or poststructuralist paradigm. His primary intellectual foil is Foucault, the majority of his other references are structuralist thinkers (Barthes, Saussure, Benveniste, and Lévi-Strauss), and he foregrounds the concepts of structuralist linguistics in his analyses in a somewhat showy manner. For Certeau, cities are texts that must be read, walking is to the city as enunciation (*parole*) is to language (*langue*), and narrative (the storytelling mode of the itinerary) is the key to escaping from the impersonal panoptic gaze embodied for him by the map. The linguistic metaphors mark him as a product of the structuralist moment, but the use to which he puts them is original and important. In order to see this, though, we need to understand his somewhat unusual use of the terms space and place, which doesn't fit neatly into either the structuralist or phenomenological camp.

When Certeau declares in "Spatial Stories" that "space is a practiced place," he reverses, very precisely and intentionally, the common-sense definitions of these terms. As Tim Cresswell notes, this reversal is "confusing" for geographers because it "stands the normal distinction on its head" (Cresswell 38). Apparently at a loss to explain why Certeau would invert standard usage in this way, Cresswell quickly reverts to the standard English use of the two terms. It seems important, though, to at least consider what would lead Certeau to use this inversion of the terms, especially in light of the more general poststructuralist preference for space previously noted.

A place, for Certeau, is a site that has a name and appears on the map. But the very traits that make a place available to the geographer bring it into the reach of institutionalized power, allowing it to be controlled. Spaces, on the other hand, can be thought of as those areas on the map that are not named or otherwise indicated on the map. Space, identified with the blank areas between and around named places, is able to escape, to some extent, the control of state power. Those who choose to inhabit these unnamed spaces find it easier to evade the panoptic gaze, while engaging in the creative activity of exploration and shaping the habitat to their liking.

What makes Certeau's terminological reversal between space and place so interesting is what it reveals about the nature of the disagreement between the humanists and the poststructuralists. Both camps are in full agreement on the fact that humans live in places that come prestructured, but they differ completely in the value they ascribe to this prestructured aspect of place. For the humanists, the prestructured nature of place is simply a constraint that must be taken into account by individuals as they go about their business. These constraints exist on both the physical and social levels (we try to avoid bumping into walls and getting arrested), but they are considered to be relatively benign and easily accommodated.

Certeau, on the other hand, defines the very stability of place as something negative: a form of rigid control and order that is associated with stasis and ultimately death. Thus the concept of place "implies an indication of stability . . . from the pebble to the cadaver, an inert body always seems, in the West, to found a place and give it the appearance of the tomb" (Certeau 118). Space, on the other hand, is considered to be the domain of motion and narrative: "Space is a practiced place" (117). For Certeau, as for Blanchot (and Deleuze), spatiality is associated with relative freedom from any kind of anchoring effect; it is deterritorializing—the domain of the nomad. In this opposition between place and space, Certeau brings to the fore what the majority of poststructuralist thinkers have in common: a deep, abiding, almost paranoid mistrust of institutionalized power structures, combined with a desire to found a new social order based on a complete revision of the humanistic assumptions that have governed social thinking since the Enlightenment.

In this sense, Certeau's counterintuitive reversal of space and place is linked to his equally counterintuitive valorization of *tactics* over *strategy*. For Certeau, individuals find themselves hemmed in by the systematic control of the state, which is aligned with the long-term, far-range perspective of strategy. Because of their limited perspective and limited access to resources, the best hope individuals have to escape from state control and surveillance is to make use of more-or-less improvised *tactical* maneuvers. This kind of behavior borders on the illicit (he speaks of it, approvingly, in terms of "delinquency") by exploiting cracks, chinks, and blind spots in the state's control apparatus. Certeau's individual is, in this sense, a kind of guerrilla fighter, flying under the radar of state control. Rather than trying to find a *place* for himself within the structures allotted him by the state, he will, so to speak, go rogue, staying off of the officially sanctioned highways and byways, avoiding the places that are named on the map, and creating his own space by wandering transversally between the established sites.

Certeau, in other words, begins with the same suspicion of the existing order as Foucault but is more optimistic about the productive potential of individual agency within that order. Rather than argue against Foucault, as a humanist might have done, by simply insisting on the efficacy of individual agency (i.e., the capacity to shape and reshape a place to fit one's needs), he decides to do Foucault one better: The individual, too weak to address the overwhelming force of institutionalized power head on, will contest that power by becoming an underground resistance fighter. By evading the control structures of hegemonic power made manifest in place, he will enter into the freer realm of space. Where are these zones of spatial freedom to be located? For Certeau, they exist in the interstitial spaces left unexploited by the existing power structures—in those zones of activity that have not (yet?) been invested by institutional power and transformed into the kinds of places that are named on maps. In this sense, Certeau is a thinker of the *entre-deux*.

Certeau accords great importance to the role of narrative in this struggle, which, in an argument that bears comparison with Entrikin's, he describes as providing a crucial bridge between place and space. Storytelling, for Certeau, creates a private space within the publicly controlled domain of place. He does not go so far as to suggest that narratives always transform place into space but says, instead, that they create the potential for a trajectory that could go either way: "Stories . . . carry out a labor that constantly transforms places into spaces or spaces into places" (Certeau 118). Depending on the *kind* of story, one side or the other will be favored. Of particular importance for him is the notion of the itinerary. The ethnographic research he has conducted suggests to him that individuals tend to represent their comings and goings in terms of first-person itineraries, which he opposes to the cartographic perspective of maps and omniscient third-person narratives.[12] Because they privilege the perspective of the individual, itineraries provide, according to Certeau, a tactic of resistance against the panoptic control of the surveillance society, which he associates with maps, conceived as an instrument of control. "What the map cuts up, the story cuts across," Certeau asserts (129). For Certeau, "the primary function [of such stories] is to *authorize* the establishment, displacement, or transcendence of limits," creating "a legitimate *theater* for practical *actions*" (125, emphasis in original). Like the representations of "lived space" that make up Lefebvre's third level, such stories participate in the process of disrupting the spatial logic of institutional power, creating the possibility for new modes of spatial practice.

Having arrived at this understanding of Certeau's inversion of the space-place hierarchy, it is interesting to note that he has not always used these terms in this way. In fact, in his essay "Walking in the City," published in the same volume as "Spatial Stories," he begins by using the terms "place" and "space" in the conventional way. Thus in a passage that sounds like a conventional lament about the dehumanizing side of city life, Certeau equates place with rootedness, presented straightforwardly as a positive value, and opposes it to walking, which is equated with exile, a lack of place: "To walk is to lack a place. It is the indefinite process of being absent and in search of a proper. The moving about that the city multiplies and concentrates makes the city itself an immense social experience of lacking a place . . . what ought to be, ultimately, the place but is only a name, the City" (103). There can be no doubt that place represents a positive value here. So how do we explain the sudden shift that leads Certeau to abandon this positive conception of place, as something that is desirable but sadly lacking in modern urban life, in favor of an unequivocally negative conception of place, as inherently oppressive? The answer is that he gradually comes to realize over the course of the "Walking in the City" essay that the desire for place is actually an atavistic desire—something we need to learn to resist if we are to free ourselves. It is nothing more than a regressive nostalgia for a plenitude that no longer exists, if indeed it ever did.

This conclusion begins to surface toward the end of the "Walking in the City" essay, after much knotty prose and a convoluted argument that seems to vacillate between the positive and the negative in its evaluation of place.[13] He had begun the essay by casting about right and left for some solution to the problem of alienation, but he ultimately decides that the real problem is not the fact of alienation itself but our stubborn clinging to the fantasy of an eventual return to a traditional place-bound sense of rootedness in the urban landscape, which has in reality been foreclosed by the social organization of modern cities. For that reason, he concludes, we must learn to embrace a harder truth: that traditional place-bound identities are illusory remnants of a bygone era and that the goal of overcoming alienation must itself be jettisoned in favor of a more gritty willingness to face up to the necessity of resisting institutional power. It is perhaps this sense of resolve in the face of a daunting reality that will lead him to adopt the guerilla warfare and insectozoid metaphors in the later "Spatial Practices" essay.

Given Certeau's explicit confirmation in this essay that place, as rootedness, is something desirable, something we all want, and that the problem with places in modern societies is that they have been taken over by the "system" of state control, the decision to abandon the search for place might seem surprising. One might, it seems, arrive at the opposite conclusion, which would entail overt political action. Isn't it really a matter of *taking back* place—of making it our own once again? Not for Certeau, because ultimately, this desire for "getting back into place" (as Casey would have it) is taken to be a retrograde fantasy, for which Certeau gives a psychoanalytic explanation:

> In this place that is a palimpsest, subjectivity is already linked to the absence that structures it as existence and makes it "be there," *Dasein*. But as we have

seen, this being-there acts only in spatial practices, that is, in *ways of moving into something different (manières de passer à l'autre)*. It must ultimately be seen as the repetition, in diverse metaphors, of a decisive and originary experience, that of the child's differentiation from the mother's body. It is through that experience that the possibility of space and of a localization (a "not everything") of the subject is inaugurated. (109, emphasis in original)

In the adult world of separation, place has become an inaccessible object of fantasy. Certeau adduces Freud's example of the *fort-da* game (played by a boy trying to compensate ritualistically for his mother's extended absences) to reinforce this point, calling the game "an 'original spatial structure.'" For Certeau, then, to "practice space," in the positive sense that he wishes to promote, is to reconcile oneself with separation from place: "To practice space is thus to repeat the joyful and silent experience of childhood; it is, in a place, *to be other and to move toward the other*. Thus begins the walk that Freud compares to the trampling underfoot of the mother-land" (110, emphasis in original). In other words, at a primitive, child-like level, we want place. But that is the very thing that is no longer available. Or rather, it may be available but only to those willing to remain in a child-like state of submission to the powers of state control. In order to achieve autonomy and selfhood, we need to sublimate that desire, mastering a compensatory skill that involves shifting one's efforts away from the inaccessible object of primitive desire and focusing them on the accomplishment of productive tasks. To grow up, socially speaking, we must renounce the rooted stability of place and accept the incessant struggle of spatial practice.

This is, we should note, a conclusion that resonates strongly with Blanchot's call to leave behind the childish games of place-bound identity and embrace the decentered perspective of the spaceman. It also resonates with Lefebvre's insistence on the need to participate actively in the production of space—appropriating and creating new spaces that better reflect our needs and values—rather than passively accepting the hegemonic forms of space that have been allotted to us by existing social and political institutions. What is perhaps less obvious is that this call for resistance to state power through one's spatial practices also moves us in the direction of Malpas's surveyor model of human subjectivity, according to which the human agent constructs its subjective identity through its spatial practices while also charting out the landscape from within. It is at this point— spatial praxis as productive of both self and world—that the poststructuralist model meets up with the phenomenological model.

Sociology and the Place Effect

The work we have done so far seems to have left us far from any intuitive, common-sense understanding of place. On the one hand, we have seen a phenomenological approach to place that treats it as a foundational component of human subjectivity but leaves aside all specifically geographical questions that might help to differentiate between and evaluate individual places; and on the other, we have seen a poststructuralist critique of place that treats topophilia as an atavistic relic of an obsolete humanist world view and urges us to set aside the sedentary comforts of place in favor of a deconstructive or deterritorializing ethic/aesthetic.

In order to make the leap from theory and Beckettian deconstruction to the more conventionally realist narratives that will be studied in the next chapter, it will be necessary to translate the epistemological questions of the preceding chapters onto a more practical sociological idiom. But how can these two theoretical approaches to place and space be applied to works that remain comfortably ensconced within the realist conventions of the social novel? Perhaps the most instructive way to make this transition is by way of the debate over what French sociologists have variously called "l'effet de territoire," "l'effet de quartier," and "l'effet de lieu" (the territory/neighborhood/place effect). This is a debate over the extent to which the immediate environment of a given place plays a determinant role in shaping the social identities and behaviors of its residents. Do certain kinds of places tend to elicit certain kinds of behavior and create certain kinds of subjects? Or should places be understood as concretizations of social structures that traverse society as a whole, creating places *and* subjects (or subject effects) as they go along? Or do we want to argue instead that, like the fully formed subject who is, to borrow Varela's phrase, "parachuted in" to an environment, humans have more autonomy than either of the first two questions seem to allow?

Both the phenomenologists and the poststructuralists reject this last hypothesis out of hand. But they split along the lines of the first two. Because the phenomenological model puts such great weight on the direct experience of one's environment, it encourages a view that emphasizes the determinant role played by the immediate environment. Taken to the extreme, this approach to place might be construed as leading to a form of environmental determinism (i.e., we are shaped wholly by our local environment). The poststructuralist approach, on the other hand, emphasizes the systemic social structures that permeate every given local situation without being directly perceptible to the local inhabitants. Taken to its Foucaldian extreme, this approach leads to a radical version of social constructionism (objects, places, and individuals have no consistency or meaning outside of the social forces that traverse them)—one that is in its own way as reductive as environmental determinism. Within the field of sociology, however, the poststructuralist emphasis on structure has been used in ways that help us to understand place in a very powerful way, notably through its interrogation of the *effet de lieu*.

Pierre Bourdieu's account of the *effet de lieu* clearly shows the influence of the poststructuralist outlook:

> Everything leads us to believe that the bulk of what is lived and seen *on the ground* . . . finds its explanation [*son principe*] in a distant elsewhere . . . One cannot break free from the false truths and errors inscribed in substantialist theories of place unless one continues on to a rigorous analysis of the relations between the structures of social space and the structures of physical space. (*La misère du monde*, 159, my translation, emphasis in original)

For Bourdieu, then, the *effet de lieu* is just that: an effect. The true causes of the local place's influence on its inhabitants are situated in an indeterminate elsewhere. To be sure, Bourdieu recognizes that the inscription of social structures into physical spaces helps to explain the frustrating "inertia" of social structures (161), which means that the materiality of the physical site cannot be discounted entirely. Nonetheless, he insists that the underlying "principle" of those physical environments can only be understood in terms of social structures that are distributed (unequally) throughout the totality of a given social system. Loïc Wacquant, a disciple of Bourdieu, explains what this outlook implies for our understanding of the contemporary urban crisis in France. "Neighborhood effects" Wacquant argues, are "nothing more than the spatial retranslation of economic and social differences" (*Urban Outcasts* 9).

The tension between this approach (which puts the emphasis on structure) and the phenomenological approach (which puts the emphasis on individual experience) is clear, and it provides a useful framework for questioning the (implicit) discourse on place that is present in all the narratives that will be studied in the following chapter. Should the reader situate "the reality" of the places represented in these texts on the level of the site itself, as it is experienced by the protagonists? Or in the "elsewhere" of the abstract social, economic, and political structures that have produced that site and its inhabitants? Framed in terms of this stark opposition, the question is no doubt a misleading one. A full exploration of the matter must include considerations of both perspectives, somewhat in the manner of the Lefebvrian trialectic. There will, consequently, be no attempt here to *choose between* these two approaches or to assert the superiority of one or the other. Rather than treating the "effet de lieu" as an either/or proposition, I understand it as a both/and proposition: We must learn how to see macrostructural forces in the subjective phenomena recounted in the literary texts under consideration and vice versa. It would be just as much of a mistake to dismiss subjective experience as epiphenomal as it would be to dismiss macrostructures as artificial constructions. My intention, then, is to use the insights of these apparently opposed approaches toward place and space as a way to bring into focus the pressing social questions opened up by the literary works, always asking how local experience is connected to social structures and vice versa.

In order to do this, we will need to adjust our methodology somewhat. Rather than treating place in the manner of Malpas (and to some extent Beckett) as an all-encompassing mode of experience, or space in the abstractive manner of Blanchot, Lefebvre, and the poststructuralists, we will be dealing with specific kinds of places, defined at the scale of the neighborhood, with an emphasis on the social interactions between the members of the communities that have grown up in those neighborhoods.

The key questions of this next chapter, then, will be questions of neighborhood and community. Of what is a neighborhood made? What transforms a group of people who happen to live in the same area into a community? How do such communities go about developing the kinds of bonds that lead them to identify themselves as a group? At what point does it become possible for the individuals who belong to that community to draw a sense of their own personal identity from that bond? Conversely, can the identification between self, neighborhood, and community be pushed too far? Does the sense of belonging that flows from participation in such a community necessarily entail exclusions of various kinds—distinctions between inside and outside and between those who belong and those who don't? And if so, does this make traditional ideas of community anachronistic or counterproductive, as Jean-Luc Nancy has argued? (See Nancy, *La communauté désœuvrée*.)

Such questions have become especially urgent in light of the ongoing "crise des banlieues" in France, which has seen a rise in ethnic and class tensions in and around France's major cities as well as a serious discussion of the spatial aspects of social exclusion. They also suggest that despite the tight focus on the local neighborhood, it turns out to be impossible to avoid consideration of the larger "imagined community" of the nation, which necessarily has a great impact on the kinds of interactions that take place within the local community. Indeed, the neighborhood-nation relationship is but one aspect of the dialectic between local experience and structural determinants I have been examining in terms of the "effet de lieu."

So long as a degree of ethnic and cultural homogeneity and a shared historical experience could be counted on, the kinds of bonds that hold together the local community are relatively straightforward, like those that Ferdinand Tönnies used in his definition of *Gemeinschaft* (community). These are apparently spontaneous bonds: organic extensions of the principle of shared kinship—the community as a kind of extended family. In a modern context, however, when the development of national and international communities has gotten us used to relying on the kind of impersonal bonds that Tönnies associated with *Gesellschaft* (society), such questions certainly need to be reformulated. The real challenge facing today's European nations is that of reconciling the traditional presumption of shared interests and goals (based on shared ancestry, cultural norms, expectations, values, and history) with the need to learn how to live with and incorporate into the community new members, who may or may not share the same interests and values and who may, as a result, be perceived as alien or inassimilable. For this reason, the upcoming chapter will focus on communities that put Tönnies's concept of community as *Gemeinschaft* to the test in their struggles to incorporate newly arrived minorities.

Such communities are interstitial in the sense that they no longer fit the traditional mold (with its presumption of at least relative homogeneity) and must stretch as they seek to accommodate the arrival of strangers with different modes of sociability. Such neighborhoods are often fragmented and may be considered (often by their own members) to be defective in some sense—not *real* communities at all but places that have lost or not yet found the kinds of advantages enjoyed by other more established communities. These are neighborhoods in need of various kinds of mending and bridge-building operations.

The search for such community building strategies has characterized many recent literary representations of France's immigrant/minority communities. It is that search that will interest me in the following chapter. My overarching goal will be to understand what literature can contribute to the formation of communities that are open enough to accommodate such diversity while remaining cohesive.

4

Beur Fiction and the *Banlieue* Crisis

To sing of Bezons, that's the challenge.

—L. F. Céline

It doesn't sing, concrete, it howls in despair.

—Mehdi Charef

Geographically speaking, the French *banlieues à problèmes* offer a prime example of the kind of emergent, interstitial spaces discussed in the introductory chapter. Despite the periodic upsurges of interest in the low-income, ethnically mixed *banlieues* surrounding France's major metropolises (which tend to follow on the periodic upsurges of violence that have occurred there), they have until very recently remained, culturally speaking, largely unmapped and depicted in the mainstream media as opaque, impenetrable *zones*. The cultural historian Anna Louise Milne has argued for the need to overcome the reductive view promoted in the mass media of "*la banlieue*" (without the plural 's') as a "singular" (i.e., undifferentiated) space of alterity, asking how we can "sunder the totalising opposition of centre and periphery, or France and misery"(Milne, "The Singular Banlieue" 60). For Milne, as for me, the best answers to such questions are provided by works of film and literature that eschew the existing interpretive paradigms and journalistic clichés while exploring the multiple, varied experience of the *banlieues* (in the plural), as seen through the eyes of those who inhabit them. Success is not guaranteed. Even those who set out expressly to come to a better understanding of the *banlieues*—like Jean Rolin in *Zones*, François Maspéro in *Les Passagers du Roissy-Express*, or Bertrand Tavernier in *De l'autre coté du périph'*—tend to leave this sense of confusion and disorientation largely intact. In this chapter, then, I will be studying several works that attempt to map out the culture of the urban periphery from the inside, providing guides that help the audience learn how to navigate these areas that have, like the *terra incognita* of Renaissance atlases, remained both spatially and culturally mysterious to those in the metropolitan center.

Since the 1980s, there has been an explosion of creative works focusing on the *banlieues*, giving rise to generic labels like "banlieue film" and "banlieue fiction" that have gained wide currency in academic circles. These genres are typically characterized not only by their setting but also by their cast of characters and tone. The prototypical *banlieue* protagonists are prematurely hardened teenagers or young adults, who have a growing awareness both of their power and impotence. Such works tend to have a hard edge and bleak aesthetic, which has led Carrie Tarr to suggest that a sense of "pessimistic realism" is the most distinctive characteristic of the *banlieue* film genre (Tarr 81). And indeed, for those who live in and write about the stigmatized *banlieues*, the geographical shift from within the city limits to the ex-urban frontier is linked to a psycho-social shift from inside to outside, from the hopeful air of multiculturalist novels like Romain Gary's *La vie devant soi*, Daniel Pennac's Mallausène series, or Calixthe Beyala's novels to the almost fatalistic sense of exclusion that inspired Tarr's notion of pessimistic realism.

Beur and Banlieue

The socioeconomic and spatial dimensions of the *crise des banlieues* are inseparable, in the popular imagination, from the question of France's minority populations. Talk of the *crise des banlieues* almost invariably turns to talk of immigration and minorities. And it is true that although the two matters are distinct, there is a great deal of overlap between the spatial relations and the racial relations that characterize such neighborhoods. (Carrie Tarr's *Reframing Difference* is structured around this overlap.) Although France's poor neighborhoods are considerably less racially segregated than their equivalents in the United States, the relative proportion of immigrants and minorities in public housing remains high—and seems to be climbing (see Levy-Vroelant and Tutin 77).[1] It is important, therefore, to consider the relationship between ethnicity and urban marginality as it plays out in the French context, despite the resistance to this approach by many in the French sociological tradition, including Loïc Wacquant, who has strenuously rejected any attempt to apply an American-style racial analysis to the problem (see Wacquant, *Urban Outcasts* 151–62).[2] For my purposes, the most pertinent way into this question is through the creative work of second and third generation descendants of North African immigrants, commonly referred to as *Beurs*. Not only does this group constitute the single biggest minority community in France; it has also produced numerous creative artists who address, in insightful ways, the geocultural concerns of this book.

The term *Beur* highlights the peculiarly interstitial identity associated with this demographic group, referred to in the unwieldy officialese of sociologists and government officials as "youths of North-African immigrant origin" (*jeunes issus de l'immigration maghrébine*). Derived from the word "Arabe" via *verlan*, or French backslang, the term was embraced in the 1980s by many youths of Maghrebi descent who, although born in France and fully entitled to French citizenship, were still, by virtue of their ethnic identity, lumped together with immigrants and foreigners. It has come to connote an energetic embrace of a stigmatized identity, somewhat similar to the way that the term "queer" has been embraced by some segments of the gay community. After having gone through some secondary iterations (such as *rebeu*, a double inversion), the term seems to have fallen out of favor and is probably used more today by academics than by the population in question. I will retain it here, nonetheless, because it provides a resonant alternative to more direct designations like *Arabe* (which is too general and too often used pejoratively) and to the official polysyllabic monstrosity. The term fills an important terminological gap, especially given the persistent use of terms like "second generation immigrant" that perpetuate the sense of alienness and otherness of the outsider, suggesting, for example, that although born in France, such people could always be sent "back where they came from."

The *Beur* community is an interstitial community in several senses: *culturally* (since they are caught somewhere between the cultural values and practices of the majority population and those of their immigrant forebears); *geographically* (since their image is tied indelibly to the impoverished suburban periphery surrounding France's cities); *economically* (since so many of them are trapped in the limbo of unemployment and dependency on social security); and also *politically* (since the officially color-blind political doctrine of French Republicanism makes it extremely difficult to provide recognition of and protections for the rights of minority groups.[3]

It is important to understand how this last, political dimension of their plight relates to their cultural and social identity. The French Republic was conceived from the beginning as "an 'abstract political society', that is, a community of equal citizens that transcends specific interests and identities" (Béland 68). In principle, the state's refusal to recognize these specific interests and identities makes it a better guarantor of equal political rights, social opportunities, and equal protection under the law. In practice, however, the last two of these elements have been difficult to achieve for "visible" ethnic minorities like the *Beurs*. The paradox of this situation is summed up nicely by Azouz Begag, the well-known novelist, sociologist, and deputy minister under Dominique de Villepin from 2005 to 2007 (who is, himself, a *Beur*):

> The French Republican model of integration, founded on the universalist affirmation of the citizen and his individual merits, has contributed to the process of tearing these youths away from their cultural moorings, without however guaranteeing them a chance of social advancement equal to that of other citizens. As a result of this paradox, it has become enormously difficult to find social regulators whose authority is accepted by these youths. (Begag, *Les dérouilleurs* 146; all translations from this text are my own)

While very good at protecting against *institutionalized* discrimination (discrimination carried out by the state), Republican-style universalism is not very good at protecting against what might be called street-level discrimination. Thus Patrick Lozès, a Beninese-born activist, points out, "People don't like it when I describe myself as black because they say that skin color doesn't count, but it's hypocrisy. I'm black in the eyes of the police, or an employer" (qtd. in "France's ethnic minorities" 32). On top of this, the republican model tends to weaken any sense of (non-French) cultural identity that an individual may have, since, as Kwame Anthony Appiah explains it, "the only publicly celebrated identity is that of the dominant culture: tolerance and full civil rights may be extended to minority groups but the national history is the history of the majority" (Appiah, "The Multiculturalist Misunderstanding").

Despite these chinks in the armor of the republican principle of abstract citizenship, resistance to Anglo-American style multiculturalism remains strong. The republican, universalist mindset is so firmly entrenched in French national culture that commentators on both the left and right tend to mistrust any gestures toward British or American styles of multiculturalism as implying a move toward *communautarisme*, which is in turn interpreted, often in apocalyptic terms, as a move toward separatism, mutual intolerance, ghettoization, and discrimination, both negative and positive. (The French term for affirmative action—*discrimination positive*—is revealing.) For this reason, no census data on ethnic identity or religious affiliation are kept by the state. This deeply ingrained resistance to the recognition of subcommunities within the state has its origins in the French revolution (which fought to overturn the privileges of the aristocracy and the Catholic church), was enshrined in the educational philosophy of Jules Ferry's Third Republic (which made cultural assimilation an official objective), and was confirmed by the memory of discrimination against Jews during the occupation. Thus Fadela Amara, founder of the women's rights group *Ni putes ni soumises* and former Secretary of State for Urban Policies (under Sarkozy), has said, "Our republic must not become a mosaic of communities . . . Nobody must have to wear the yellow star again" ("France's ethnic minorities" 32).

How, then, does one reconcile the laudable ideal of a color-blind society with the realities of street-level discrimination and a *de facto* lack of equal opportunities? Is it possible to combat such inequalities effectively without betraying the republican principle of *laïcité* (secularism) and giving in to the potential social costs of a turn toward *communautarisme* and particularism? One solution has been to frame such problems in geographical terms, identifying geographical pockets of economic and social deprivation (rather than defining exclusion in terms of ethnic or religious communities) and promoting the collective well-being of an *area* rather than a group. The French *politique de la ville* since the 1980s has relied on this approach to develop geographic responses to widespread socioeconomic problems, creating categories like the ZUP (zones à urbaniser en priorité), ZUS (zones urbaines sensibles), ZRU (zones de redynamisation urbaine), and ZFU (zones franches urbaines). Some of the limits of this approach will be discussed later, but it has an important role to play in a society where resistance to anything resembling ethnic or religious preferences has been strong: Whatever limits the republican model may have, the French, on both the Left and the Right, have remained committed to it.

Hybridity or Interstitiality?

The official refusal to recognize specific identities does not mean, of course, that identity politics have not played an important role in the arguments used by minority writers to advance their cause. But they have taken on a particular flavor in the republican context. The most significant attempt to bring minority identities into the national conversation without adopting the kind of particularistic mindset that is so anathema to the republican heritage has involved an emphasis on the concept of *métissage*. The advantage, in a republican context, of *métissage*, or cultural hybridization, is that it puts the emphasis not on the particularities of any given community—whether ethnic, religious, or other—but on the mixing of identities that inevitably goes on when two or more communities intermingle. Rather than proposing that France should abandon the traditional conception of itself as a single, undifferentiated political body, it offers a historical narrative that attempts to explain how this kind of social unity arises from and is enriched by cultural diversity.

Things like this are never simple, however, and areas of incompatibility between the theory of *métissage* and republican ideology have since appeared. Mireille Rosello, among others, has pointed out that the idea of *métissage*, conceived as a combination of two preexisting cultures, may in fact unwittingly reinforce essentialist notions of identity. She sees this as part of a deeper ideological bias that has permeated identity politics of all stripes. The problem, as Rosello sees it, is the tendency to pose the question in binary, oppositional terms, presuming the existence of easily opposable, monolithic cultures and forgetting the importance of individual variation within a given cultural sphere. Thus,

> The difficulty of conceptualizing the "Beur" community in other than binary terms (i.e., as being bi-cultural, bi-national, and bi-religious) is less a proof of the empirical validity of this approach than an indication that notions of dual allegiance and dual origins constitute a hegemonic ideology that permeates the discourses of people whose own opinions are radically opposed to each other. (Rosello, "The 'Beur Nation'" 14)

However well-intentioned the theory of *métissage* may be, she concludes, it may actually play into the hands of those who would discriminate against minorities, since it accepts the underlying premise of their argument: the existence of distinct groups that are culturally and ethnically opposed to each other. This critique is part of a much larger wave of revisionist thinking in postcolonial studies that began in the 1990s. Apart from the essentializing tendency Rosello critiques, there is the risk, noted by Christopher Miller and emphasized by many in the French Republican tradition (like Pierre-André Taguieff and Jean-Loup Amselle), that this emphasis on hybridity risks turning it into a prescriptive value no less exclusionary than the ones it has sought to replace (see Miller, *Nomads and Nationalists* introduction; Taguieff; and Amselle, *Logiques métisses*). *Métissage*, in this view, risks becoming a new, perhaps more sophisticated—but no less essentialist—identitarian category.

We can allay some of these concerns if we take the term *métissage* to mean simply that people from different cultures inevitably borrow practices (and beliefs and values) from each other when they come into contact with one another. It is only when we attempt to define *métissage* in a stronger sense—as implying an organic fusion of two monolithic entities—that we run into problems. We need to distinguish, in other words, between a *strong* theory of *métissage* (implying a fusion of monolithic blocks) and a weak theory (involving any kind of cultural exchange or appropriation). This distinction is important, because the strong theory presupposes a kind of organic necessity that makes it vulnerable to accusations of essentialism, while the weak theory leaves much more room for individual choice and variation in its explanation of cultural evolution.

That France's *Beur* population is a product of *métissage*, in the weaker sense just described, is undeniable. In their dress, speech, and religious and cultural attitudes, young *Beurs* display a variety of influences from both North African and French customs as well as many other influences from around the world (of which North American hip-hop culture is an obvious example). But if we pay attention to what *Beur* writers and filmmakers have to say, it quickly becomes apparent that the strong theory fails. They tend to describe their own cultural position in terms of interstitiality, in-betweenness, and lack—the lack of a secure cultural perch around which to organize their lives, leaving them with *le cul entre deux chaises*. They find themselves forced to come up with their own creative solutions in order to fill the cultural in-between space they inhabit. The narrator of Mehdi Charef's *Le thé au harem d'Archi Ahmed* makes this point about his protagonist Madjid:

> [He has] long been convinced that he is neither Arab nor French. He is the son of immigrants, lost between two cultures, two histories, two languages, two skin colors, neither white nor black, left to invent his own roots, his anchoring points, to make them for himself [*à s'inventer ses propres racines, ses attaches, se les fabriquer*]. (Charef 17; all translations from this text are my own)

As we see in this passage, there is a perceived need for roots (he uses the word *racines*) and anchors (*attaches*), but neither the North African culture of the parents nor the host country's culture provide a fully satisfactory model. So the search for roots becomes a process of *invention* and *fabrication*. Madjid believes that he must "make them for himself." In this sense, it is more accurate to say that *Beur* culture has grown up in the space *between* its source cultures—not as some kind of fusion of the two. Notions of hybridity are of little use to characters like this as they try to navigate the minefields of daily life.

We must also recognize that France's *Beur* population has already become so inextricably entangled in the social and cultural fabric of mainstream French society that the theory of *métissage* begins to sound quaint—like something that is in many respects just a given—but that may also seem irrelevant or worse as individuals seek to work through the specific problems they confront in their daily lives. Indeed, despite much noise on the far Right about the inassimilability of North Africans and despite much fretting on the Left about the failure of the French model of integration, the picture one gets from the vast majority of *Beur* literary and filmic representations of their experience is that such institutions as the public school system and the mass media have been highly successful in carrying out the work of integration. Or, to be more accurate, the *cultural* integration of these minorities has proceeded apace. It is on the level of *economic* integration that things have gone wrong. And it is this lack of economic integration that has created social disorders of the kind that burst forth in 2005 and 2007.

Finally, we must not forget that the kinds of cultural exchanges that define *métissage* do not only apply to those who define themselves (or are defined by others) as bicultural. On the contrary, one has only to listen to the radio to grasp how much mainstream French culture has been and continues to be influenced by intercultural exchange—not only with the culture of the *Beurs*, of course, but also by that of its other minority communities and with cultural influences from around the world. What the weak version of *métissage* leaves us with, then, is simply a local instanti-ation of an axiomatic law of cultural interaction: Wherever there is contact between cultures, there will be some kind of exchange. But the modalities of that exchange cannot be predicted in advance with any certainty.

In order to illustrate this point, we can turn to the film *Salut Cousin!*, by Merzak Allouache, which offers a postcolonial update of the city mouse–country mouse fable. There, the city-mouse character, Mok (Messaoud Hattau), who has grown up in France and seems (initially) entirely at home in Paris, is continually singing the praises of *métissage* to his newly arrived Algerian cousin Alilo (Gad Elmaleh). Mok, it turns out, is an aspir-ing musician whose great artistic ambition is to rap the fables of La Fon-taine to a hip-hop beat. He explicitly theorizes this project as a way to bring about a hybrid mixture of high French culture and the pop culture of the streets. But this project leaves him exposed to derision from every quarter. His rhymes and flow are, by any standard, terrible, and he finds himself mocked by most of the people who hear him—including a multiethnic group of suburban teens (who openly ridicule him), a karaoke bar full of middle-class whites (who politely, but also perhaps condescendingly, applaud his school-boy earnestness), and us, the viewers of the film, who are meant to understand that this is a case of failed *métissage*: an artifi-cial, contrived *superimposition* of two cultures driven by a flawed theory rather than an organic synthesis driven by good taste, talent, and common sense.[4] Implicitly, of course, we are meant to contrast Mok's failed attempt at cultural synthesis with the kind of cultural *negotiation* that is carried out by Allouache himself in the film we are viewing. That Allouache sees the negotiation of the area between cultures as more important than contrived attempts at synthesis is brought home by the dénouement of the film. Mok, due to a case of mistaken identity, is deported—sent off to Algeria despite the fact that his status is entirely legal. Meanwhile, Alilo (who has no residence visa and had, at any rate, planned to return to Algeria) falls in love with Fatoumata (Magaly Berdy), a dark-skinned African beauty, and so he makes a last-minute decision to stay on in France, illegally. Everything leads us to believe (following the genre conventions of comedy) that Alilo's alliance with Fatoumata will work out and that his very innocence will enable him to thrive in his new homeland. Ironically, then, Mok's project of cultural *métissage* is superseded by the unsophisticated and untheorized but more organic, nimble, and *adaptive* tactics of Alilo, his naïve cousin, so recently arrived from Algeria.[5] Alilo's alliance with Fatoumata could be considered a kind of *métissage* (between a North African man and a Black African woman), but if so, it is one that defies the expectation of a French-African hybrid. This *métissage* can only be considered French in the sense that it takes place on French soil. France provides the setting for the alliance (the environmental constraints, we might say) but does not enter into the reproductive arrangement.

This film, then, provides a striking example of the central argument I will be making over the course of this chapter: that those in the *Beur* community who have been most successful in finding solutions to the social, cultural and economic problems that they face as they seek to integrate fully into French society have tended to eschew established models of cultural interaction like *assimilation* and *métissage* and to adopt an improvisational, opportunistic cultural practice close to the kinds of tactical and spatial practices promoted by Certeau. Azouz Begag calls those who know how to navigate in this interstitial space between cultures *dérouilleurs*. Derived from the term *dérouiller* (literally: to de-rust; figuratively: to limber up one's joints), this is a term that emphasizes the interstices or joints between existing social and cultural categories, extolling those who exercise their ingenuity in the development of gap filling solutions.

The Interstitial Morality of the *Banlieue* Protagonist

In order to show what this interstitial theory of *Beur* culture contributes to our understanding of the *crise des banlieues* in its geographical and sociological dimensions (and how it might help to address those problems), I would like to explore the ways in which it is set forth in several exemplary works of *Beur* film and literature. I'll be focusing primarily on three works: Mehdi Charef's novel *Le thé au harem d'Archi Ahmed* (1983, adapted for the screen by Charef in 1985), Malik Chibane's film *Douce France* (1995), and Akli Tadjer's more recent novel, *Bel-Avenir* (2006). The first of these works represents the nascent moment of the *Beur* movement in the 1980s, at a time when it was strongly focused on questions of cultural difference and alienation. The second work represents the 1990s, which shifted away from this kind of identity politics, soft-pedaled questions of ethnic difference, and put the emphasis on demands for recognition of the basic civil rights promised to all by the republican model. (This is the era of the *black/ blanc/beur* trio in such films as Kassovitz's *La haine*.) The third work is emblematic of the growing sense of disenchantment and frustration of the 2000s. This is a disenchantment that can take the forms of irony, fantasy, and escapism, as it does in Tadjer's novel, but can also manifest itself in the impulsive violence seen on the streets in 2005 and 2007.

More than simply illustrating this historical progression, I see these works as promoting a vision of France's immigrant *banlieues* as laboratories of social and cultural innovation. By emphasizing the tactical spontaneity and deterritorializing tendencies of the *dérouilleurs*, who disdain both the assimilationist and *métissage* models of cultural adaptation, they portray their protagonists as explorers on the cutting edge of French social evolution—innovators who are deeply, and sometimes successfully, engaged in the search for new solutions to the ongoing social malaise of the *banlieues*. In so doing, they show how the *banlieue* setting—which provides the environmental constraints within which these characters must operate—plays an active role in shaping their evolution. It is in this sense that they can be considered place narratives.

One of the most interesting and widespread (but also troubling) traits of the typical *Beur/banlieue* narrative is the obsession with the theme of *casual criminality*, which tends to be presented in a titillatingly offhand way. This offhandedness implies, of course, familiarity, which is no doubt to be expected in stories set in economically deprived communities. But these narratives sometimes seem to present the crimes of their protagonists in a benevolent, even approving and almost gleeful light—a fact that seems to call for explanation. In what follows, then, I would like to analyze this theme of casual criminality, in terms of the *entre-deux*, as exemplifying an interstitial morality that rises up in the grey zones between social strata, where established legal codes must be broken and the ethical codes that underlie them must be tested so that the minority protagonists of these works can reach out and enter into the mainstream community. Although most of the crimes in question are relatively minor, they do imply allegorical extensions suggesting a number of provocative lines of reflection on the nature of the ongoing *crise des banlieues*. For example, might the street violence of 2005 and 2007 have been a *legitimate* manifestation of grievances against the entrenched inequalities of French society? Are they best understood as part of the long republican tradition of popular uprisings, which includes the barricades of 1968, 1871, 1848, 1830, and 1789? And if so, might the real impediment to the social integration of France's minorities be on the side of the French majority?[6] I will be coming back to these questions in the conclusion to this chapter, but I raise them now as a way to suggest that the relatively lighthearted treatment of petty criminality in the works studied here resonate at a much deeper level.

My first example is Akli Tadjer's recent novel, *Bel-Avenir* (2006), whose protagonist, Omar, gets his first job—as a journalist in a high-profile weekly magazine—in a flamboyantly unethical manner. He is accorded a job interview on the merits of a comically padded CV in which he makes all kinds of outrageous claims about his qualifications (i.e., that he has earned not one but two doctorate degrees, that he is a multilingual world traveler and philanthropist, etc.). All of these inflated claims are presented with a naïve confidence that is, as one can imagine, entirely unconvincing. These claims are immediately debunked in his job interview—and yet, he is hired: not because he succeeded in impressing his future boss, who is a right-wing, neoliberal admirer of Nicolas Sarkozy, but through a perverse application of the principle of affirmative action. The boss's real goal is to shore up, politically speaking, his left flank, polishing up his progressive credentials, and so he is willing to hire any minority, no matter how unqualified. Of course affirmative action, *discrimination positive*, is frowned upon in France and is outright illegal in the public sector, but this is just one of the many ironies of this situation, which seems only to lead to a satisfactory conclusion because all the negatives cancel each other out. And crucially, this initial twist—the perverse application of the principle of affirmative action—will lead directly to the happy ending of the novel, which, following the twisted logic of the romantic comedy, enables the protagonist to make a name for himself as a journalist while also, in the process, saving an entire community of *sans papiers* from a dire fate and, of course, getting the girl.[7]

In a similar vein, Malik Chibane's film *Douce France* begins with a morally troubling stroke of good fortune. The two protagonists—Moussa and Jean-Luc—happen to witness the armed robbery of a jewelry store. The robber is immediately caught but manages to ditch the jewels in a garbage can before being hauled in by the police. Our protagonists see their opportunity, and rather than cooperating with the police investigation, they retrieve the jewels, take them home, fence them, and then use the cash to set themselves up in business. One buys a neighborhood café, while the other opens a law office, although it is not clear that he has any legitimate legal credentials. His specialty, of course, will be immigration law.

Before exploring the significance of these two examples of casual criminality, let's look at one more example, taken from Mehdi Charef's *Le thé au harem d'Archi Ahmed*. Unlike the Tadjer novel and the Chibane film,

Charef's novel is not a comedy but instead an example of what Tarr calls pessimistic realism. Like Mathieu Kassovitz's *La haine* or Fabrice Genestal's *La squale*, Charef's novel focuses on more muscular characters but also takes a much dimmer view of the future of the *banlieues* and of the possibilities for successfully integrating France's minorities. In a key scene from *Le Thé au harem*, the two protagonists, Madjid and Pat, decide to go "do themselves a metro" (*se faire un métro*), by which they mean go pickpocketing in the metro. After targeting an appropriately contemptible looking—and white—victim, Madjid, a *Beur*, steals his wallet and passes it to Pat, who is white. The victim, noticing that his wallet is gone, sees Madjid standing next to him and immediately assumes, correctly, of course, but also, presumably, for racist reasons, that Madjid took his wallet. This is exactly what Madjid was waiting for. Accused publicly of theft, Madjid launches into a long—and loud—tirade about the racist tendencies of the French, who always assume that the Arab did it. The deliciously multiple ironies of this scene are apparent. Madjid gets both the wallet and the right to complain about the injustice of racial profiling, and the victim, who was right all along but for all the wrong reasons, winds up apologizing publicly to his tormentor, despite the fact that he is, in reality, the aggrieved party.

This scene is played for laughs and makes an interesting, although complicated, point about the nature of stereotypes, their effects, and their uses. But it is important to note also that this scene is just one in a long series of crimes committed by Madjid and Pat, which range from recreational drug use to burgling a tennis club, stealing a car, prostituting one of the neighborhood girls, and giving a beating to an unsuspecting gay john that they have targeted at a local cruising spot. It is the last two of these crimes that interest me here. What differentiates them from the petty larceny in the metro scene just discussed is that these crimes are presented in a way that makes it abundantly clear that there is nothing about them that can be considered cute, funny, or clever. Narrated in a way that recalls Hubert Selby Jr.'s *Last Exit to Brooklyn* in their sordidness and violence, they involve deep betrayals of trust and a kind of inhumanity that seems unforgivable. And yet they are presented without comment by the narrator—as if they were simply a fact of life and no ethical judgment was called for. This apparently amoral aspect of the novel has troubled many of the novel's critics, who have wondered if the ultimate effect of this refusal to judge or explain isn't precisely to reinforce the negative stereotypes that so many French already have of minorities and the *banlieues*. Is this, then, a cynically sensationalistic novel? Or are we perhaps meant to conclude that the author is simply "telling it like it is," without judgment or explanation? Otherwise, how *are* we supposed to interpret this egregious refusal to condemn such unambiguously despicable behavior?

This question takes on particular resonance when we consider it in relation to the comic narratives discussed earlier, which clearly seek to overcome the influence of such stereotypes and to bring *Beur* culture into the mainstream, defending the rights of *Beurs* by combating such images of violence and lawlessness and replacing them with a more comforting message of compassion and a shared, if flawed, humanity. Unsurprisingly then, the problem represented by this novel has been obsessed over by almost all the critics who study *Beur* narratives. But none of them is able to arrive at a completely satisfactory response to this larger question. Alec Hargreaves, for example, tries to shift the terms of debate from the cultural realm of ethnic stereotypes to the socioeconomic realm of material deprivation: "The life of petty crime which Madjid shares with Pat has nothing to do with his ethnic origins"; rather, "the motivation of both youths lies in the material deprivation which they share" (Hargreaves, *Voices* 106). This may well be true, but it does not help to understand why Madjid himself draws attention to his own ethnicity in the metro scene. Carrie Tarr, who examines the film adaptation of the novel, goes one step further, explaining the role that these crimes play in the larger symbolic economy of the story, emphasizing that the stereotypical stigma of *banlieue* criminality that the crimes seem to reinforce is counterbalanced (for readers) by what we know of the characters' positive traits—specifically, their "sympathetic nature," which is "demonstrated by their inter-racial male camaraderie and their protection of the estate from drug dealers" (Tarr 59). This seems fair enough—Tarr is certainly right to say that we feel sympathy for these characters—but does not go very far toward explaining the gratuitous, attention-getting nature of the metro theft nor excusing the sadistic, humiliating nature of some of their other crimes. It is Mireille Rosello who seems to get closest to the fundamental essence of the metro scene, which she interprets as being a scene that is not so much about criminality as about the play of stereotypes. She concludes that "if Madjid is the undeniable winner of the stereotypical game, it is not because he is right, or because he is innocent, but because he knows how to manipulate the dangerous weapon of stereotypes while his adversary is not even aware that he is using it" (Rosello, *Declining the Stereotype* 61). In other words, we are not meant to justify Madjid's crime or accept the legitimacy of his motives but, instead, asked to enjoy the fact that Madjid is quite simply better at playing a crooked game than those around him. Whatever admiration we have for him in these scenes is admiration for his ability to get away with it—and to do so with style. If true, this would imply a strikingly amoral vision on the part of Charef—and one that has important ethical consequences for readers. Indeed, for Rosello, one of the strengths of this novel is its ability to implicate readers in the crimes of the characters: "This text turns us unto accomplices," she argues.

"We readers are forced into a position that I would compare to the possession of stolen (discursive) goods and to the concealment of criminals" (59).

Even if we agree, following Hargreaves and Tarr, that Madjid and Pat's
socioeconomic hardships explain their departures from the laws of conventional morality or that Madjid's likeability and cleverness outweigh his
violent streak, it is hard to imagine excusing some of their other crimes—
one of which can only be described as a hate crime (targeting a gay victim
for a beating) and another of which involves the complete degradation of
a close personal friend (by prostituting her to a large crowd of workers
at a nearby squatter city). These are not unfortunate lapses in judgment
or youthful indiscretions; they are profound betrayals. However much we
might wish to find excuses for characters that we find ourselves liking, à la
Tarr, we cannot shy away from the very serious ethical issues raised by the
commission of such crimes.

I think that another approach to this issue is required if we are to come
closer to a satisfactory resolution of this conundrum. I will address it by
reframing Charef's treatment of casual criminality in relation to the comic
narratives discussed earlier and by thinking of it in terms of the interstitial morality of the *entre-deux*. This will involve an understanding of the
generic conventions that are in play in each of these works and will, moreover, help us to understand the place-bound nature of these narratives and
the role that place plays in shaping the destiny of these characters.

Geography as Destiny

In the comic narratives of Tadjer and Chibane, the crime, for as morally
suspect as it may be, is justified (or at least justifiable) as part of a larger
strategy for social and economic integration into mainstream French society. Balzac famously asserted that all great fortunes are founded on great
crimes, and the crimes in these novels often represent the stroke of good
fortune that alone, it seems, makes it possible to escape from the ghetto.
In a first phase, this means personal advancement—getting off the dole,
moving into a better neighborhood, and finding a mate—but these protagonists then turn around and project their good fortune back onto the
old community. Both of these comic works are quite explicit about this.
For Omar, the protagonist of *Bel-Avenir*, the fake CV and hypocritical boss
launch him into a career that enables him to do some good by successfully
mobilizing the group of *sans papiers* living in his old neighborhood. His
professional *departure* from his old life enables a *return* to his old neighborhood that takes the form of a much needed political intervention—one
that simultaneously helps his clandestine friends enter into a more tolerable

physical and legal situation while also teaching mainstream French society a thing or two about the real plight of the *sans papiers*. Similarly, in *Douce France*, Jean-Luc and Moussa ultimately use their stroke of good fortune—the discovery of the stolen jewels—to help their neighbors. Moussa helps by opening a café that becomes an important gathering spot in the community while Jean-Luc provides legal support for the residents. As in *Bel-Avenir*, this return also involves a media lesson given to mainstream French society: Jean-Luc becomes a kind of media star on behalf of the exploited and victimized members of his community. In both cases, the personal good fortune of the protagonists is leveraged into an improvement in the physical and spiritual health of the community and also, perhaps just as importantly, an improvement in its public image. Indeed, one of the primary lessons of these works is that the real battle, in many respects, is a media battle—a battle against entrenched but unwarranted negative stereotypes. This makes the question of *Le thé au harem d'Archi Ahmed*'s apparent amorality stand out with even greater urgency.

For Pat and Madjid—this is one of the crucial differences between *Le thé au harem* and the other two works—any meaningful departure from their *banlieue*, whether spiritual or physical, turns out to be impossible. For this reason, Pat and Madjid are never able to convert the spoils of their exploits into any kind of constructive project. We are meant to understand Pat and Madjid, in other words, not as exemplary figures but as failures—products of the desperation of the suburban cultural environment. Or to put it more starkly, Pat and Madjid *are meant to* reinforce the stereotype of *banlieue* criminality. But why would Charef write a novel that confirms so many of the negative stereotypes that have emerged around immigrants and the suburban poor? Ultimately, I would argue, because this novel is not so much about ethnicity as about place, and more specifically, about the "effet de lieu" (as defined by Bourdieu) pushed to its deterministic extreme.

This point is made quite forcefully in the novel but in an indirect way that might not be consciously registered by a reader who is not attuned to the poetics of place. Two otherwise puzzling episodes that occur toward the end of the novel will help us to understand Charef's point. In one, Pat and Madjid get a chance at a job in a factory located a couple towns over. Madjid learns the job quickly and actually takes pleasure in it, but Pat quickly fails and is fired. Madjid, despite his apparent inclination for the work, immediately quits and rejoins Pat. Pat asks if Madjid did this out of loyalty to him. But Madjid evades the question:

— They threw you out too?
— Think what you want, says Madjid.

— Don't tell me it's because you don't want to leave me in the lurch that you took off!

— I didn't say that, says Madjid.

— What an idiot! [. . .]

— Okay . . . let's just drop it. (Charef 171)

Then a few pages later, in the final chapter of the novel, there is an apparently unrelated incident: Pat and Madjid get a chance to go on a road trip to Deauville with a group of friends in a stolen car. Inexplicably though, as soon as they have left their neighborhood, Madjid goes into a kind of semicatatonic state. There is no clear explanation for his immobilization, but a couple scenes later, when the stolen car, parked with Madjid inside, is discovered by the police, he is so incapacitated that he doesn't even attempt to escape. Meanwhile, Pat, who *had* initially escaped, returns to the scene of the arrest and turns himself in. Was this out of loyalty to Madjid? Once again, the question is raised but not answered, and the novel ends with an image of Pat and Madjid face to face in a paddy wagon rolling through the night.

The symmetry of these two episodes is clear. On the most obvious level, they suggest that given a choice between freedom and friendship—between autonomy and each other—Pat and Madjid will always choose each other. Pat and Madjid, it seems, are destined to remain together. But there is a further, geographical dimension to this relationship. They are, for all intents and purposes, bound together within the prison-like confines of their home territory. Whether for work or for pleasure, they find themselves unable to stay away from their *cité* for any period of time. They do make occasional forays into Paris and into other neighborhoods, but the farther they get from home, the less able they are to function and the less able they are to do without each other. As for their refusal to leave their friend and strike out on their own, it is of course possible that it is simply out of personal loyalty that they stay. And it is possible that it is solely out of modesty and a kind of masculine reserve that they refuse to declare openly any such loyalty. This "fraternal" reading of these passages would no doubt prevail within the generic conventions of the buddy film adduced by Carrie Tarr. But there is another possible reading of this silence. I think that the fact that Charef twice *raises* the question of personal loyalty and then refuses to *answer* it, whether positively or negatively, suggests that he wants us to consider another kind of response to the question—one that works on a symbolic or allegorical level. From this perspective, the most likely explanation for their apparent inability to leave each other is linked to their inability to leave home. They do not have the confidence to strike out on their own, and fear themselves unable to function away from each other and from their home environment. Indeed, if we take *seriously* Madjid's strange catatonic state in the Deauville episode, it becomes possible to say that he is constitutionally unable to survive in the outside world. Madjid at the seashore (Deauville) is like a fish out of water: Leaving the *cité* means symbolic death. Pat and Madjid are almost literally unable to conceive of life outside of their *cité*, however terrible it has been for them and however unlivable it has become. They would rather be big fish in a small, dangerous, polluted pond than anonymous members of the larger mainstream society, whose rules and power structures remain mysterious and threatening to them. For as terrible as life in the city is, "It seems easier to give yourself a scare while giving others a scare by staying cloistered at home with a German shepherd at your feet, than to go out before strangers in order to better understand oneself and them" (Charef 23).

We could reframe this conclusion in more properly generic terms by saying that *Le thé au harem* is not exactly, or at least not only, an example of pessimistic realism but rather a tragedy—and I mean to use that term in a fairly strict sense, as implying a deterministic sense of inevitable submission to an implacable destiny. It is the tragedy of those who have become so stunted by life confined in their neighborhood on the margins of society that even leaving their neighborhood feels threatening.[8] Location has become destiny and the internalized sense of inferiority has become the tragic flaw of these characters, the mechanism through which their fate imposes itself. *Le thé au harem* is, in this sense, a novel about geographical determinism.[9]

Lest this emphasis on the tragedy of immobility seem too forced, we must recall at this point that the thematics of mobility and immobility are central to the novel. I've already discussed the abortive road-trip to Deauville with which the novel ends. But the novel opens with an equally explicit symbol of immobility: Madjid's broken down motorcycle.

> The old cycle, a Norton, was left breathless at each difficulty. You practically had to push it up a hill like the one at la Défense, and on the Pontoise freeway Madjid had panicked the night he was overtaken by a truck. It just couldn't take it any more, his old machine. To fix it up would take money, and Madjid didn't have any. (Charef 9)

Given the strongly anthropomorphic tenor of this passage, it seems fair to interpret it as a metaphorical portrait of Madjid himself: the difficulty in surmounting obstacles, the inability to make an effort without being pushed, the sense of panic at being overtaken, and a feeling of being prematurely over-the-hill—an old machine. We're told that it's a lack of money that keeps him from getting the bike working right. But we also learn over the course of the novel that Madjid, thanks to his various criminal exploits, regularly finds himself in possession of more-or-less significant amounts of money. Of course, somehow the money never goes toward getting his machine rolling again. Any question of actually leaving, it seems, is always deferred. It's not insignificant, in this light, that a big part of the informal uniform of Madjid and his buddies is the brand of boots that most of them wear: Santiagos, a well-known brand of motorcycle boots. We quickly come to understand, however, that whatever these boots were made for, they will not be used for going anywhere. They have been reduced to a purely decorative function.

This is, then, ultimately a story about stasis—even entrapment. But it is also a story about the *banlieue* as a specific type of environment that creates certain kinds of people. It is in this sense that we can speak of environmental determinism in Charef's novel. This becomes apparent in an important chapter that evokes the stark austerity of the suburban landscape and suggests that it plays a determinant role in shaping the personalities of those who grow up there:

> It's in the concrete that they grow, the children. They grow up and resemble it, this dry, cold concrete. They too are dry and cold, hard, apparently inde-structible, but there are also cracks in the concrete. When it rains, you see them better, it's like tears that run down the pale cheeks of a kid . . . It runs in rivulets on the skin, and it surprises and it goes down like a river on one of the maps they tried to get us to learn in geography . . . So many fissures in the concrete: on the heart, on the forehead, already at such a young age. (Charef 62)

For these children, the *cité is* nature (concrete is the soil in which they grow), and they are themselves the tenacious-but-frail, beautiful-but-brittle reproductions-in-miniature of an arid, cracked, desert landscape. They have been marked by this environment both spiritually (on the heart) and physically (on the forehead).

Given the generally negative connotations of the housing projects that make up this universe, it is surprising to note how morosely lyrical the passages devoted to describing the *cité* and its inhabitants really are. We sense a deep bond with this landscape alongside the recognition that it is shaping a generation of emotionally stunted youths who will most likely never be able to overcome the damage done by such a harsh environment: "You don't get over concrete. It is all around you, heavy, in your gestures, your voice, your language . . . It will follow whoever is born into it, even to Peru . . . Concrete has an odor too . . . How to get rid of that odor? Fat Chance! [*Oualou*] They've tried everything, all the beer in the world, all the drugs too" (Charef 63). Ultimately, Charef suggests, it is this environment that has created the predatory attitude that we find even in otherwise likeable characters like Madjid. Like wolves starving in a wintry forest, the children of concrete become aggressive out of desperation:

> It doesn't sing, concrete, it howls in despair like the wolves of the forest, paws in the snow, without even the strength to dig a hole to die in. They wait like jerks, to see if someone won't come lend them a hand. They wait, just like the kids of the concrete. They're intimidating too. People stay away from their territory. When someone decides to pay attention to them, it's to find a better, cleaner, way to destroy them. To isolate them. It's as a pack that they attack. Sowing their mischief. (Charef 63–4)

Passages like this one help us to better understand why we find the strange mix of endearing traits and outright inhumanity that characterize Madjid and Pat. Charef's intention, it turns out, is not to discredit the stereotypes of ghetto criminality but to lament the tragic plight of the children of concrete and to emphasize the extent to which their antisocial behavior is the direct consequence of the inhospitable environmental conditions they must endure. Cut off from mainstream society, isolated on the outskirts of the city, and herded into unlivable housing blocks, they are like the victims of Foucault's carceral society. And Charef, who seems to share Foucault's pessimism about the ability of individuals to overcome the gravitational force of such conditions, seems less interested in excusing, justifying, or putting an end to such behavior as in diagnosing the underlying condition, which is the *banlieues* themselves, encapsulated in the almost elemental image of concrete.

Mobility, Immobility, and the Place Effect

This diagnosis of the *banlieue* problem emphasizes the themes of alienation and lack of belonging that Tarr identifies as most characteristic of the first phase of *Beur* cinema in the 1980s (Tarr 15, 17), although I would argue that it is the geographic, spatial problem more than the ethnic problem that is foregrounded here. Indeed, I would argue that one of the things that makes Charef's novel important is the way it pivots from the ethnic to the geographical theme. After all, Pat, the truly vicious one of the pair, is white, and although Madjid does lament his cultural in-betweenness in the first pages of the novel, Charef increasingly uses passages like the ones just examined to push the novel in the direction of an indictment of inhospitable living conditions. In this way, the novel, published in 1983, provides an early attempt to examine from the inside a set of spatial problems that is all too easy for the comfortable classes to forget when the populations in question have been geographically and socially isolated.

At the most obvious level, Charef's diagnosis highlights what I have been calling the place effect. It suggests that the stultifying material conditions of the *cité*, symbolized by its grey concrete landscape, play a crucial role in explaining the stultified outlooks of young people like Madjid and Pat. In this, Charef's novel resonates with the work of sociologists like Catherine Bidou-Zachariasen, who have emphasized the *effet de lieu* (or *effet de territoire*, as she calls it) in their analyses of suburban dysfunction. In her article, "La prise en compte de l'effet de territoire' dans l'analyse des quartiers urbains," Bidou-Zachariasen examines two neighborhoods that have comparable economic and ethnic profiles but are opposed along geographical lines. One is a more traditional urban *quartier* near the city center, which she describes as functioning well despite the low economic status of its inhabitants. The other is a social housing project in the *banlieue*, judged to be lacking the positive qualities of the more traditional neighborhood. From this contrast, she draws the conclusion that the physical infrastructure of the *banlieue* environment plays the determinant role in explaining the relative lack of dynamism and social cohesion of the suburban social housing projects. While taking into account the larger structural forces that weigh upon the urban poor (primarily in relation to underemployment, economic globalization, and the passage from a Fordist to a post-Fordist economy), she suggests that, unlike the mixed-use neighborhoods still found in city centers, the monofunctional residential neighborhoods of the suburbs are inherently prone to problems: "This type of built space has revealed a double layer of rigidity: that of the lifestyles to which it is linked and that that of the functions that it fosters" (Bidou-Zachariasen 105, my translation). Geography trumps structure.

If, however, we pay close attention to the mobility/immobility theme examined above, we begin to see another, equally if not more important, spatial element that needs to be taken into account. This is the question of mobility. To develop the implications of this reading, we might turn to Azouz Begag, who has devoted his career as both a novelist and sociologist to addressing the question of social mobility, which he tends to link, quite literally, to the need for geographical mobility. In *Les dérouilleurs* (2002), Begag speculates on the origins of the tragically circumscribed sense of self we've just seen. For Begag, youths like Pat and Madjid identify so strongly with their home territory because they lack the richer sense of identity and self-worth that would come from a strong sense of belonging to a larger community of some kind, be it the kind of tightly knit ethnic community that first-generation immigrants often still have or the larger national community from which minorities so often feel excluded. Such youths, according to Begag, become territorial and adopt a street-gang sense of turf as a kind of substitute. As Begag explains it,

> These youths are more fragmented on the social plane and lack any sense of multiple belonging. The fusion of their personality and of the place—the *cité*, the neighborhood, a housing block, a building—takes up the majority of their internal identitarian space. They no longer have any sense of an ethnic community: that belongs to a past that has left few traces in them. (*Les dérouilleurs* 146)

Begag, although a strong supporter of the French tradition of republican universalism, clearly believes that a sense of one's ethnic identity and traditions can be an important source of stability for those threatened by social and spatial marginalization. But rather than contesting the French model of assimilation, he emphasizes the need for these youths to break the spell of the attachment to home. (This is an outlook that resonates strongly with Certeau's theory of spatial practices: identification with the ethnic community and home is desirable but no longer feasible.) Begag, in a sense, draws from the link between geographical immobility and social immobility established by Charef the conclusion that increased geographical mobility is a necessary first step toward social mobility, arguing that it can lead to greater levels of intercultural contact and exchange beneficial to all.

If we return now to the Tadjer and Chibane narratives in light of this question of mobility and immobility, it becomes clear that for them the most fulfilling sense of place—the sense that one has a deep, organic relationship with one's home base—comes not from turning inward and remaining snugly sheltered within the confines of one's home territory but in looking outward and strengthening the ties between that place and the outside world. A productive sense of home and rootedness is strengthened by the ability to come and go, to see the place from the outside, and to get away from it and come back with fresh eyes. (This is something that anyone who has lived abroad knows very well.) Departure without the possibility of return is exile; but the inability to leave at all is either imprisonment or solipsism.

We see this same dynamic of home and away at work in many other *Beur* narratives. In Begag's *Le gone du Chaâba*, for example, the denizens of the shantytown initially prefer the sense of security they find there, despite the squalor, over the thought of moving elsewhere. Being surrounded by one's own people seems preferable to living apart, even if living apart results in vastly superior conditions. It is only when they are forcibly evicted that the hero's family begins to appreciate the advantages of a real apartment in the city, where they can live in greater comfort and have contact with people outside their own ethnic group. The novel ends ominously, however, with the family being shunted off into a newly constructed housing project—one that will no doubt have many of the comforts of their city apartment and where they will also perhaps regain contact with the immigrant community but that will also have the effect of isolating them from the mainstream society of the city center.

Similarly, the drama of Zouina (Fejria Deliba) in Yamina Benguigui's film *Inch'Allah Dimanche* (2001) is that of her attempts to break out of her imprisonment in the family apartment and enter into contact with members of the community around her. (This is, of course, a theme that has special resonance for women, especially within the context of conservative Muslim families and the tradition of cloistering.) And to cite one last example, Abdellatif Kechiche's 2003 film *L'esquive* (which might be translated as "getting away") emphasizes the importance of social mobility by translating it into the discursive realm of eloquence and expressivity. The crucial trait that decides which characters will be successful is their discursive range—their relative ability (or inability in the case of the sensitive but hapless protagonist Krimo) to talk one's way into and out of different social situations. This involves being able to switch rapidly between different linguistic and rhetorical registers, from the impenetrable argot the kids use among themselves to the kind of politely submissive tone necessary to deal with the cops, to the language of Marivaux's *Game of Love and Chance* (the play being put on by the students).

What all of these works have in common is their emphasis on the need to reach outside of one's comfort zone, traversing that eminently unfamiliar (and therefore uncomfortable) space between communities—Bhabha's Third Space or *entre-deux*—in order to build a more extensive map of the world, to better understand one's place in it, and to master the art of navigating its social and political complexities, which is, in this context, strictly synonymous with the art of (social) survival. The ethically suspect gesture that set the story of Moussa and Jean-Luc into motion, like that of Omar (the hero of Tadjer's *Bel Avenir*), has the effect of pushing the protagonists out of their comfort zone and into what is, for them, unmapped territory, which forces them to improvise solutions without preestablished guidelines to help them navigate. This improvisatory ability is the mark of their success and also, apparently, what Pat and Madjid lack in Charef's novel.

We might think of this entry into the *entre-deux* in terms of Certeau's emphasis on tactics and his insistence on the need to leave behind the attachment to place (seen as an atavistic clinging to home) in order to engage in the liberating practice of space. We could also think of it in terms of the spatial metaphors favored by Deleuze and Guattari: deterritorialization and nomadism. But, and this is the crucial point, if Certeau makes a virtue of tactical thinking as a way of life, which he opposes to strategic, institutional thinking, and if Deleuze and Guattari make a virtue of deterritorialization to the point of seeing reterritorialization as the weak moment of thought, then we must realize that the suburban narratives studied here have a more conservative agenda. The interstitial phase of their search is understood as being justifiable only to the extent that it ends in a final reterritorialization, which is often conceived in rather conventional, strategic, terms: marriage, economic success, social integration, recognition, and the return home.[10] The protagonists of these narratives do not seek to found a radically new social order or promote revolutionary violence—although other *banlieue* filmmakers, like Jean-François Richet, do—or to use tactical maneuvers as a way to foil the panoptic gaze of hegemonic power. Their project is, rather, fundamentally reformist. It is an attempt to repair the existing system from within so as, precisely, to become visible within that system as full partners in the social project of the French Republic, a republic whose legitimacy they do not contest in any fundamental way.

This is clearly a lesson aimed directly at the youths in question. But it is also a lesson that has important implications for policy makers. Rather than focusing exclusively on the *banlieue* problem at the neighborhood level, an approach that assumes the determinant role of the immediate environment ("l'effet de lieu") and that does little to promote communication between periphery and center, it is important to think more about how bridges can be built between these peripheral communities and the centers of power. The state has in important role to play in helping suburban youths to break out of this impoverished form of self-identification, notably by shifting the emphasis of lococentric urban renewal projects onto projects that enhance mobility (both social and geographic) and communication between communities. Much of the French "politique de la ville" in the last thirty years has been focused on improving the conditions within underprivileged neighborhoods. This is no doubt a necessary part of any egalitarian urban policy, but in the course of his research Begag interviewed many *dérouilleurs* (those inhabitants of the *banlieues* who have succeeded in breaking out of the defeatist mindset of the urban underclass) and was repeatedly reminded of the need to leave the familiar but stifling cocoon of the home territory. As one of his informants put it,

What I hate in today's urban planning is its territorial politics: everything has to happen in the shadow of the buildings, and the catch-word of the elected officials is "proximity." I say that proximity kills . . . Today, we have to fight to give kids a chance to go elsewhere. Proximity only gives the illusion that we're going to tighten up the social bonds of the community. (Begag, *Les dérouilleurs* 148)

After thirty years of a *politique de la ville* focused on the construction and rehabilitation of neighborhoods conceived in isolation, more emphasis on the connections between those neighborhoods and the centers of power would be welcome. This is a message that seems to have gotten through on some level to the planners of Nicolas Sarkozy's signature project for *Le Grand Paris*, which was, at least as initially formulated, designed around the idea of better connecting the Parisian suburbs with each other and with the city center, both through infrastructural improvements (a train system) and an integrated administration that would cover Paris and the Petite Couronne of suburbs around it.[11] Of course in order for such a project to be implemented, it would first have to overcome the resistance of those in the city centers who feel more comfortable with the spatial and psychological barriers between periphery and center left in place. The question of urban renewal and reform is as much a cultural and ideological battle as an administrative or practical one.

The vast majority of *Beur* youths are products of the French *Education nationale* and have been successfully inculcated with the dominant values of the French republic. The works of *Beur* authors are all but unanimous on this point—at least as it applies to second and third generation immigrants. There are, of course, exceptions to every rule—sometimes spectacular ones—but the more extreme assertions of analysts like Christopher Caldwell (author of 2009's *Reflections on the Revolution in Europe*) about the general disinclination of Muslims to assimilate strike me as needlessly alarmist. Vigilance is no doubt necessary on the subject of Islamic extremism, and the lure of extremism can make use of the feelings of alienation and exclusion experienced by many minorities (and many adolescents!), but the categorical projection of suspicion onto the entire community of Islamic immigrants and their descendants is unconscionable.[12] Indeed, recent developments, including the mainstreaming of the *Front National* and the cooptation of many of its arguments by Sarkozy's UMP (*Union pour un Mouvement Populaire*) and other Center-Right parties suggests that, if anything, the greater impediment to the social and economic integration of France's impoverished minority populations is coming from the mainstream French side. It is that possibility—and possible reactions to it—that I would like to explore in the conclusion to this chapter.

Of Riots, Republicanism, Resistance, and Reform

The recent waves of urban violence in France's suburbs—especially the riots of 2005, which spread throughout the country—bring these issues into sharp focus. The journalistic hullaballoo around these events gave rise to a thousand theories on the root causes of the problem, ranging from the inassimilability of Muslims (Caldwell, *Reflections on the Revolution in Europe*) to a weakening of the French social network due to the penetration of neoliberal economic principles (Wacquant, *Urban Outcasts*), to the failure of the French model of assimilation (Tshimanga, Gondola, and Bloom), and to (bizarrely, given France's adherence to its universalist, assimilationist principles) the failure of European multiculturalism (formulated in recent high profile statements by Angela Merkel, David Cameron, and Sarkozy).[13]

From another perspective, though, these riots were very French. Street violence has a long and storied role in the history of French political action. Moreover, although the rioters were not part of an organized movement with clearly formulated political goals, commentators like Didier Lapeyronnie have shown how the disorganized, spontaneous, apparently pointless violence of rioters may actually provide, in certain circumstances, a rational response to a set of legitimate grievances: "These primitive rebels make an appeal to the *values* of society against a social *order* they judge immoral and, at the same time, demand to become part of that order, to be acknowledged" (Lapeyronnie, "Primitive Rebellion" 26, emphasis added). The resort to violence is justified by an appeal to ethical values that transcend the legal order, because that order is, itself, judged to be the problem. Moreover, because they feel themselves to be locked out of the political process and to be actively targeted rather than protected by the state (in particular the police), they feel that their only option is this kind of inchoate violence, which Lapeyronnie presents as an *expressive* and occasionally *effective* mode of action: "The populations that engage in [rioting] remain on the outside and erect their 'us' against the institutions, but nevertheless intend to provoke an institutional reaction or bring about reforms" ("Primitive Rebellion" 26).[14]

We might give a similar reading to the apparently senseless violence of Pat and Madjid. Like many ghetto youth, they feel locked out of mainstream society and unable to access the officially sanctioned tools of the political process. As a result, they lash out against that system while simultaneously longing to join it. In fact, it is on this level that we find, I think, the true meaning of the casual criminality that is so pervasive in *banlieue* narratives: that criminality and expressive rage may be the only available recourse for youths who find themselves trapped in the double bind of a society that tells them they must (culturally and socially) integrate but then doesn't make available the tools necessary for (economic and geographical) integration. The real question is whether that activity can subsequently take on a socially productive valence. For Omar, Moussa, and Jean-Luc, the answer is yes. For Madjid and Pat, it's no.

If, as I have argued, the primary lesson of these narratives is the necessity of entering into the interstitial zone between established cultural and value systems in order to reform the existing social order from within, we must remember that this message is directed not only at potential *dérouilleurs* but also at the mainstream French public. The process of deterritorialization and reterritorialization cannot result in true reform if it is embraced only by those without much political power. Short of a revolution, then, a meaningful search for real solutions to the endemic problems at issue here will necessarily involve the participation of the dominant community, too. The ideologues of the far Right will never be open to such arguments, of course. But there is perhaps a group on the Left and Center who would be receptive to these arguments that is large enough to make a difference. What would this entail?

For one thing, it might be necessary to rethink some of the sacrosanct principles of color-blind republicanism—or at least the ways in which they are deployed. This is emphatically *not* to say that the French should simply turn to an Anglo-American multiculturalist model of social interaction but rather that a rigid application of 230-year-old republican principles to problems they weren't designed to handle may be more useful as a way to find political cover than to seek real solutions. At some point, the practical question of the greatest common good becomes compelling enough to override an established principle.

Is the French public—Left, Right, or Center—open to such a challenge? An interesting test case for this question is the somewhat less remembered mass uprising that took place in the year between the 2005 suburban riots and the riots of 2007. I'm referring to the wave of protests that were sparked by the passage of the *Contrat première embauche* (CPE) as part of the Equal Opportunity Act (*Loi sur l'égalité des chances*) of 2006. The CPE amendment purported to lengthen the probationary period governing hiring/firing of youths in exchange for some financial guarantees for the employees. The idea is that the law would create new entry-level job opportunities for youths—enabling more of them to gain an early foothold in the job market—by giving employers substantially more flexibility in hiring and firing. Introduced less than a year after the suburban riots of 2005, this initiative was proposed as a way to facilitate the social insertion of marginalized youths. But it provoked such a massive wave of protests that the amendment was eventually repealed. There certainly were legitimate reasons to oppose the CPE (such as maintaining the exceptionally high level of job security that employed workers have long enjoyed in France and suspicion that Chirac's prime minister Dominique de Villepin was using the urban unrest of the preceding months as a wedge for a neoliberal attack on French labor laws). But this event could also be construed as a case where the reflexive rejection of all forms of special treatment had an antiegalitarian consequence, quashing a legitimate attempt to bring more chronically unemployed but willing workers into the labor force. Coming as it did on the heels of the suburban unrest of the year before, the student mobilization had, for many, the appearance of a privileged group fighting to protect its privileges against the underprivileged. In this respect, it is comparable to the resentment against corporate outsourcing of jobs to foreign countries—except that the recipients of the new jobs would have been compatriots. This ungenerous aspect of the demonstrations led some commentators to make unfavorable comparisons between the 2006 demonstrations and the 1968 student movement: "The middle-class youth revolt is not about getting more, as was the case in the 1968 student uprisings, it's about keeping what it has" (Portier).

We have already examined some of the ways in which the universalist principle of color-blindness makes it difficult to protect minorities against street-level discrimination. The anti–CPE demonstrations also suggest that the putative impartiality of the "abstract citizenship" dimension of republican ideology can become a screen for attitudes that may not be discriminatory per se but that serve to perpetuate de facto inequalities—in this case by allowing those who had access to recognized forms of political pressure (e.g., strikes and demonstrations) to overturn a law that was already on the books and might have contributed to a real reduction in social inequality and the tensions that go along with it.

These are not, however, the only reasons to call into question the almost religious veneration for the principles of French Republicanism, which some have termed *intégrisme laïque* (secular fundamentalism). We also need to question the putative universality of these principles, which in practice often have a hidden localist bias. As Kenan Malik has argued, the republican emphasis on assimilation, although laudable in principle, can become in practice a tool of discrimination:

> In principle, the French assimilationist resolve to treat everyone as a citizen, not simply as an inhabitant of a particular ethnic box, is welcome. Yet as evidenced by police brutality against North African youth and the state ban on burqas, France continues to tolerate, and even encourage, *policies that polarize society in the name of colorblindness.*" (Malik, "Assimilation's Failure," emphasis added)

The universalist principle of color blindness, designed to protect citizens against institutionalized discrimination, can become a kind of alibi, a cover for tolerance of discrimination, which Malik terms "racism blindness": "We also need to make a distinction between color blindness and racism blindness. The two have become confused, so that in France, for instance, arguments against multiculturalism have become an argument in defense of racism. Discriminatory policies . . . have been defended on the basis that they are necessary for assimilation" (Malik, "Multiculturalism"). The French pride themselves on this principle of universalism and many of them, like Wacquant, insist on making a clear-cut distinction between American-style ghettoes (which have their origins in institutionalized racism) and the French *banlieues* (in which the concatenation of minority status and economic deprivation is seen as an incidental result of the fact that most immigrants begin at the bottom of the economic ladder). But the current conjuncture seems to be moving in the direction of the American ghetto, creating an underclass of racialized "others" that has been largely "contained" in the *banlieues* (as Lapeyronnie argues in "Primitive Rebellion"). To be sure, as Wacquant insists, racial segregation in France is much less severe than in the United States, but recent census data suggests that the geographic and economic separation between *français de souche* and minorities is becoming an increasingly pervasive phenomenon. Moreover, the level of anti-immigrant, antiminority sentiment is just as high in France (and Europe) as in the United States and has been mounting in recent years across the continent, under the combined weight of economic crisis and a growing perception of a demographic threat to the "traditional" (i.e., white) culture of Europe coming from (mainly Islamic) minorities. Such arguments always seem to carry more weight in times of economic stress, when the logic of scapegoating is most likely to kick in. And the recent attacks on multiculturalism by Merkel, Cameron, and Sarkozy feed into this dynamic. It is in this way that the *banlieues* have increasingly become segregation machines even as the French government and most French intellectuals, on the Left as well as Right, insist on maintaining the strictest principles of republican universalism.

This is not to say that there has been an irreversible ghettoisation of the country but instead that, given the current political and economic atmosphere, France finds itself at a critical juncture. What, then, can be done about it? What concrete measures can be taken to encourage the social, cultural, and economic integration of France's suburban poor that (a) do not violate the egalitarian spirit that gave rise to the color-blind principles of the republican system; (b) are economically viable, despite the ongoing "post-Fordist" restructuring of Western economies; and (c) can gain sufficient support from the voting populace? The key goals of such a plan would be to increase the opportunities available to those living in the *banlieues à problèmes*, to promote contact between the *banlieue* populations and the rest of France, and to break the us-versus-them mentality characteristic of the *banlieues*. As a literary scholar, I am not particularly well placed to offer authoritative advice on such issues, but there are a few proposals that flow naturally from my readings of the literary works.

1. *Mobility.* It is time, as Begag suggests, to move the *politique de la ville* away from a lococentric model to a model emphasizing (social and geographic) mobility.
2. *Police reform.* Since, as Lapeyronnie shows, much of the suburban rage is due to poor relations with the police, it will be necessary to improve police training to create a more disciplined, culturally sensitive police force, with more emphasis on community building and conflict resolution techniques. A community-based policing model would be preferable to one involving officers who only show up when there is trouble.
3. *Jobs corps.* High unemployment and the grim economic outlook are, of course, among the most intractable structural issues facing the *banlieues*. Simply calling for more job creation serves no purpose. But there may be ways to stimulate job creation that would help the *banlieues* by promoting a higher degree of social and geographical mixing. Something like a jobs corps—modeled on the principle of the *service militaire* (which was abolished in 2001) but oriented toward community building and public service projects—could promote this goal.
4. *Culture wars.* Putting an end to the ongoing culture wars over the veil, burqa, mosques, and other infringements on the expressions of minority identities would help to reduce the sense of victimization among those minorities. Practices like polygamy and female circumcision, of course, are more complicated, since they conflict directly with French law.
5. *Racism blindness.* As Malik shows, the principle of *laïcité* can be used as an alibi for tolerating discrimination, notably in the job market and police enforcement. How could this problem be resolved? The recent (but apparently abortive) movement to make the "anonymous CV" a central part of the hiring process provides food for thought. This is also a question of intercultural sensitivity. There are certainly adjustments to school curricula that would, over time, foster a greater sense of tolerance and inclusiveness without violating the universalist imperative (through, for example, the addition of an ethnic studies component to civics or history courses).

6. *Parité géographique.* Passage, of the June 6, 2000 law on *Parité* ("l'égal accès des femmes et des hommes aux mandats électoraux et fonctions électives") shows that the French public will consider certain forms of preferential treatment for subgroups. How can this model be adapted for use in the *banlieues*? Perhaps it would be possible to encourage a geographic or socioeconomic form of *parité* that would ensure that disadvantaged neighborhoods benefit from more direct political representation at the regional and national levels.

These are not cure-alls, obviously. Some of them may not be able to pass all the necessary political, economic, and administrative tests (e.g., voter approval, affordability, and implementation), while some are currently under debate. I consider them here as part of an effort to find ways in which the social problems of the *banlieues* could be addressed from within the current republican framework.

Achille Mbembe writes, "The question posed today to the secular republican democracy of France is that of knowing how to liberate the notion of difference from its negative connotations and introduce into it other norms and values" (Mbembe, "Décoloniser les structures," my translation). France (and Europe in general) has become, whether it likes it or not, a postcolonial country—shaped, at its metropolitan core, to an extent it could not have predicted two hundred years ago by questions of difference that are a direct consequence of its colonial past. An important part of the future development of its national character will be determined by its ability to negotiate the current social and spatial crisis in terms that are more compatible with its republican ideals than with its colonial history, while also keeping in mind that a *rigid* application of those principles (i.e., a "foundationalist" or "originalist" application, as opposed to a historically informed one) does not make sense in the current conjuncture. With such thoughts in mind, then, I turn now to the question of postcolonial place, asking how postcolonial history, theory, and literature can contribute to a renewed understanding of the national space that is cohesive but not exclusionary and that could, moreover, be universal in its application, in the sense that it would be as relevant to the former colonial powers as to their former colonial territories.

Part III

Postcolonial Place

5

Place after
Postcolonial Studies

Implied in the title of this chapter are two symmetrically related questions. First, how has our understanding of place changed since the advent of postcolonial studies? That is, what do the central themes and methodologies of postcolonial studies contribute to the theory of place? Second, to what extent has it become necessary today to move beyond postcolonial approaches to the study of place? This second, more controversial question is motivated not by some desire to contest the legitimacy of postcolonial studies as a field but by my sense that it might now be necessary to think about how to reintegrate the themes, problems, and methodologies associated with the field into the larger discipline of cultural studies, making possible a *post*postcolonial phase of the field or, better yet, making it possible to drop that frustratingly backward-looking "*post*" prefix altogether, moving instead in the direction of world literature or transnational or global studies.

Place, as we have seen, had come to be perceived as a somewhat dubious object of inquiry by the middle of the twentieth century, derided by postwar geographers of a positivistic bent as unscientifically subjective and then, in the 1970s, by poststructuralists as essentially a humanist myth. The 1970s also saw, however, the beginnings of a struggle to reassert place as a legitimate object of geographical inquiry, with the humanist geographers in particular emphasizing the need to defend geographically bound identities and cultural heritages from the delocalizing, homogenizing, destructive forces of modernity and postmodernity (Fordist standardization, suburbanization, environmental degradation, media saturation, etc.).

It so happens that this period also marks the rise of postcolonial studies as a distinct academic subdiscipline. Within the field of postcolonial studies, however, the concept of place has been subject to at least as much suspicion as it has in the poststructuralist tradition. This is due in large part to the strategic uses to which the notion of place has been put over the course of colonial history. If "myth consists in turning culture into nature," as Roland Barthes famously put it (Barthes 65), then the very efficacy of localizing imagery as a way "to naturalize the rhetoric of national affiliation and its forms of collective expression" (Bhabha, "DissemiNation" 295) suggests the need to question such images in terms of their motives.[1] For this reason, postcolonial spatiality has most often been theorized in terms of the artificiality of the conventions governing representations of the colonized territory. The relatively direct experience of place postulated by the humanist geographers is subjected to a critique of the various levels of mediation that intervene between a given place and its representations. The section devoted to place in the influential *Postcolonial Studies Reader*, edited by Ashroft, Griffiths, and Tiffin (1995), is symptomatic of this tendency. The editors preface this section with a warning that place as understood in postcolonial studies has less to do with location or spatial *experience* as with language and ideology: "The theory of place does not simply propose a binary separation between the 'place' named and described in language, and some 'real' place inaccessible to it, but rather indicates that in some sense place *is* language" (391).[2]

This theoretical suspicion of the "naturalness" of place has not kept it from playing an important role in postcolonial literature. There can be no doubt that the attachment to place, usually defined in terms of the homeland, has been a central preoccupation of writers and artists from former colonies. From the Martinique of Aimé Césaire's *Cahier d'un retour au pays natal* to Ahmadou Kourouma's Horodugu in *Les soleils des indépendances*, to the Somalia of Nuruddin Farah's *Maps*, and to the Vietnam of Anna Moï's *L'écho des rizières*, expressions of affection for the landscapes and landmarks of one's homeland play a prominent role. But one of the particularities of these evocations of the homeland is their insistence on the need to recover an originary identity that has been lost or covered over by colonization. This creates a powerful sense of ambivalence about the true nature of one's attachment to the homeland. The political struggle to establish the territorial autonomy of the colonized land is often enmeshed with the symbolic struggle to establish the identity of the postcolonial nation in terms of a recovery of a precolonial past. As Edward Said has argued, "For the native, the history of his or her colonial servitude is inaugurated by the loss to an outsider of the local place, whose concrete geographical identity must thereafter be searched for and somehow restored" (Said, *Nationalism, Colonialism and Literature* 77).

How, then, can the postcolonial tradition of place (as something that must be uncovered and/or restored) enrich the phenomenological approach to place (as direct experience) and vice versa? Can the humanist emphasis on the phenomenological experience of place even be reconciled with the postcolonial suspicion of colonial misrepresentation and cartographic manipulation? The answers to such questions have varied over time, so it will be helpful to examine here the evolution of postcolonial studies, which has its origins in the anticolonial activism of the 1950s and 1960s but evolved over the course of the 1970s into a distinct field whose disciplinary specificity is defined by its focus on the ideological machinery of colonialism and its legacy. It is a field founded, to quote Achille Mbembe, on the principle that "the colonial project was not reducible to a simple military-economic system, but was underpinned by a discursive infrastructure, a symbolic economy, a whole apparatus of knowledge the violence of which was as much epistemic as it was physical" (Mbembe, "What Is Postcolonial Thinking?"). This discursive emphasis of the field has been construed both as a strength (making it particularly adept at deconstructing the myths of official power and subjugation) and a weakness (since it tends to privilege refined, and sometimes abstruse, cultural analyses over more directly political forms of action).

The Evolution of Postcolonial Studies

Building on this definition of postcolonial studies as a form of discursive critique, we can divide the history of the field into three main moments or phases: a long anticolonial phase, which culminates in the massive wave of decolonizations in the 1960s; the "classical" moment of postcolonial critique, which lasts from the mid-1970s to the early 1990s; and an aftermath or mutated form of the field, which is ongoing and marked by a preoccupation with globalization. The first phase is primarily activist in orientation and is intertwined with the rise of identity politics; the second is deconstructionist in outlook and focused on understanding the role of colonialism in shaping the social and cultural institutions of the modern world; and the third has been shaped by an understanding of globalization that emphasizes its origins in the colonial system and its neocolonial avatars.[3]

The first (anticolonial) phase of this tradition is embodied in the work of writers like Fanon, Césaire, Memmi, and Sartre and is often powered by essentialist identitarian programs like those associated with negritude, Panafricanism, Black Power, and Hindu Nationalism. Then, as the unifying struggle against external domination gave way in the 1970s to the more complex dynamics of the postcolonial era, texts like Derek Walcott's "The Muse of History" (1974) signaled the turn toward postcolonial studies *proprement dit*—the second phase in my chronology.

This second phase of postcolonial studies is often said to begin in earnest with the publication of Edward Said's *Orientalism* in 1978, which marks a distinct change in orientation, as direct political opposition gives way increasingly before the analysis of culture and ideology. The anticolonial origins of postcolonial studies ensured that this work would continue to have a strong activist dimension, with questions of social justice at the fore (as well as outstanding issues of decolonization, like the Palestinian dispute, South African Apartheid, and the French Overseas Department question), but the focus in western academic circles is increasingly on cultural oppositions rather than oppositional politics. Accordingly, these writers are less focused on colonialism per se (direct colonial domination has increasingly become a thing of the past) and more focused on the internal dynamics of postcolonial societies and the ideological legacy of colonialism.

Some, like Arif Dirlik, have taken a dim view of this tendency, seeing in it a sign that postcolonial intellectuals serve as a comprador intelligentsia, wittingly or unwittingly facilitating the neocolonial exploitation of their homeland while improving their own social status by focusing critical attention on cultural questions of secondary importance instead of on the more pressing questions of economic and social justice.[4] There is no doubt some truth to such claims, and many, like Dirlik, Spivak, and Ahmad, have sought to push the field back toward its activist origins. Still, this discursive turn in postcolonial studies corresponds to a real change in conditions on the ground. In this new phase of postcolonial studies, the kinds of battles that must be fought have changed, and cultural critique has become an indispensable part of the progressive struggle for justice. Gone (for the most part) is the ideological clarity of the anticolonial period, and the tools of postcolonial studies have had to adapt to the more nebulous, subtle modes of domination and exploitation characteristic of neocolonialism. The head-to-head conflicts of the decolonization era have been succeeded by an ever more complex web of interdependencies, fostered in part by large-scale migration and by the influence of international institutions like the World Bank and the International Monetary Fund (IMF). In a world where former enemies have often become (at least nominally) friends, benefactors, and/or trade partners, armed conflict has given way to economic competition, enslavement to indebtedness, occupation to extraction, forcible expropriation to forced market liberalization, and indoctrination to mediatization. Given the indirectness and (relatively) noncoercive nature of these modes of control, often combined with the complicity of local ruling elites and the willing participation of large segments of the populations in question, the shift from an anticolonial to a postcolonial perspective requires a corollary focus on indirectness, complexity, interrelatedness, and the big picture. It is in light of such considerations that

Timothy Reiss has declared himself to be "against autonomy." How, he asks, "using instruments presupposing confrontation, separateness and isola-tion . . . are the spaces between cultural places to be bridged? How can one even envision homes, places, and times in their own particularities" if everything is conceived in the oppositional terms of class conflict and monolithic ethnic identities? (Reiss, "Mapping Identities" 122.)[5]

In this context, the events of 1989 mark a real turning point. The fall of the Berlin wall and the crumbling of the Soviet empire bring about the moment of neoliberal triumphalism, facilitating the spread of economic globalization and accelerating the "financialization of the globe" as Spi-vak has called it (364). This event, more than any other, marks the change that will bring about the third phase of postcolonial studies, which might be thought of as a *post*postcolonial iteration of the field in the sense that, focused increasingly on the economic and cultural problems associated with globalization, the ties between such problems and the history of colo-nialism are less direct and more intertwined with other developments. Thus if the central preoccupation for the first generation of anticolonial thinkers was putting an end to colonial domination, and that of the classi-cal phase of postcolonial studies was understanding how colonial domina-tion continues to shape the world we live in, then the central question for the third phase of the field has become this: how can the smaller, weaker players on the world stage find justice and make a place for themselves in the global marketplace? This new question fundamentally changes the ground rules by which postcolonial studies had traditionally played.

Michael Hardt and Antonio Negri have emphasized the extent of the new challenge that globalization puts to (phase two) postcolonial studies, which they see as unable to cope with the realities of the contemporary world: "The post-colonialist perspective remains primarily concerned with colonial sovereignty . . . This may make postcolonialist theory a very pro-ductive tool for rereading history, but it is entirely insufficient for theoriz-ing contemporary global power" (Hardt and Negri 148). For Hardt and Negri, Empire (which is their term for the new neoliberal world order that has arisen in the era of globalization) "is not a weak echo of modern impe-rialism but a fundamentally new form of rule" (148). It is "a global order, a new logic and structure of rule—in short, a new form of sovereignty" (xi) that has grown up to fill the void left by national sovereignties, which are no longer able to control the flow of capital and production within or out-side of their borders. Thus the "basic hypothesis" of Hardt and Negri is that "sovereignty has taken a new form, composed of a series of national and supranational organisms united under a single logic of rule. This new global form of sovereignty is what we call Empire" (xii). This new state of affairs makes it imperative to discover a new mode of (legitimate) sovereignty able to give control back to the People, a collective entity they prefer to call "Multitude." It is this kind of political project that governs, implicitly or explicitly, the objectives of many postcolonial studies in the era of globalization while also complicating the relationship between the field and its traditional focus on colonialism and its aftermath. Emblematic of this turn of events is Achille Mbembe's decision to substantivize the adjective "postcolonial" itself. He writes of "the postcolony" as if postcolonial states were no longer societies in transition but rather a new kind of society that had been thought transitory but now seems to have implanted itself in the geopolitical landscape for good (see Mbembe, "Provisional Notes" and *On the Postcolony*). Thus we could say of the postcolony what Mbembe says of the refugee camp: It "ceases to be a provisional place, a space of transit that is inhabited while awaiting a hypothetical return home. From the legal as well as the factual point of view, what was supposed to be an exception becomes routine and the rule within an organization of space that tends to become permanent" (Mbembe, "At the Edge of the World" 270). This formulation acknowledges the hegemonic power of the neocolonial world order, but it also makes it clear that the resolution of such problems will require the development of a new strategic outlook. It is not that the post-colonial moment has ended for these thinkers, then, but that it is increasingly considered to be something that has no end and that is now simply part of the way the world is. They have begun to emphasize an understanding of colonialism that sees it as an instantiation of larger, transhistorical forces—not as a historical event *sui generis*. We have, it seems, taken up permanent residence in the *entre-deux*. What we had thought to be a transitional phase or interregnum has turned out to be the way of the world, making it necessary to understand even the horrors of the slave trade as, in Derek Walcott's turn of phrase, "men acting as men" (Walcott 27).

Neo-Marxist and Culturalist Geographies of Globalization

In response to this new state of affairs, the field of postcolonial studies has mutated. The anticolonial wing of the field, dominant during phase one, has evolved into a radical left or neo-Marxist critique of economic globalization, while the discourse-oriented wing of the field, dominant during phase two, has given rise to a culturalist response to globalization that deals with it in terms of the unprecedented levels of intercultural contact it has made possible. The first is political and activist in orientation, emphasizing the problem of (economic and political) justice, while the second strives to develop a cosmopolitan vision able to address the question of how to get along in a world characterized by increasingly pervasive transnational cultural flows.

The first tendency has its origins in the Marxist vein of anticolonial activism mentioned above and includes the work of Dirlik, Ahmad, and Spivak. In the aftermath of 1989, they have responded to the triumphalism of neoconservative thinkers like Fukuyama and Huntington (who interpreted 1989 as confirming the superiority of Western capitalistic modes of social organization and discrediting Marxist teleology), by reorienting their thinking to focus on globalization. The World Systems Theory of Immanuel Wallerstein provided a powerful model for this vision, as did the growing tendency in social geography to emphasize the extent to which localities are enmeshed in global networks of power, money, and information characterized by uneven development (see Smith). The second tendency, which I call culturalist, is carried forward by thinkers like Kwame Anthony Appiah, Simon Gikandi, Abiola Irele, Homi Bhabha, and Edouard Glissant. It maintains the traditional humanist emphasis on culture and literature, highlighting questions of intercultural understanding and individual subjectivities.

This opposition between neo-Marxism and culturalism can be reformulated in terms of the theoretical split studied in Parts I and II of this book: the neo-Marxists tend to think in terms of space, while the culturalists think in terms of place. Still, of central concern to both groups is the same fundamental ethical question: Can we conceive of a new kind of community in the era of globalization—one that is able to resist the corrosive, derealizing power of globalized capital without falling back into the ethnic nationalism and identitarian essentialism that marred so many of the national agendas put into place by the liberation movements of phase-one anticolonialism? On the need for such a vision, both the neo-Marxists and the culturalists can agree. But their respective approaches to this problem differ in ways that have important consequences for the spatial theme of this book.

The neo-Marxists tend to subordinate all questions of cultural difference and particular identities to the universalizing questions of economic and social justice. Thus Mbembe, haunted equally by the specter of interethnic violence on the African continent and by the increasing dominance of the "indirect private government" of transnational corporations, argues that it is only through a Marxian emphasis on class that such a community can be formed:

> It is indeed possible to propose new visions of community that are not necessarily biological, to invent new kinds of social bonds [*formes de parentés*] that transcend lineage and tribe. It is this kind of imaginative space that

must be opened up . . . It is necessary to translate the very idea of democracy into ordinary language . . . *to revive the sense of class consciousness* if we wish to escape from the trap of racialism *[aux rets de l'ethnisme].* (Mbembe, "Pour l'abolition des frontières," emphasis added)

Mbembe, to be sure, is not a Marxist—at least not in any doctrinaire sense. (He espouses a Foucauldian theory of power that tends to emphasize the structural constraints on human agency and, like Certeau, puts his hope in the "microstrategies" of social actors rather than in a concerted class based social strategy.) Nonetheless, his work is emblematic of the neo-Marxist position in its embrace of the abstract category of class as the most viable alternative to atavistic forms of social organization, which is conceived as an extension of ethnic or tribal thinking. In a related move, Fredric Jameson has insisted on the need to understand culture in terms of class, praising the "forced materialism" of third-world writers, which, he believes, prevents them from falling into the bourgeois sin of autoreferentiality (see Jameson, "Third World Literature" 65–88). Some neo-Marxists, like Peter Hallward, a self-proclaimed "neo-Jacobin," go so far as to actively condemn any emphasis on cultural difference as a distraction from or impediment to the fight for social and economic justice (see Hallward).

This outlook has important consequences for the neo-Marxist approach to questions of space and place. Such thinkers tend to think in the abstractive terms of space, at the expense of any particularist emphasis on place. They describe a global space segmented into geopolitical territories but shaped increasingly by an abstract network of economic forces that is able to cross national borders with ease. This tendency implies a top-down, "cartographic" perspective that emphasizes an abstractive understanding of the global situation rather than the particularities of the local situation. Thus, even though Mbembe is closely attuned to specifically African realities and to regional variations within the continent, his solutions to the continent's various problems entail a passage through the abstractive analysis of power, class, and "structural elements."

Hardt and Negri go even further in their deployment of this cartographic perspective, preferring to think on a global scale that tends to lose sight of all local struggles in the haze of generalities: "The forces that contest Empire and effectively prefigure an alternative global society are themselves not limited to any geographical region. The geography of these alternative powers, the new cartography, is still waiting to be written—or really, it is being written today through the resistances, struggles, and desires of the multitude" (xvi). The vagueness of their attempt to formulate an all-encompassing strategy for resistance on a global scale is no doubt understandable given the magnitude and scope of the project, but it leaves them ill equipped to envisage pragmatic solutions to the political and economic struggles they seek to foreground, insofar as those struggles are necessarily embedded in local political and economic conditions. They leave us with a need to bridge the gap between local tactics and global strategy. It is on this point that the culturalist branch of postcolonial studies can complement the work of neo-Marxist activists, provided that its insistence on cultural differences and local identities can be made to feed into consideration of political and economic realities. And it is around such questions of convergence—convergence of the local and the global and between the cultural and the political—that many of its activities have been focused.

Unlike the neo-Marxists, this second group, which I have been calling culturalist, tends to think first in the localized terms of individuals, communities, and places. It emphasizes the concerns of individuals belonging to geographically situated communities with their own distinct cultural identities and traditions, and it struggles with the problem of how to situate those localized cultural experiences within the larger web of global cultural interactions. To what extent, it asks, must the relationship between an individual and his or her local community be reconceived in an era of televisual and economic interconnectedness? This has given the question of cosmopolitanism renewed importance in the work of these thinkers and has led them to question, with renewed urgency, the promise as well as the problematic nature of the universalist aspirations of humanism in the Enlightenment tradition.

Simon Gikandi, for example, examines the same scourge of ethnic violence that leads Mbembe to choose class as the rallying point for a new model of African community—but arrives at very different conclusions. Like Mbembe, Gikandi argues for the need to leave behind the identitarian focus of so much postcolonial theory. (Indeed, he sees the contemporary rise of ethnic violence in Africa as a consequence of the European introduction of totalizing theories of racial difference into the African context.) But if this dimension of his thinking suggests a turn away from postcolonial theories of difference, it does not keep him from recognizing the central role played by local differences in the practical deployment of ideas. Thus he emphasizes "the simple fact that theories that appear imperative and liberating in one situation have no agency, or are quite dangerous, in another" (Gikandi 16). Local specificities, in other words, count, not only because people value their local affiliations and traditions, but also because the specific mix of conditions prevailing in any given place has the potential to fundamentally change the meaning of any given message. Theories of difference, for example, may play a liberatory role in a society characterized by powerful institutions and a dominant national culture (as in many Western countries), but they may have disastrous consequences in societies that lack institutional stability and that are struggling to forge a cohesive national identity in the face of conflicting demands from rival subcommunities (as in many African countries). What is needed, to put it chiasmatically, is not a theory of difference but more finely differentiated theories. Any totalizing theory claiming to have universal jurisdiction is bound to have unintended consequences and unforeseen implications when transported from one cultural context to another. This makes sensitivity to local conditions and recognition of jurisdictional limits a crucial element of any theory that takes its ethical obligations seriously. The law of unforeseen consequences must be factored into any attempt to generalize. This is why, for Gikandi, postcolonial studies must remain wary of the destabilizing power of Western theories of difference and find a way to revitalize the exploration of such old-fashioned "essentialist categories as community, being, and morality" (17). Those categories, he argues, are more pertinent to the present needs of African societies than any fashionably deconstructive or deterritorializing theory of difference would be.

It is worth pointing out here that what Gikandi is formulating is, at least in part, a theory of place: the same theory will have different actualizations from place to place, depending on local conditions. And lest there be any confusion on this point, we should note that this view is diametrically opposed to the kind of essentialist thinking that gave rise to the ethnophilosophy of Paulin Hountondji and Placide Tempels. Gikandi's point is emphatically *not* that different cultural groups have fundamentally different world views (ethnophilosophies) that are organically shared by all within the community. On the contrary, he believes that there are universals—including the concepts of community, being, and morality that are foregrounded in his article. His point is that those universals will express themselves differently in different places, depending on local circumstances. The differences between cultures are *conjunctural* not ontological; they are due to the ongoing interaction of various historical, geographical, and social forces rather than the result of some deeply ingrained common essence.

In a similar vein, Appiah emphasizes the need for legal and moral principles to be adapted to fit local circumstances. This principle is illustrated in such anecdotes as the "fender-bender" incident recounted in *In My Father's House* (8–9), which Appiah uses to show how different social sensibilities might lead to different but equally legitimate legal outcomes. But he also prefers the "modernist" emphasis on universal principles to "postmodernist" cultural and ethical relativism. This belief in the need to reconcile local differences with universal principles leads him to formulate his ethics in terms of an "Archimedean" search for an objective (nonethnocentric) vantage point outside of all existing cultures. Such a vantage point is by definition impossible to achieve (hence Archimedean), but we can none-theless make an *asymptotic* approach toward the formulation of universally applicable principles of truth and value. This involves, for Appiah, a dialecti-cal process of grappling sincerely with the cultural practices of others in an open but discriminating manner and being willing to put one's own cultural assumptions in jeopardy by taking seriously the practices of others.

Using this line of reasoning, Appiah sees the "primitivist" appropria-tion of African art practiced by Picasso, the Surrealists, and other European modernists as a positive development. Where other postcolonial critics have dismissed it as an illegitimate expropriation of cultural practices akin to Elginism or as a superficial domestication of alien forms, Appiah sees it as part of a struggle to overcome local cultural biases (see *In My Father's House* 137–57). This outlook is what gives rise to Appiah's later definition of cosmopolitanism as "universality plus difference" (*Cosmopolitanism* 151). It is not just a matter of finding a happy medium between the two extremes of universalism and particularism; rather, his approach requires an understanding of the ways in which close attention to the particular can lead us to universal truths—or at least beliefs that can make an asymptotic approach to the truth.

It is this insistence on the dialectic of difference and universality that makes the work of the culturalists so important for the question of place in a postcolonial context. Their work on the universality/difference dia-lectic opens up a third path—a middle way or *entre-deux*—between the extremes of ethnocentrism and universalism, in which the concept of place has a crucial role to play. By emphasizing the ways in which geographi-cal identities cut transversally through ethnic and social (class) affiliations, their work makes it possible to conceive of place as a base from which cul-tural differences can be preserved in the face of globalization and stan-dardization without succumbing to the exclusionary and discriminatory temptations evoked by both the neo-Marxists and universalizing human-ists like Gikandi and Appiah.

Toward a Postpostcolonial Poetics of Place

Before moving on to the literary analyses of the following chapter, it will be useful to provide a brief preview of the ways in which the three-stage evo-lution of postcolonial theory has influenced the representation of place in postcolonial literature. Schematically put, this evolution brings about suc-cessive shifts in the way the local place is conceived—of which the emblem-atic images might be the *nation* (phase one), the *neighborhood* (phase two), and the *niche* (phase three). In saying this, of course, I do not mean to imply that phase-one postcolonialism produced no neighborhood narratives, that phase two was not interested in the nation, or that the niche is exclusive to the third phase of postcolonial studies. Given the diversity and richness of this body of literature, such broad categorical claims would be pointless. What I do mean to suggest is that these three emblematic images of place help to isolate important trends in the way place is conceptualized in the postcolonial sphere. I propose them, then, as heuristic models that help to highlight the changing preoccupations of postcolonial writers of place as the field evolves.

The first image—that of the nation—corresponds of course to the nationalist aspirations of the anticolonial moment of postcolonial studies. The nation is defined, often against its external enemies and/or rivals, as a unified and even monolithic entity, and it is given consistency through the kinds of "naturalizing" strategies that will later be critiqued by Bhabha and W. J. T. Mitchell . The strategic advantage of this equation of place and nation is easy enough to understand: it projects a sense of the nation as a unified, organic, indivisible entity whose necessity is inscribed in the territory itself. This model tends to essentialize the nation, however, evacuating divisions within the body of the nation—and it is that presumption of unity that begins to break down in the second phase, under the stress of internal pressures.

In phase two, the image of the *neighborhood* arises in response to a growing awareness of the need to recognize the diverse subcommunities of which any nation is composed. The place in question might be a city neighborhood or a village within a larger populated region, or it might be conceived on a larger scale—as a member of a larger geopolitical community—as in the image of the archipelago (Glissant; and Benítez-Rojo) or the borderland (Anzaldúa). Whatever the case, this conception of the neighborhood treats it as a community that has a more-or-less recognizable collective identity (i.e., with a name, a location, and distinctive qualities) but that is understood to be composed of a disparate group of individuals (of various backgrounds and with competing interests) and to open up onto and interconnect with the larger region. This image of the neighborhood corresponds to the increasingly fine-grained understanding of difference in the second phase of postcolonial studies, which distances itself from monolithic or essentialist notions of collective identity exemplified by the militant nationalism characteristic of the anticolonial struggle. The neighborhood provides a way to deconstruct the unitary image of the nation and show greater sensitivity to the needs of the subcommunities of which it is composed (which have so often found themselves excluded from monolithic definitions of national identity). Homi Bhabha's emphasis on interstitial communities and hybrid identities in *The Location of Culture* is exemplary in this regard. (See esp. 1–18.)

As for the *niche* figure, it corresponds to the preoccupations of postcolonial communities in the era of globalization, in that it redefines the local place with respect to its situation within the larger global order. It does so, moreover, in a way that suggests strategies for coping with the complexities of globalization, which it does by building on analogies with the biogeographical concept of the ecological niche and the economic concept of the niche market. In both the economic and biogeographical models, the niche helps to explain how relatively weak or small players can survive in a competitive environment. The pertinence of this model for postcolonial societies, which so often find themselves surrounded by more powerful neighbors, is clear. The key to success is to carve out a space for oneself between already occupied sectors. By finding an area that has been left unoccupied or unexploited by the dominant players in any given system (whether natural, economic, cultural, or otherwise), a small or weak but adaptable player can survive and perhaps thrive.

This survivalist aspect of niche theory might be construed as implying a depressingly defensive or subservient posture, but that is not the only possible interpretation. Both evolutionary and economic theory conceive of the niche as a kind of testing ground or incubation chamber from which a newer or weaker player can build strength and, given the right circumstances, break out of its niche, perhaps even becoming a dominant player in its own right. In this way, the image of the niche recognizes the relatively weak position of most postcolonial societies in the contemporary geopolitical landscape while suggesting the need to develop strategies for maximizing their potential and also holding out the possibility of future preeminence. Rather than wishing away the reality of the neoliberal global marketplace, niche thinkers seek to face up to that reality and adapt to its challenges. As Edouard Glissant has put it,

> No matter where you are or what government brings you together into a community, the forces of this market are going to find you. If there is profit to be made, they will deal with you. These are not vague forces that you might accommodate out of politeness; these are hidden forces of inexorable logic that must be answered with the total logic of your behavior. (*Poetics of Relation* 152)

It is in its willingness to work within the framework of global economic competition that the niche metaphor can be considered postpostcolonial. It provides a way to think through the challenges facing postcolonial societies that is conceived in terms of the general laws governing world

markets. Rather than focusing on the injustices of the colonial past or fil-
tering everything through the lens of relations between the formerly colonized and the former colonizers, it seeks to find a way forward for today's
postcolonial societies by formulating its questions in the more general
terms of survival in a competitive environment.

Having sketched out in this chapter a three-stage history of postcolonial
studies and suggested some ways in which it helps to understand the postcolonial poetics of place, I will be turning in the next chapter to the French
Caribbean tradition of place writing in order to illustrate and substantiate
this argument. This chapter will culminate in an examination of Edouard
Glissant's poetics of place, which marks a kind of apotheosis of this tradition and provides a powerful model for understanding the social and cultural dynamics of contemporary postcolonial societies.

6

Evolution in/of the Caribbean Landscape Narrative

And in all those escapes he could not help being astonished by the beauty of this land that was not his. He hid in its breast . . . and tried not to love it . . . tried hard not to love it.

—Toni Morrison, *Beloved*

Is the homeland the place where I am not? I am sick and tired of not being in my place and not knowing where my place is. But homelands don't exist, anywhere, no.

—Bernard-Marie Koltès, Le *retour au désert*, my translation

Soon after starting preschool, the young hero of Patrick Chamoiseau's autobiographical novel, *School Days*, begins to bring home pictures he has drawn of the family house. But the house depicted in the drawings—which always features a smoking brick chimney—bears little resemblance to the house in which he actually lives. Nor do the oaks and firs he draws around it seem to belong in a Martinican landscape. The boy has, it seems, taken images seen in school textbooks and transposed them, innocently and unconsciously, onto his own environment—a development that causes some consternation in the boy's family: "S'cuse me?!"[1] If, after just a few weeks of school (learning French fairy tales and the history of "our ancestors the Gauls"), the boy has already begun to view those things most familiar to him through the lens of French pictorial conventions, then what will be the long-term effects of continued schooling and reiterated contact with institutions that are scornful of his native culture?

This little fable, which is recounted by Chamoiseau with tender humor, is just one of the countless anecdotes to be found in French Caribbean literature about the perils, both major and minor, of an assimilationist education and the need to develop a specifically local sensibility. It stands out, nevertheless, for the concise way in which it uses the landscape to make a point about the effects of even well-intentioned and relatively benign forms of ideological manipulation on the individual's relationship to his surroundings. Chamoiseau's *négrillon* has, without realizing it, been thrust into the dialectic of home and away that is such a persistent and troubling feature of West Indian cultural life. The very education that will provide him with the tools for his future success as a writer risks estranging him from the people, traditions, and places that have shaped him up to this point.

Edward Brathwaite has linked education to the landscape in a similar way: through the problem of cultural alienation. Brathwaite characterizes the Caribbean intellectual as someone who suffers from a sense of "not belonging to the landscape":

> The most significant feature of West Indian life and imagination since Emancipation has been its sense of rootlessness, of not belonging to the landscape; dissociation, in fact of art from the act of living . . . The problem of and for West Indian artists and intellectuals is that having been born and educated within this fragmented culture, they start out in the world without a sense of "wholeness" . . . Disillusion with the fragmentation leads to a sense of rootlessness. (Brathwaite 29–30)

By linking the West Indian cultural predicament to the landscape, Chamoiseau and Brathwaite enter into a long tradition. In the French-Caribbean context that is Chamoiseau's, this landscape tradition can be traced back to the earliest Creole (i.e., native born) poets, continues through Saint-John Perse to the writers grouped around Aimé Césaire and the journal *Tropiques*, and on to the generation of Edouard Glissant and his disciples in the *Groupe de la Créolité*. For all these writers, the landscape and natural environment of the islands have been seen as key symbols for the development of a specifically Caribbean cultural identity. Indeed, there is a recurrent tendency among these writers to depict the landscape as an active player in the drama of postcolonial history, with some, like Daniel Maximin, going so far as to treat the natural environment not as mere setting but as "a character in our history . . . a character with its own revolts and cowardice" (Maximin, *Lone Sun* 10).[2]

What is the significance of this tendency to attribute such an active role to the landscape? What do these writers hope to achieve by depicting the environment as an active agent of Caribbean history? And what can the history of this treatment of the landscape teach us about the evolution of West Indian culture and cultural theory? Such questions are intimately bound up with questions of place, since they are linked to the problem of defining the island space as "our sole place" (*notre seul lieu*)—that is, as that which might have the power to forge a locally determined rather than externally imposed sense of shared identity (Glissant, *Traité du Tout-monde* 176).

The natural environment has been a major source of inspiration and a focus of narrative attention across the arc of the Caribbean islands, from Cuba and Haiti (e.g., Carpentier, Benítez-Rojo, Roumain, and Alexis) to Saint Lucia, Barbados, and Trinidad (e.g., Walcott, Brathwaite, and Hosein). Continental writers have also turned to the landscape, from turn-of-the-century nationalists like the Brazilian Euclides da Cunha, to "boom" generation writers like Colombia's García Márquez, to experimental environmentalists like Wilson Harris, to African American writers like Toni Morrison. But the landscape narrative does seem to have played a particularly important role in the postcolonial French-speaking Caribbean territories—perhaps because of their status as Overseas Departments of France, which has left them in a strange kind of political, economic, and identitarian limbo, neither oppressed (at least not in the overtly coercive colonial manner) nor free (of outside control), but in an interstitial state somewhere between a colonial possession and a self-determined state. In order to trace the evolution of the genre, I have organized my argument around a reading of five major exemplars of the landscape narrative: Aimé Césaire's *Cahier d'un retour au pays natal*, Edouard Glissant's *La Lézarde*, Patrick Chamoiseau's *Texaco*, Maryse Condé's *Crossing the Mangrove*, and Glissant's *Tout-monde*.[3]

Where does this obsession with the natural landscape come from? If we think of other prominent place-bound genres like the American "Western," the French (and French-Canadian) "*roman de terroir*," or the British pastoral tradition studied by Raymond Williams in *The Country and the City*, we are reminded that the natural landscape has long played an important role as a source of emblems useful in the construction of local (national, protonational, or regional) identities. In all of these cases, the question of collective identity is at stake, and the relationship between man and landscape is taken to be definitive of critical elements of a national or regional character, be it American pride in its frontier mentality, French insistence on character as an expression of *terroir*, or Victorian nostalgia for Britain's agrarian past. It seems clear that the same kind of process is at work in the Caribbean. These writers seek in the local landscape emblems of the historical forces that have forged a new civilization out of a disparate mix of populations.

There is, however, an important distinction to be made here. As Brathwaite suggests, the founding crimes of Caribbean history (i.e., slavery, forced migration, and the eradication of the islands' original Amerindian inhabitants) have tended to weaken any sense of geographical rootedness, belonging, or entitlement among the populace. They have also complicated the sense of aestheticized reverence for the tropical beauty of the islands that might be expected there. Thus writers from Suzanne Césaire to Daniel Maximin have been suspicious of the landscape's seductive appeal, treating it as a kind of "camouflage" that serves to hide the social misery of the islands' Black population (see S. Césaire) or as a lulling, soporific force—"a womb hostile to rebirth," as Maximin has put it (*Lone Sun* 10). These writers seem to have what amounts to a love-hate relationship with the natural landscape.

What does seem to be an ongoing motivation for this use of the landscape is the sense that the particularities of local history, from Columbus to *départementalisation*, have given rise to an entirely unprecedented kind of society—one that is still in the process of emerging and that has not benefited from the sense of commonality that has traditionally bound individuals to their community. The theoreticians of Caribbean nationalism have found themselves asking what, if anything, could provide a common ground upon which a society that has its origins in a series of historical crimes could be united. And the natural environment is one of those things that fit enough of the criteria of a shared common good to fill the bill.

These preliminary considerations are not, I think, particularly new or controversial, but they help to frame the principal argument of this chapter, which can be summed up in a few sentences. The symbolic use of the natural landscape just described has entailed the embrace of a number of theoretical presuppositions that have remained remarkably consistent over the course of this genre's history. Chief among these is the adoption of what can best be described as an evolutionary logic—one that is closely, albeit metaphorically, related to the Darwinian principle of natural selection. The underlying presupposition behind this narrative use of the landscape, in other words, is that societies evolve, like species, in accordance with the constraints and resources of the environment in which they find themselves. It is the second part of this proposition that is most telling, because what is new about this genre is not the idea that civilizations might evolve and interact like species but, rather, the emphasis that these writers place on the active role played by the natural environment in shaping the features of the cultures in question. Rather than taking a heroic view of Caribbean identity as the result of an act of collective will (as nationalists often do), these writers put the emphasis on the contextual factors that have driven this evolution in particular directions.[4] Of particular importance to this genre, then, is the concept of *adaptiveness*. Whether this evolutionary view of cultural change is consciously embraced or unconsciously assumed, whether it is explicitly stated or simply implied, it uses the principle of adaptiveness as the primary criterion of value and worth. But unlike Spenserian theories of social Darwinism (i.e., "survival of the fittest"), which (mis)used evolutionary theory to justify a political hierarchy dominated by Europeans, the Caribbean version of the evolutionary argument emphasizes the importance of unpredictable mutations, ecological niches, and biodiversity. And unlike Foucauldian theories of power (which leave little room for effective human agency), this tradition is closer to Certeau in emphasizing the creative force that those struggling individually to survive in oppressive circumstances are able to muster. In this way, the Antillean landscape tradition has been able to serve as the starting point for a larger strategic reflection on how small, relatively powerless but inventive entrepreneurial societies like those found in the Caribbean can not only survive but also carve out a satisfying place for themselves in the world and compete successfully in the global marketplace.

Aimé Césaire and the Volcanic Origins of the Postcolonial Landscape Narrative

It is, without doubt, the publication of Aimé Césaire's *Cahier d'un retour au pays natal* that marks the foundational moment of French-Caribbean letters in its postcolonial mode. And it is with Césaire's *Cahier* that the genre of the landscape narrative is inaugurated within this tradition. It would be hard for even a distracted reader to dip into the *Cahier* without being struck by the profusion of references to the local environment. Presiding over Césaire's environmental imagery are two central figures: the tree and the volcano.

The volcano imagery of Césaire's poem has an obvious local referent: the eruption of the Mont Pelée volcano in 1902, which destroyed Martinique's capital, Saint-Pierre, along with its population of over thirty thousand souls. As it is used in the poem however, the volcano, along with the other cataclysmic forces of nature (e.g., storms, earthquakes, and epidemics), is a revolutionary image: It reflects Césaire's Marxist view of history and cultural change as involving sudden, violent shocks of opposing forces. It symbolizes Césaire's desire to sweep away the injustices of the past in a cataclysmic moment of renewal and to start over from scratch—to return to a state of nature and rebuild society along more just lines.

Given this clearly allegorical violence of the volcano imagery, we might be tempted to say that Césaire's poem is not really concerned with the local environment at all—let alone with the gradual, long-term processes of evolutionary change. The same could be said of the poem's tree imagery, which serves principally as a metaphor for negritude's primal bond with nature ("my negritude . . . takes root in the red flesh of the soil . . . it takes root in the ardent flesh of the sky," etc. [Césaire, *Collected Poetry*, 67–69]).

However, Césaire's poem does begin to explore Antillean culture in specifically environmental terms, and it is arguably his attunement to the geographical, ecological, social, and cultural specificity of the Caribbean archipelago that kept him from adopting the more strongly essentialist vision of negritude promoted by Senghor. This consideration provides us with another way to understand the cataclysmic imagery I've been associating with the volcano.

As we saw in the Chamoiseau *School Days* anecdote that opened this chapter, one of the central preoccupations of Caribbean cultural theory has been the problem of disalienation. Before claiming the ability to speak for and of the island, it is necessary to do away with the mediating filters of colonial ideology. Thus the "return" in Césaire's title is not a simple matter of travelling back to his homeland but rather a matter of excavating a lost homeland that had been buried under centuries of colonial domination. The violent destruction of the city symbolizes not only the revolutionary potential of the island but also the need to (re)discover a more authentic vision of the homeland. We can begin to see, then, how—despite the strongly delocalizing tendencies of Césaire's version of both negritude and Marxism (which involves allying a pan-African sensibility to the struggle of a global proletariat)—Césaire's text also contains a powerfully localist message: that the poet's first allegiance is to his Caribbean *pays natal*. To be sure, the trip home involves a passage through Africa, but the espousal of negritude is not for Césaire the endpoint of the quest. Negritude, rather, is conceived as a *tool* that is useful for stripping away the blinders of colonial ideology.[5]

It would seem that Césaire's Marxist-inspired view of social change leaves little room for the evolutionary outlook outlined earlier. It is interesting to note, nonetheless, that Césaire's political activities and social policies diverged sharply from the revolutionary vision expressed in the *Cahier*. Césaire is, after all, the statesman who successfully fought for the integration of Martinique, Guadeloupe, French Guyana, and Réunion into the French nation as Overseas Departments in 1946. Césaire willingly embraced a gradualist approach to the problem of decolonization, opting for a rapprochement with France that would leave open the possibility of a gradual move toward political autonomy and eventual independence. In a sense, Césaire's cultural program and political rhetoric called for revolutionary changes that his political decisions pushed off into an ever receding future. Why this discrepancy? I would argue that it was a simple matter of geopolitical pragmatism. Having surveyed the political landscape of the era (in the immediate aftermath of the deprivations of World War II and more than a decade before the era of massive decolonization that spanned the 1960s), Césaire determined that this gradualist route was in the best interests of the local populace.

Subsequent generations of writers have been grappling with the consequences of *Départementalisation* ever since. By some measures, this approach has been largely successful. The French Caribbean *Départements d'outre mer* (or DOMs, as they are commonly known), have avoided the levels of economic deprivation and political instability that have plagued many decolonized nations. By other measures, however, this route has been less successful, as it has fostered a mentality of dependency and has stifled the development of autonomous economic structures and of a distinct political identity. Indeed, for some, like the Creole nationalist Raphaël Confiant, *départementalisation* was Césaire's great sin (see Confiant, *Aimé Césaire*). But others have been more willing to recognize the imperatives of *Realpolitik* that drove Césaire's decision. Chief among these is Edouard Glissant, who picked up on this evolutionary logic and made it explicit in his first novel.

Glissantian Hybridity, from *La Lézarde* to *Malemort*

Edouard Glissant began his career as a novelist, poet, and cultural theoretician in the 1950s, moving into a cultural landscape dominated by Césaire. His first novel, *La Lézarde* (1958), still showed strong signs of Césaire's influence but tempered it with a strikingly new theory of cultural evolution through hybridization. Indeed, one way to read this novel is to see it in terms of an agon between the revolutionary rhetoric of Césaire and the still-emergent theory of cultural hybridization (*métissage*) that was to become such a central feature of Glissant's thinking in *Caribbean Discourse*.

The plot of *La Lézarde* is a revolutionary one: it is organized around the activities of a group of radicalized young intellectuals who carry out a successful plot to assassinate a political opponent. The evolutionary component of Glissant's argument surfaces in the way he deals with the relationship between country and city. Like Césaire, Glissant uses the city as a symbol of alienation, but he envisages a mode of cultural and social change that will work through the progressive hybridization or *métissage* of city and country rather than the sudden annihilation of one by the other as in Césaire. This emphasis on *métissage* has a powerful effect on the poetics of place of the novel. At first glance, *La Lézarde* seems to offer a basic, even simplistic, use of the landscape as an allegory of Martinique's coming of age. As Michael Dash puts it in his useful introduction to *The Ripening* (Dash's translation of *La Lézarde*), "It is the story of the familiar tensions between the values of the plain and those of the hills, between the slave who revolted and the one who remained in bondage" (Dash, "Introduction" 9). I would go further, however, and argue that this use of the landscape is motivated at a more fundamental level by its larger epistemological project, which could be summed up as learning how to think *with* the land—to act in accordance with its dictates rather than trying to dominate it in colonial fashion. The allegorical framework is given weight and substance through this epistemological project.[6] Mankind is explicitly presented as acting as a part of nature rather than as a force that is in some sense outside of or above it. In fact, the search for a national identity is conceived in precisely these terms: the task of Glissant's heroes is to help the local environment express itself. "What is at issue here is a country not men," says one of his characters (Glissant, *The Ripening* 20). In this sense, the task of asserting legitimate territorial and political control over the landscape can only succeed if it is conceived as flowing from the needs of the landscape itself. Much of the novel is devoted to trying to understand what that means.

For Glissant, the relation between the human plot line and the environmental imagery is more than metaphorical; it is also causal. The genius of his characters, that which makes them heroes, is to have understood the nature of their link with the land. This sets them above the rest of the population of Lambrianne, which fails to understand that the town in which they live is not so much an assemblage of people and buildings as a particular manifestation of general laws determined by the natural environment. As Thaël puts it,

> [This town] grows out of the ground like a flower. It's full of people who think they are special because they have salons, services and go for a stroll every Sunday afternoon. But this is not the truth of the town! Deep down inside they are aware of the land around them . . . this town is a product of the land, not cut off, there is no wall, it's part of everything, pulling it all together . . . a continuation of the land . . . There is no town; houses have simply sprouted from the land and men from the land who, enter the houses . . . both land and town are nourished in the same way, survive in the same way. (Glissant, *The Ripening* 97–100)

Like the town itself, the populace suffers from being subjected too strictly to the rationality of an urban model that has no link with the local environment. Dominated by asphalt, Cartesian rationality, and European colonizers with their mulatto imitators, the town lacks life. This lack is particularly apparent when contrasted with the life of the river. The town's main road, for example, is presented as a kind of rationalized imitation of the river:

"another Lézarde but this time infertile" (96). Repeatedly, in his descriptions of the town, Glissant uses words like "inflexible," "flat," "banal," and "monotonous" to oppose the town to the supple curves and resplendent proliferation of the natural landscape. The river, on the other hand, seems intent on protecting, reassuring, and helping people "to unfold a little humanity, to reassure men and help them" in their struggle against the inhumanly linear inflexibility of the town's streets (33). This opposition between the "humanity" of the river and the "linear inflexibility" of the town has a provocatively paradoxical quality: the natural landscape, it seems, is more human than the man-made urban environment.

To the extent that the town is associated with the values of Western rationalism and territorial domination and the mountains are associated with a mystical view of nature, it is tempting to interpret such analogies in Césairean terms: as an opposition between European and African values, implying the need for a return to more authentic values. But the point of the many images like these in the novel is to argue for a hybrid mixture of the two worldviews—not for a racialized competition between them. Thus the intradiegetic narrator of *La Lézarde* comes to understand over the course of his narrative that he has been given a great historical task, which is to develop a new aesthetic mode capable of synthesizing these two complementary forces, addressing the political realities of the city without losing contact with the obscure natural forces embodied by the legends of peasant mythology and the mountain landscape. Whereas Césaire symbolically destroys the town, allowing a reemergence of pristine nature, Glissant seeks a reconciliation—a symbolic mating (*métissage*) of the two cultures. The Thaël-Mathieu couple embodies this reconciliation, and Glissant's narrator takes on the task of disseminating and explaining it in order to show, as Thaël puts it, that "the only true wealth . . . is that of a country which had freely chosen a set of values in keeping with its essential nature" (Glissant 141).

We can see, then, both continuity and rupture in the passage from Césaire to Glissant. Like Césaire's poem, Glissant's novel involves an activist call for renewal (his characters are, after all, militants); unlike Césaire, however, Glissant adopts an approach that involves a preference for cooperative effort rather than a conflictual outlook. This is not to say that there won't be conflict or revolutionary violence (including Garin's assassination), but the real center of interest of the novel is the budding relationship between Thaël and Mathieu and the deepening of their ties with the land. It is the relationship between these characters (along with that of Mycéa) that will be pursued in Glissant's subsequent novels, from *Le quatrième siècle* to *Tout-monde*. In a very real sense, then, it is only after the assassination of

Garin that Glissant begins to develop his own distinctive voice, moving decisively away from the Césairean, Marxist model.

This evolutionary project is further developed in Glissant's subsequent novels, with the themes of history and landscape intertwining in complex ways. The revolutionary argument of *La Lézarde* is abandoned almost entirely in these later novels, which adopt an increasingly dark and at times almost despairing outlook that reaches its lowest point in the novels of his middle period—especially *Malemort*. The novels of this period reflect the political stasis and ongoing economic dependency that gripped Martinique in the decades after *départementalisation*. The sociopolitical autonomy that Glissant had prophesized in *La Lézarde* did not materialize, and Glissant's characters spend increasing amounts of their time brooding, in Faulknerian fashion, on the past, with particular emphasis on the traumatic legacy of slavery and the plantation system and their ongoing effects on the Martinican psyche.

Novels like *Malemort* show Glissant combing through Martinican history, looking for elements that could be used in the formation of a new sense of Martinican identity. But they tend to present history in negative terms, as a "black hole" symbolizing the trauma of the middle passage or as the "rocks of opacity" of isolated memories lost in a sea of forcibly imposed collective amnesia. This novel comes to the demoralizing conclusion that such a sense of identity rooted exclusively in the history of the island might be more of a prison-house than a tool for community building or progressive politics. In a sense, then, the lesson of texts like *Malemort* is that the search for answers to the question of Martinican identity in history (which is not only traumatic but also ultimately irrecoverable) must give way before a search for answers in space—answers that are both internal (learning to understand what the island has to offer) and external (learning to understand the relations that link Martinique to the Caribbean archipelago and, ultimately, the rest of the world).

It is this realization that leads to the next phase in Glissant's work, initiated by the publication in 1981 of both *Le discours antillais [Caribbean Discourse]*, which remains Glissant's most widely read work of nonfiction, and *La case du commandeur*, which is perhaps his best (and most difficult) novel. In both of these works, we see a new emphasis on the need to look outward in the search for a more productive sense of collective identity. This new outward focus is symbolized by Mycéa's sudden awareness of the neighboring islands at the end of *La case du commandeur* and by the concept of *Antillanité* (Caribbeanness), which Glissant articulates in *Caribbean Discourse*, presenting it as a way for Martinique to free itself from its current status as essentially a French client state by strengthening its economic, political, and cultural ties with the other islands of the Caribbean archipelago.

As we shall see, however, that emphasis on *Antillanité* will not outlast the 1980s. It is with his *Poétique de la Relation* [Poetics of Relation] (1990)—his first full-fledged inquiry into the underlying processes that govern cultural evolution (which he calls creolization)—that Glissant's work will enter its mature phase. This will entail leaving behind the pan-Caribbean theory of *Antillanité* and, perhaps more important, fundamentally revising his theory of *métissage*, which he now considered incomplete. But that turn in Glissant's thinking might never have occurred without the intervention of the writers identifying themselves around the banner of Creoleness. It is to these that I now turn.

Chamoiseau's Urban Mangrove

By the 1970s, Glissant had become the dominant figure on the Martinican cultural scene and had gained quite a following among the younger generation. Among these were Patrick Chamoiseau, Raphaël Confiant, and Jean Bernabé, who would publish, in 1989, their *Eloge de la créolité*, a manifesto in praise of Creoleness. Their theory of Creoleness, which builds on Glissant's earlier work on *métissage*, begins, famously, with the pronouncement, "Neither African, nor European, nor Asian, we proclaim ourselves Creole" (Chamoiseau, Bernabé, and Confiant 75)." The authors then go on to argue that it is this hybrid aspect of Creole culture—and not the African or European source cultures—that is central to the identity of the Caribbean islands as well as to other regions in the world that have been through the colonial ordeal.

The role of the natural landscape as an emblem of the forces that shaped Creole culture can be seen in all their works, from Confiant's autobiographical *Ravines du devant jour* (1993) to Chamoiseau's recent culturo-ecological fable, *Les Neuf Consciences du Malfini* (2009). But nowhere has the relationship between Creole culture and the natural environment of Martinique been worked out more thoroughly than in Chamoiseau's 1992 novel *Texaco*. This relationship is expressed most vividly in the metaphor of the urban mangrove, which designates the blend of rural traditions and modern adaptations that have given rise to a specifically Creole form of urbanism.[7]

The debt of the Creolists to the thinking of Edouard Glissant is clear and explicitly avowed. Nonetheless, the contrast between their understanding of Creole culture's significance and Glissant's understanding of it is revealing. Whereas the Glissant of *La Lézarde* saw the development of an authentically Caribbean culture as an ideal to be achieved with the help of visionary leaders, the Creolists see it all around them, in the Creole culture and folk traditions of the islands. To be sure, they understand as well as Glissant the social and cultural problems that threaten Caribbean societies—the persistence of a color-bound social hierarchy, economic and political dependency on France, the loss by attrition of local cultural traditions, and so forth—but they explain the genesis of such problems in a different way. The real problem as they see it is not that an authentic Martinican culture has not yet evolved but that Caribbean intellectuals have either not known where to look for it (in the popular culture of the islands) or have not been able to understand its vitality. The Creolists suggest that the intellectual elites of the islands, including Glissant, have misconstrued the significance of the islands' Creole culture because of a perhaps unconscious Eurocentric bias toward high culture, which makes it appear to the intellectual elites as rustic and uncouth—as, at best, a protoculture. The corrective to this attitude, the Creolists believe, is to embrace this vernacular culture and work to establish its legitimacy on the world stage. Or, to put it in terms of the urban metaphor that governs *Texaco*, "People have only moaned about the insalubrity of Texaco and other such quarters . . . [but we must] take in their poetics without fear of dirtying our hands in its mud" (Chamoiseau 143). Their hope for establishing a coherent Caribbean identity does not lie in some future hybrid but instead, in the existing folk traditions of the islands. Thus they turn to the local popular culture for inspiration, embracing not only its stock of legends but also its manners, idioms, style, and history—warts and all.

In *Texaco*, the spatial implications of this cultural program appear most explicitly in the notes of the urban planner character, who is modeled on Serge Letchimy.[8] The urban planner initially comes to Texaco (a squatter city on the outskirts of Fort-de-France) to prepare for its demolition. As a representative of the city government, he initially sees it only as a menace to the public health. But having been convinced by a well-aimed rock to spend a few days in Texaco, he has time, while recuperating, to hear an account of the place's history, which is recounted to him by Marie-Sophie Laborieux, the informal head of this impoverished community. She is able to convince him not only that Texaco provides an important repository for the history and culture of the island but also that it plays a key role in the continued survival of Fort-de-France itself. Without places like Texaco, the urban planner finally concludes, the city would die from the excessively rigid rationalization of its social infrastructure:

> In its old heart: a clear, regulated, normalized order. Around it: a boiling, indecipherable, impossible crown, buried under misery and History's

obscured burdens. If the Creole city had at its disposal only the order of the center, it would have died. It needs the chaos of its fringes . . . Texaco is Fort-de France's mess; think about it: the poetry of its Order. The urban planner no longer chooses between order and disorder, between beauty and ugliness; from now on he is an artist. (Chamoiseau, *Texaco* 184)

The urban planner repeatedly describes Texaco as a cross between town and country. And we might notice here that this alliance—between periphery and center, order and disorder, urban and rural—bears a strong resemblance to the type of *métissage* Glissant theorized in *La Lézarde*. But there is a crucial difference: Texaco has grown up spontaneously, whereas the project that Glissant's narrator set forth was to involve a centrally planned domestication of the natural landscape (via the construction of dams, dykes, and other public works). This point must be emphasized, because for Chamoiseau it is the spontaneous nature of Creole culture that is the best guarantor of its authenticity and vitality.

Chamoiseau sees Creole culture as a fully constituted, coherent response to the challenges posed by the environment and history of the Caribbean. Significantly for my purposes, his justification of this view makes an implicit appeal to an evolutionary argument. For Chamoiseau, the very fact that Creole culture has managed to survive in the crucible of West Indian history—an ordeal comparable to Darwin's process of natural selection—proves its viability and worthiness. Creole culture is, in other words, an eminently *adaptive* response to its environment (both natural and social). For this reason, it is possible to say that Chamoiseau is, in a very real sense, an environmental determinist: The mark of authenticity of Creole culture is the fact that it has evolved autonomously, without centralized planning or coordinated effort, in response to pressures beyond the control of individuals and governmental agencies and, indeed, in spite of the best efforts of the colonial system to crush the spirit of the slaves who cobbled together the first iterations of this culture.

The Texaco neighborhood is not, however, simply a metaphor for Creole culture. The novel has an important message about the urban environment that is directly relevant to the geographical inquiry of my study. For Chamoiseau, impromptu developments like Texaco have an important role to play in the island's ecosystem as it becomes increasingly urbanized. Such neighborhoods do not destroy nature, as the bulldozers of the *en-ville* would, because the Creole culture that reigns there encourages them to maintain an organic, symbiotic relationship with nature. Creole gardens, construction techniques, folklore, and folk remedies work because they entail a certain complicity with nature—an ability to understand its dictates, which is absolutely essential for a population deprived of the resources of the city center. Thus as the character Esternome puts it (echoing a passage from Glissant's *La Lézarde*, quoted previously), "The Creole Quarter is like a native flower" (Chamoiseau, *Texaco* 132).

A big part of the significance of neighborhoods like Texaco is their interstitial character. The Creole *quartier* as Chamoiseau describes it is an intermediary, hybrid form of urbanism—a transition zone between the rural and the urban. It is "what City kept of the countryside's humanity" (Chamoiseau, *Texaco* 281). It is this transitional status that explains the vitality of the Creole *quartier* and also guarantees its usefulness for the city center itself. The epiphany experienced by the city planner is his realization that places like Texaco are actually necessary if the city is to survive the demographic pressures it is facing. This is what makes it possible for him to see the *quartiers* as something more than a defective variant of the center and what inspires the urban mangrove metaphor:

> Texaco was not what Westerners call a shantytown, but a mangrove swamp, *an urban mangrove swamp* . . . Texaco is neither City nor country. Yet City draws strength from Texaco's urban mangroves, as it does from those of other quarters, exactly like the sea repeoples itself with that vital tongue which ties it to the mangroves' chemistry. (Chamoiseau, *Texaco* 263, emphasis in original)

If the mangrove swamp is a place of transition and exchange where ocean and dry land meet and replenish each other, then the urban mangrove is where exchange between city and country takes place. It provides a kind of buffer zone for the city that provides two crucial services. On the one hand, it provides a refuge for those who have been squeezed out of the city center by the fierce economic competition that reigns there. The poor, sick, tired, old, and weak can eke out a living on the (rent-free) margins of the city while awaiting better opportunities or a change in fortune. On the other hand, the ring of shanty towns around the city helps to manage the constant flow of new arrivals from the countryside, as the island's economy shifts from an agrarian to an urban model. It provides a staging ground for those who have left the countryside in search of economic opportunities but have not yet been able to gain a foothold in the city's economy.

Chamoiseau's emphasis on this interstitial geographic zone between city and country enables him to stress an aspect of Creole culture that is often left out of less sophisticated theories of hybridization and *métissage*: the extent to which all hybrid cultural forms are products of the milieu in which the source cultures meet. In order to understand why any given culture evolved the way it did, we need to understand the environmental constraints under which the variously interacting populations were operating.

This is where the evolutionary dimension of the environmental metaphor comes into play. What Marie-Sophie's narrative emphasizes is the adaptive process that new arrivals go through when they arrive at the outskirts of the city and find themselves seeking shelter in places like Texaco. They are forced to adapt their rural living patterns and values to an (ex)urban setting that requires the development of new survival tactics and new modes of dwelling. This process of adaptation is akin to what would happen if we moved, say, a tropical species to a temperate climate: its struggle to adapt to that environment would give rise, over time, to a population displaying new adaptive features. In the case of Texaco, the need to adapt rural practices to the new semiurban environment of the *quartier* gives rise to a new variant of Creole culture. Those practices are at first ill adapted to the new setting, but after some modifications they enable the inhabitants of the *quartiers* to thrive, relatively speaking. In so doing, they create what amounts to a new form of culture: an urban-rural hybrid that gives rise to the cast of characters that populate the novels of Chamoiseau and Confiant (the *djobeurs, crieurs, majors, pacotilleuses*, etc.).

To illustrate this principle—the active participation of the milieu in the creation of Creole culture—we need only refer to the historical periodization that is superimposed by the novel's narrator (the *marqueur de paroles*) onto Marie-Sophie's story. Spanning several generations, the story is organized into a series of four "eras" or "ages," each of which is defined by the primary building materials used in the construction of the dwellings that make up the Creole *quartier*. This organization is made explicit in the table of contents, complete with start and end dates and page numbers:

The Age of Straw	(1823(?)–1920)	[p. 33]
The Age of Crate Wood	(1903–1945)	[p. 161]
The Age of Asbestos	(1946–1960)	[p. 252]
The Age of Concrete	(1961–1980)	[p. 316]

What do these materials have to do with these dates? Simply that they were the materials that were ambiently available at the time. Whether scavenged from other sites or made available by the city government, they all reflect the need of the denizens of squatter towns like Texaco to make do with whatever materials were at hand. In a sense, then, the industrially produced materials like asbestos and concrete have become, by the end of the novel, as much a part of the natural environment of the Creole *quartier* as the wood and straw used by previous generations. This gives us an indication of the extent to which today's Creole culture must be understood as a product of past necessity. Hunger and scarcity have long been central features of life in poor Creole communities, and these features, more than anything else, explain why such typically Creole institutions as the Creole garden, *case* (shack), *quartier*, and *djobeur* [odd-job man] took the forms that they did. They are nothing other than the local versions of more general practices that are typical of impoverished populations: small-scale subsistence farming, informal "vernacular" architecture based on scavenged materials, squatting on open or underutilized land, and hustling for piecemeal jobs.

The evolutionary bent of Chamoiseau's defense of Creoleness has important implications for the future of Creole culture. It is clear that the nature of the Creole struggle for survival has changed dramatically since the *départementalisation* of Martinique. Thanks to the modern French social-security network now in place there, adequate nutrition and shelter are no longer the desperately urgent preoccupations they once were. Freed to a great extent from the day-to-day struggle for individual survival, contemporary Martinicans have begun to develop new cultural practices in response to the new challenges and opportunities facing them. For better or worse, many of the most typical features of traditional Creole culture—including the Creole gardens, oral traditions, and shanty-town neighborhoods described in such loving detail by Chamoiseau—are mutating into new and often unrecognizable forms, while others have already devolved into folkloric shadows of their former selves. (Witness the madras displays and dance demonstrations featured at the tourist resorts.)

One of the underlying convictions that motivate Chamoiseau's depictions of the Creole *quartiers* is his belief in the sheer vitality of such informal communities. He constantly emphasizes the ways in which the informal, bottom-up decision-making process that guides their actions gives rise to creative solutions to apparently intractable problems. This emphasis on the vitality of informal communities is a lesson that Chamoiseau seems to have learned from Letchimy, whose research into the sociology, geography, and architecture of squatter communities like Texaco helped legitimize them in the eyes of the region's political authorities (see Letchimy, "Tradition et créativité," and *De l'habitat précaire*). If Chamoiseau's novel has helped to cement the image of places like Texaco into the popular imagination, it must also be said that Letchimy's work has helped literally to cement communities like Texaco into the landscape. As the head of a locally financed private-public development alliance (SEMAFF, the Société d'économie mixte d'aménagement de Fort-de-France), he helped to preserve the vernacular architecture of Texaco, saving the neighborhood from the bulldozers, supplying its residents with more durable building materials like concrete, and integrating the neighborhood into Fort-de-France's grid of utilities and services. (The work done by his group earned it a "SEM d'or" award from the French government in 1999.) The kind of work carried out by people like Letchimy and Chamoiseau, in other words, has left a significant imprint on the landscape. By helping to build aesthetic appreciation for the informal, vernacular architecture that is characteristic of such communities, they have helped to fight against the standardization and alienating scale of the high-rise towers and housing blocks of institutional public housing.

In this respect, Chamoiseau and Letchimy's work has contributed to a much broader movement—one that has sought to gain recognition for the vitality and social importance of these kinds of marginal communities and the informal economies they sustain, while also seeking ways to integrate them into the mainstream and to alleviate the often appalling conditions they must endure. The roster of this movement spans the globe and would have to include the names of scholars, journalists, and activists like Janice Perlman, Hernando de Soto, and Robert Neuwirth (see Perlman, *The Myth of Marginality* and *Favela*; De Soto; and Neuwirth). It would also include creative writers like Vikas Swarup, Athol Fugard, Paulo Lins, and Azouz Begag, who have helped to bring the dynamics of informal squatter communities to the fore of public consciousness and overcome—or at least complicate—the public nuisance stigma associated with them. In this way, their work has contributed to the recognition of squatter cities as an important and dynamic, albeit difficult and unsatisfactory, form of urban dwelling.

Condé's *Crossing the Mangrove*

Given the type of link between landscape and cultural identity examined so far, along with the suggestive title of Maryse Condé's *Crossing the Mangrove*, it seems reasonable to expect to find in this novel yet another study of the environmental determinants of identity. This is, in a sense, what *Crossing the Mangrove* offers, but anyone who has followed Maryse Condé's career knows not to expect the type of monolithic cultural program that we've looked at so far. Condé does not share the Creolist desire to promote a normative vision of Creole culture or Caribbean authenticity. Nor does she believe that West Indian literature should seek its identity within the confines of the cultural and natural environment of the islands. On the contrary, Condé has published strongly worded articles condemning this obsession with the local landscape and calling for a stop to what she sees as authoritarian attempts to regulate West Indian society by using localness as a test for cultural authenticity (see esp. Condé, "Order, Disorder, Freedom"). This critical stance reflects the path she has taken in her creative work, much of which is set outside of the Caribbean—in Africa, Europe, and North America. However, neither the fact of her refusal to submit to the dictates of the theorists of authenticity nor the fact that she has lived much of her life away from her native Guadeloupe has kept her from writing novels that explore the culture and landscape of her island. *Crossing the Mangrove* offers what may be the most notable example of this aspect of her work.[9]

How, then, does Condé use the landscape in *Crossing the Mangrove*? Like Chamoiseau and Glissant, she presents her characters, the inhabitants of an isolated village named Rivière au Sel, in terms of their relationship with the local landscape. For example, Mira claims the Gully (Condé capitalizes the word, suggesting allegorical possibilities) outside of town as a kind of personal refuge. Her brother Aristide is a self-proclaimed man of the mountains who spends his time seeking out the edenic, precolonial landscape about which his father told him. Then there is Xantippe, one of the most shadowy figures in the novel, who is also the one most closely identified with the landscape. Indeed, Xantippe has almost completely given up human companionship, has taken up residence in the forest like the maroons of old, and goes so far as to claim to have personally named the elements of the landscape in a primal, Adamic gesture: "In a word, I named this land. It spurted from my loins in a jet of sperm" (202). But the central figure of the novel is Francis Sancher, and his link to the land is more complex.

Crossing the Mangrove is structured around the wake of Francis Sancher. Although he lived among the villagers for several years, he died as a stranger to them, and each of the inhabitants of the village spends the duration of the wake trying to piece together the secret of his identity. In this, *Crossing the Mangrove* calls to mind Chamoiseau's *Solibo Magnifique*, which also centers on a wake. But whereas Chamoiseau's novel memorializes a way of life (Solibo is taken to represent the last of the great Creole *conteurs*), Condé's novel offers no such evaluation of Sancher's cultural role. He remains an enigma, at once a symbol of Guadeloupe and someone who undermines received notions about what Guadeloupe is and how it can be defined. He seems to have longstanding ties to the local village through his ancestors, but the nature of these ties remains mysterious, and this mystery gives rise to the notion that they are supernatural in some way and perhaps linked to the slaving past of the island.

Who, then, was Francis Sancher? Even his name is uncertain. (He gets mail addressed to Francisco Sanchez.) The only thing that can be said with certainty is that his presence among the villagers has irrevocably upset the life of the village, disrupting the balance of power and changing the lives of its inhabitants forever. This identitarian mystery extends to the novel as a whole. Condé writes in such a way as to avoid imposing any univocal meaning on the town, its inhabitants, its natural surroundings, or on

Guadeloupian identity in general. As in Faulkner's *The Sound and the Fury*, each of the characters in the novel examines the same limited set of facts but draws different conclusions about their meaning. The landscape around Rivière au Sel, in particular, is subject to this kind of contradictory scrutiny. The village is seen as a prison by some, a refuge by others, and for others still, it is simply the only place they have ever known. The same uncertainty hovers over Mira's Gully. She goes there to find solitude and escape from her claustrophobic home life, but Sancher discovers the place and goes there, believing it is there that his destiny will be revealed. For others, gullies simply represent lurking danger (rape), while for others still, the Gully's waters embody a threat to the town (flooding). Other features of the local landscape (mountains, springs, beaches, the Soufrière volcano, etc.) receive the same range of divergent interpretations. All judgments in the novel are inconclusive, because they are based on dubious information or coupled with other, contradictory interpretations. And even where we have no information explicitly contradicting a given judgment, we are often led to question its pertinence. Carmélien, for example, has spent his life searching for a hidden spring—not because he has any special affinity for springs, but because he has read Jacques Roumain's *Masters of the Dew* and is determined to follow in the footsteps of that novel's protagonist.

What, then, does this novel have to say on the question of Guade-loupian (or Creole or Caribbean) cultural identity? At first reading, it is extremely difficult to tell, because Condé so consistently puts individual variation before theoretical generalization. The indeterminacy described earlier makes it difficult for the critic to forward any univocal statements. Indeed, I would argue that if her novel seems to offer no clear-cut identi-tarian theory of the type promoted by Césaire, Glissant, and Chamoiseau, it is precisely because it is written in response to their cultural theories, in what reads, at times, almost like a point-by-point rebuttal. For each ste-reotypically "classic" Caribbean figure, Condé offers her own problematic counterfigure—one who, without exactly undermining its right to enter into the Caribbean pantheon, flies in the face of received conventions. Thus there is the classic figure of the *mento* or *homme fort*, to whom she opposes Xantippe (who seems be believe he is an *homme fort* but is, if his neigh-bors are to be believed, simply a half-deranged old hermit); to the figure of the supportive daughter and/or wife, she opposes the fiercely independent Vilma and Mira; to the cruelly assimilationist schoolteacher, she opposes Léocadie Timothée (whose cruelty stems from her difficulty relating to men, not her difficulties relating to her native culture); to the politically committed writer, she opposes "the writer," Lucien Evariste, who is politi-cally committed but for all the wrong reasons (and who never manages to get any writing done); to the masterful historian in the C. L. R. James mold, she opposes Emile Etienne, who, instead of writing history with a capital "H," has his own, more humble, documentary project, called "Let's talk about Petit Bourg"; to the masterful storyteller or *conteur Créole*, she opposes Cyrille, who gets outtalked by Sancher and then seems to have lost his touch at Sancher's wake; and so on.[10] Finally, there is Francis Sancher himself, who, despite his heroic stints abroad and his ambition to write a novel called "Crossing the Mangrove," does not become a heroic leader in the Césairian mode but just an aging man with a history who is haunted equally by his personal demons, by a sense of historical guilt (his ancestors may or may not have been involved in a slave massacre), and by a bad case of writer's block.

What links all these characters to the poetics of place is Condé's careful attention to situating them within the dialectic of imprisonment and exile. Several of the characters see the village as a prison and insist on their need to escape. Some wonder why a man such as Sancher—who has fought with Castro and seen the world—would choose to settle in a backwoods village like Rivière au Sel. And when Vilma hears the title of Sancher's novel and replies "You don't cross a mangrove. You'd spike yourself on the roots of the mangrove trees. You'd be sucked down and suffocated by the brackish mud," Sancher concurs (Condé, *Crossing the Mangrove* 158). Unlike Chamoiseau, who had used the mangrove swamp as a life-affirming symbol of cultural vitality and nourishment, Condé's novel presents it as a mesmerizing but bewildering wilderness—a symbol of confusion and potential entrapment. In this, it serves, along with the town of Rivière au Sel, as an emblem of Guadeloupian society, conceived as insular and impenetrable in every sense of the words.

Interestingly, one of the refrains of the novel—used by Mira, Aristide, and others—is "partir" (to leave). Readers of Césaire's *Cahier* will recognize an important motif of that text, but whereas the Césairean departure prepares a more complete and satisfying return to the native land, this is by no means assured in Condé's text. The few glimpses that we get of locals who have actually left the island show us pale and depressed, if relatively affluent, exiles who miss their home but cannot return without giving up the standard of living and freedoms to which they have become accustomed. This, Condé seems to be saying, is the dilemma facing all those who have grown up in a small island community: Life at home offers only limited opportunities, but life away from home is exile. Lucien Évariste's thoughts upon returning to Rivière au Sel after his studies in Paris are typical of Condé's approach to this theme: "Lucien was glad to be back home as soon as he had finished his MA. More often than not, though, he poignantly bemoaned the torpor of this sterile land that never managed to produce a revolution" (Condé, *Crossing the Mangrove* 180). Lucien bemoans the lack of revolutionary spirit of the people, while others hate the insularity, xeno-phobia, or lack of economic opportunities of Rivière au Sel. But all share this kind of love-hate relationship with the village and with Guadeloupe in general. It's what they know, it's home, and it feels comfortable, but it's not enough.

Given all of this, *Crossing the Mangrove* is perhaps best understood as an iconoclastic response to the cultural program of Chamoiseau and the Créolistes. Condé does not object to Creole culture itself but rather to the Creolist habit of promoting Creoleness as the absolute arbiter of authenticity and worth. By contrast, her message seems to be that there is no single shared Guadeloupian or Caribbean or Creole identity. The les-son she has drawn from environmental science is one emphasizing not the quasi-deterministic pressures of natural selection but, rather, the irrepress-ible diversity of nature. For her, the infinite variability of individual dif-ferences is more important than the construction of a collective identity.

Condé's approach to studying the cultural ecosystem of Rivière au Sel might best be understood in light of Lucien Évariste's idea for a literary project built around Francis Sancher:

> Instead of hunting down Maroons or nineteenth-century peasants, why not, as an urban son of the twentieth century, put together Sancher's memories end to end, as well as snatches of his personal secrets, brush aside the lies and reconstitute the personality of the deceased? Oh, this idealist without an ideal was not going to make it easy for him. He would have to reject the power of generally accepted ideas. He would have to look dangerous truths in the face. He would have to displease. He would have to shock. (Condé, *Crossing the Mangrove* 188–89)

This is a call for writers to resist imposing their ideological programs onto their subjects and get back to the equally important task of paying close empirical attention to their surroundings. From Condé's perspective, the ideological demands of theories of negritude, *Antillanité*, and Creoleness can be just as blinding as the distorting influence of colonial ideology decried by Saïd, Chamoiseau, Brathwaite, and the others.

Sancher, then, does turn out to be a personification of Guadeloupe, but one whose purpose is not to promote a certain vision of what the island is, should, or can be but, instead, to force the reader to question received wisdom, generalizations, and theory-driven assertions about what is and is not authentically Caribbean. Condé's novel sends out a call to Caribbean writers that it is important to work as empiricists, telling the story of the private side of Guadeloupe in its multiplicity and without imposing an authoritarian interpretive schema on them. In this sense, for Condé, the humble oral history envisaged by Emile Etienne, "Let's Talk About Petit Bourg," is potentially of greater import than Sancher's *Crossing the Mangrove*, Glissant's *Discours Antillais*, or the *Eloge de la Créolité* of Chamoiseau, Bernabé, and Confiant.

Creolization and *Tout-monde*

At about the same time that Condé was writing *Crossing the Mangrove*, Edouard Glissant was going through a kind of conversion experience. Sparked by some of the same concerns that motivated Condé's novelistic rebuttal to the Creolists, Glissant began to distance himself from them and also from some of the positions he had espoused earlier in his career. The last two decades before Glissant's death gave rise, as a result, to an important new phase in his work, which also marks one of the major turning points in the history of West Indian cultural theory. This transformation occurs in his most important work of cultural theory, *Poetics of Relation* (published in 1990, one year after *In Praise of Creoleness* and *Crossing the Mangrove*), and is further elaborated in his subsequent publications, especially in the novel *Tout-monde* (published in 1993, one year after *Texaco*) and the related *Traité du Tout-monde* (1997). As the term *Tout-monde* suggests, this project is no less totalizing in ambition than his previous efforts, but it does open up a substantial space for individual variation, diversity, and unpredictability that responds to many of the points made by Condé in "Order, Disorder, Freedom, and the West Indian Writer" as well as those explored in *Crossing the Mangrove*.

This new phase in Glissant's thought can be understood in part as a critical response to the theory of Creoleness. As we saw, the Creolists share Glissant's insistence on the hybrid nature of Creole culture. But by making Creoleness their cultural ideal, they place their bet on an already achieved hybrid—they attempt, in a sense, to stop the clock and to invest their energy in a particular historical state of Creole culture, as if they could put an end to its evolution. In *Poetics of Relation*, Glissant comes out strongly against the Creolist position, noting that however generously multiculturalist its rhetoric may be, it implies an inherently normative, and therefore potentially exclusionary, view of Caribbean culture. In response, he proposes that the implicitly static, normative concept of Creoleness must give way to the more properly processual concept of "creolization," which puts the emphasis on the processes of cultural evolution rather than on the "contents" (i.e., specific manifestations) of a given culture. For Glissant, the Creole culture extolled by Chamoiseau and the Creolists must be understood as no more than a point on a continuum—one moment in a long history of adaptive cultural evolution:

> Creolization, one of the ways of forming a complex mix . . . is only exemplified by its processes and certainly not by the "contents" on which these operate. This is where we depart from the concept of creoleness . . . We are not prompted solely by the defining of our identities but by their relation to everything possible as well . . . Creolizations bring into Relation but not to universalize; the principles of creoleness regress toward negritudes, ideas of Frenchness, of Latinness, all generalizing concepts—more or less innocently. (Glissant, *Poetics of Relation* 89)

The mistake of the Creolists, in this view, was to take a certain state of the culture for its essential being—to imagine that the contents of any given culture could be defined once and for all.

The novel *Tout-monde* is clearly meant as a defense and illustration of the ideas set forth three years earlier in *Poetics of Relation*. This makes *Tout-monde* an important test-case in Glissant's oeuvre—a narrative demonstration of the discursive arguments first put forth in *Poetics of Relation*. The novel builds on the mythos of Glissant's previous novels in quasi-Faulknerian fashion, bringing back the central figures of the previous novels and extending their stories into the present day.[11] Of particular importance are Mathieu Béluse (the writer, who happens to be writing his own *Traité du Tout-monde*), Raphaël Targin (the adventurer, whose travels provide much of the narrative glue of the novel), and Marie Celat (who is variously referred to as "la folle" [the madwoman] and "the one who stayed home" and who seems to have become, since *La case du commandeur*, the character most closely identified with the contemporary identitarian crises of the island's populace).[12]

Given the novel's sprawling six hundred pages, multiple globe-trotting protagonists, and habit of interweaving different historical periods and geographical locations—ranging from the colonial era to the present day and from Martinique to Italy to North and West Africa to North and South America—there can be no question of trying to give a comprehensive overview of the novel here. In fact, that resistance to summary—the novel's unruly sprawl—is central to its message and is part of a strategy for representing the *Tout-monde*, which requires both an openness to the chaotic proliferation of world events (major and minor) and an ability to create a certain kind of nonlinear order out of them. In what follows, I will draw out the spatial significance of the novel's central theme—the concept of *Tout-monde*—and its relation to the identitarian malaise of the French Antilles. This will then enable us to consider how the concept of *Tout-monde* enriches our understanding of the experience of place and marks what I consider to be the culmination of this Caribbean tradition's contribution to place theory.

How, exactly, are we to understand the concept of *Tout-monde*?[13] As always with Glissant, clear-cut definitions are hard to come by. But it is possible to piece together a working definition of the notion from the novel and the subsequent *Traité du Tout-monde*. In a preliminary, approximative way, we can say that it involves the development of a globalized vision—an attempt to reconcile the particular and the universal—without reducing the infinite number of particulars found in the world to being merely members of abstract categories. It is important to note in this regard that *Tout-monde* is not so much a geographical concept as an epistemological concept. The *Tout-monde* is most emphatically not the world itself, in the geographical sense of the planet's spatial configuration. It implies, rather, a certain *vision of* the world in the phenomenological sense of a consciousness that is simultaneously aware of and awash in the world around it. As Longoué puts it in the novel, "the world is not the Tout-monde . . . Because the Tout-monde is the world that you tossed around in your thoughts while it was tossing you in its swell" (*Tout-monde* 208; all translations from this text are my own).

In order to understand why this particular mode of global vision has so much importance for Glissant, we need first to understand the relationship between two of the central concepts of his cultural theory: opacity and relation.[14] Opacity is a concept that has long been dear to Glissant. It designates the fundamental core of our identity—that kernel of absolute difference that guarantees our individuality and cannot be communicated to others. A helpful metaphor here is that of translation from one language to another. My opacity as an individual is like the remainder that is always left over whenever I translate a word from one language to another. The opaque is, by definition, that which cannot be communicated to others—at least not in its own right. Nevertheless, analogy—the *mise en contact*, or *mise en relation*, of different elements—makes it possible to get an approximate sense of other people's zones of opacity by relating what we observe to comparable phenomena that we know from our own experience. "You do not illuminate the obscure, there is no recipe for it; instead you relate it to what you know in the surroundings" (Glissant, *Tout-monde* 305). Analogy, then, plays a critical role in Glissant's project. Accordingly, one of the central preoccupations of all the travelers in Glissant's novel is to relate what they see in their travels to what they know from home—as a way to better understand both. This process of putting distant phenomena into relation with each other reveals what Glissant's characters repeatedly refer to as subterranean passages, linking different cultural realities, much as volcanoes are linked by subterranean fault lines. (This idea of the invisible but very real underground channels that link volcanoes to each other is a recurrent image in the novel. Once again, Glissant takes an image with a Césairean pedigree—the volcano—but puts an entirely different symbolic spin on it.)

Tout-monde, then, is a mode of cognition, founded on analogy, that is able to give us a sense of the meaning of objects, events, and people by emphasizing their participation in the interconnected web of *relation*. And this is exactly the kind of program that the novel puts into play in its narrative structure, which explains why this novel had to be Glissant's most sprawling and undisciplined and also most cosmopolitan, globetrotting novel. Although his protagonists still identify strongly as Martinicans, they come to realize that all those things they had initially thought to be specifically Martinican or Caribbean (or French or anything) are in fact tied to analogous phenomena all over the world. They are constantly struck, in their travels, by the uncanny sensation that an object encountered in Egypt or America is closely related to something they had thought specific to their homeland and that, in fact, to *fully* understand those typically Martinican things, they must understand their relation to analogous phenomena in other parts of the world, at other times, and in other languages.

One clear example of the kind of double vision that Glissant's characters develop is triggered by the realization that Nile reeds bear a more than passing resemblance to sugar canes. (This is a motif that is used several times in *Tout-monde* and *Traité du Tout-monde*.) The traveler, abroad in Egypt, is looking at reeds along the Nile when he suddenly realizes that what he is *seeing* is the sugarcane of his youth.

> I am this mangrove country around Lamentin in Martinique where I grew up, and at the same time, through an infinite imperceptible presence, which does not subjugate the Other, this shore of the Nile where the reeds turn to pulp like sugarcanes. The aesthetics of Relation have made obsolete the illusions of exoticism, which standardized all it touched. (Glissant, *Traité du Tout-monde* 178; all translations from this text are my own)

It is this uncanny ability to see the familiar in the unfamiliar, and vice-versa, that separates the true heroes of Glissant's novel from all others. These heroes are "those who could put into relation such distant landscapes . . . which make contact through evanescent appearances and at the same aching depth. In this way the indefinable mornings of the Mississippi . . . came to encounter the traces of faded mud on the flanks of our local hills" (Glissant, *Tout-monde* 194). What we come to realize over the course of the novel is that the theory of *Tout-monde* promoted there is, in a very real sense, a theory of the representation of place—one based on the principle of dual or stereoscopic vision, which is the ability to see both the local thing and the larger global context. This implies that any true understanding of "our own place" requires a better understanding of the global totality: "we would no longer be able to sing, for example, or labor [travailler à souffrance] from within our own place without also plunging into the imaginary of this totality" (Glissant, *Traité du Tout-monde* 176). This is an outlook that, carried to its logical limit, suggests the need for a new kind of vision—a kind of multilayered vision that enables one to perceive the singularity or opacity of what is there before us while also putting that thing in relation to the entire realm of related phenomena. This is a kind of second sight that would enable us to see "all these countries at the same time and in the same moment" (Glissant, *Tout-monde* 234). That, in its utopian form, is what *Tout-monde* implies: the ability to see everything everywhere, at the same time—in the object before us.

This renewed understanding of the relationship between the local culture of "our own place" and the *Tout-monde* has important implications for the theory of place studied in Chapter 1. Before bringing this chapter to a close, then, I would like to explore the contribution of Caribbean landscape narratives to the theory of place in the humanist tradition of Malpas, Casey, Entrikin, and Tuan.

Glissant, Malpas, and Place Theory

Le lieu est incontournable, Glissant writes: "there is no getting around place." This formula, repeated several times over the course of *Tout-monde* and the *Traité du Tout-monde*, could serve as the motto of Glissant's literary aesthetics (see *Tout-monde* 31, 153 and *Traité du Tout-monde* 59).[15] Indeed, in many respects it is the central premise of the entire tradition of Caribbean landscape narrative studied in this chapter. But what exactly does it mean? At first glance, the term *incontournable*—which translates roughly as "unavoidable"—seems only to insist on the *importance* of place. Some commentators have pushed Glissant's thinking on place no further than this, construing the idea of place as a way to emphasize the more general concepts of local specificity and the particularities of individual cultures.[16] But to stop there would be to miss the whole point of Glissant's exploration of the *Tout-monde*. If we look more closely at Glissant's use of the word *incontournable*, it becomes apparent that he takes great care to activate the secondary, etymological implications of the term, which, built around the root *contourner*, is related to the idea of tracing the *contours* or outline of something.[17] In other words, place is *incontournable* in the sense that you can't avoid or replace it—but also in the sense that you can't circumscribe it; you can't get around it because it has no outer limits. Glissant quite explicitly activates this secondary meaning of his motto: "Place. There is no getting around it, since you can neither replace it nor travel around it" [*Le lieu. Il est incontournable, pour ce qu'on ne peut le remplacer, ni d'ailleurs en faire le tour.*] (*Traité du Tout-monde* 59). Why is it that we can't circumscribe our place? Because, following the epistemological program of *Tout-monde*, whatever place we wish to define as ours is inextricably interconnected with every other place. There is no inviolable border to the place we wish to define as our own but rather a highly permeable peripheral zone that blends into the larger order of relations with other places and radiates out toward infinity.

This more complex definition of place is presented in one of the entries to Mathieu Béluse's *Traité du Tout-monde* in a manifesto-like statement.

> PLACE.—There is no getting around it. But if you would like to take advantage of this place that has been given to you, remember that henceforth all the places in the world meet up with each other, right out to the astral spheres . . . Then you will come to this realization, which is powerful knowledge: that the place grows from its irreducible center as much as from its incalculable margins. (Glissant, *Tout-monde* 31)[18]

Our sense of the homeland ("this place that has been given to you") is enriched not only by an exploration of its center but also by a willingness to look outward to the rest of the world, exploring the ebb and flow of exchanges between inside and outside—between the "irreducible center" and its "incalculable margin." This is, we might say, a definition of place designed for the era of globalization. And it has important ethical consequences: "So, there is no getting around place. One doesn't live suspended in an indefinite space. This is the question: How to drink at your spring, without depriving others? . . . [It is] not just a place, but also a commonplace, overturned [*chaviré*] by anxiety" (Glissant, *Tout-monde* 513–14). "Our place" is not autonomous ("we do not live suspended in an indefinite space"). Events in the wider world are constantly at work in shaping the place in which we live, and to pretend otherwise would be vain. Conversely, we must also be aware of how the choices we make at home flow out and affect people elsewhere in the world. Every drink of water that I take from the local river is one less for those who live downstream. This was already understood in Glissant's first novel, *La Lézarde* (which was organized around a struggle for control of the source of the Lézarde river), and it has become the central axiom of the poetics of *Tout-monde*.

This newfound vision of place *as* interrelatedness is cosmopolitan in the sense that Appiah gives to the term in *Cosmopolitanism*. It implies a sense of interdependence with and also responsibility toward others. As a consequence of this enhanced global awareness, Glissant is able to follow through on a promise that Jeff Malpas made in his theory of place. Malpas, as I pointed out in Chapter 1, insists strongly on the "nested" quality of place—the fact that my immediate environment, however clearly defined, always opens up onto a larger context, such that any place in which I find myself is itself situated within an ever-receding horizon of awareness that stretches off to infinity. Ultimately, then, every place is permeated by the influences that impinge on it from all points of the world, although the distant influences will only be felt obscurely and will soon fall below the threshold of perceptibility.

Malpas clearly recognizes the importance of this principle, yet, as we saw in Chapter 1, he tends in his evocations of place to emphasize the immediately perceptible environment. When, for example, he writes that "the landscape in which we find ourselves, and through which we are defined, is thus as much a part of what we are, of our minds, our actions and our selves, as is the food we eat and the air we breathe" (Malpas 189, quoting Schama 578), he seems to have forgotten to factor in the influence of the distant places in which our own place is "nested." If "the landscape in which we find ourselves" is as immediately accessible as the air we are breathing or the food we could eat, then this is a tightly circumscribed definition of place indeed. That vision, I would argue, underplays the extent to which, in the globalized, media-saturated world of today, knowledge of the most remote corners of the world impinges in very direct ways upon our sense of the local landscape. Malpas would certainly not deny this, but he gives us little help in understanding the mechanisms through which our (often indirect) experiences of the wider world impinge on our understanding of the local environment. Glissant, on the other hand, foregrounds the ongoing interplay between the immediately accessible and the distant and mediatized dimensions of the world in which we live. Glissant's theory of *Tout-monde* develops Malpas's intuition about the nested nature of place by emphasizing the importance of relationality and by studying the ways in which knowledge of different places can be brought (analogically) to bear on the place we are in and enrich our understanding of even those places we know the best, like our homeland. His novel provides us with a detailed illustration of the processes through which the nested, complex quality of place experience manifests itself in our changing relations to the loci of our formative experiences.

Glissant puts this tentacular, rhizomatic conception of place front and center in his theory of *Tout-monde*, in contradistinction to many philosophers in the phenomenological tradition of place—from Heidegger to Bachelard to Casey—who, intentionally or not, privilege Schama's inherently conservative emphasis on rootedness in an original or authentic place. Moreover, Glissant's work suggests how limiting—even damaging—such a theory of self and place can be. As with the characters that populate his novels, the more contact we have with the wider world—be it through traveling, talking to outsiders, reading books, watching television, and so on—the more we will be impressed by the complex interrelations between any given place, object, or event and the networks of similar phenomena that permeate other places. This is especially true in the current era of globalization and is all the more important in a region like the Caribbean, where migration is the norm and not the exception. More often than not, migration has been dealt with in postcolonial literature in a minor mode, under the heading of exile and estrangement from the homeland. But Glissant's novels make it clear that this is not the only way this experience can be lived. Indeed, one of the objectives of *Tout-monde* (both as a novel and as a concept) is to help us rethink the dynamics of home and away in a more constructive way that enables us to visualize ourselves as citizens of, as Anastasie had put it, "all these countries . . . at the same time in the same moment" (Glissant, *Tout-monde* 235 and passim). This is, again, a fundamentally cosmopolitan vision—an attempt to reconcile allegiance to the homeland with openness to contact with others. Glissant has been criticized by some on the nationalist Left for this openness, which they interpret as a lack of commitment to the needs of the homeland (see Hallward), but, as I have argued elsewhere (Prieto, "Edouard Glissant"), such critics seem to have underestimated the extent to which conditions have changed since the 1960s. The militant strategies that were appropriate for the decolonization struggle no longer make sense in the era of globalization.

I see this Glissantian conception of place as the culmination of the entire history of Caribbean landscape narrative (so far). The result of an ongoing dialogue between Caribbean writers that passes from Césaire to Glissant, to Chamoiseau, to Condé, and then back to Glissant, this tradition has given rise to an exceptionally sophisticated view of what makes a territory a place and what makes a group a community. By emphasizing the need for communities to evolve adaptively in response to the resources and constraints of their local environment, this tradition of place writing has made possible a fuller awareness of how limiting the reliance on essentialist or universalist definitions of self, race, class struggle, the nation, and other absolutes can be.

As we saw, this tradition begins with Césaire and the project of disalienation and involves a desire to discover the specificity of Caribbean culture. However, this desire to plunge into the local soil and discover the elements that are most uniquely Caribbean leads, in time, to the following paradoxical discovery: that what is most deeply revealed by the search for a specifically local identity is precisely the impossibility of finding any such identity that can be walled off from the outside world. Glissant's discovery of the *Tout-monde* dialectic is already implicit in Césaire's *Cahier*—in the tension between the local nature imagery and the pan-African theory of negritude—but is subordinated to the immediate project of disalienation and the search for political justice. It is also implied in Chamoiseau's use of the urban mangrove metaphor: The urban mangrove is its own kind of place but is also a transitional site—a kind of capillary membrane, allowing exchanges between the country and the city. This same vision is also central to Condé's depiction of Rivière au Sel, in which the dialectics of home and away, of imprisonment and exile, and of shelter and escape play such an important role in determining the ambivalent attitudes the characters maintain toward their hometown. But this idea is given its fullest expression in Glissant's *Tout-monde*, in which the characters, thanks to their travels, come to the realization that even the most characteristic features of the local landscape are held in common with other landscapes throughout the world—the commonality of the sugarcane and the Nile reed as well as the subterranean fault-lines that link the volcanoes of the world into invisible but very real rings of fire.

The historical trajectory of the Caribbean basin seems to have made this truth stand out with more clarity there than in other parts of the world. From its inception, the local context has been penetrated in highly visible ways by global processes, beginning with the fact that the main elements of the population came from elsewhere, whether by choice or by force. This has remained true throughout the history of the Caribbean, which long sat at the center of the worldwide sugar trade and has been subject to wave after wave of immigration and emigration. This dynamic is more visible than ever today, in the era of globalization, as fragile Caribbean cultural ecosystems find themselves inundated by foreign cultural products while also playing an outsize role in the creation of a world culture. (Think of the importance of rumba and reggae in the evolution of world music or the importance of magical realism in world literature.) This may be why, as Glissant believed, Caribbean cultural theory has been so eminently exportable: The Caribbean region's historical experience dealing with the cross-currents of global exchange has situated it at the vanguard of globalization theory, enabling it to develop a number of viable strategies for dealing with the geocultural and geopolitical challenges of globalization.

Of central importance to the success of these strategies is the evolutionary model that governs so many aspects of Caribbean place theory. The emphasis on the natural environment serves as an implicit reminder of something that is often forgotten in rudimentary theories of cultural hybridization, which is that environmental pressures determine the various forms that the local culture will take. If a cultural hybrid is not *adaptive*, in the sense that it can compete successfully against other cultural formations, then it will not survive. Because of this, the evolutionary emphasis of this tradition has provocative implications for the future development of postcolonial studies. In a world in which direct colonial domination has given way to indirect modes of domination, new forms of resistance are needed, and the evolutionary principle of the struggle for scarce resources seems to provide a better model for understanding this situation than the old-fashioned, anticolonial model of head-to-head combat or the multicultural myth of a world of placidly cooperative interactions. In particular, the evolutionary outlook of these writers has enabled them to provide important principles and strategies to keep in mind as we seek to respond to the identitarian challenges posed by the ever greater levels of intercultural contact in the era of globalization.

Nation, Neighborhood, and Niche

I offered, at the end of Chapter 5, a chronology of postcolonial place models that mirrored the evolution of postcolonial theory as a whole: to the first, anticolonial phase of decolonization and emergent nationalism corresponds an emphasis on the nation as the primary scale of place narrative; to the second, postcolonial phase corresponds an emphasis on the neighborhood as a way to contest essentializing visions of the nation as an undifferentiated whole; and to the third phase, which is that of globalization theory, corresponds the theory of the niche, which emphasizes the place of that society within the global cultural ecology. We are now, I think, in a better position to understand how this progression meshes with the evolution of French-Caribbean literary history.

There can be no doubt that Césaire begins his career as an anticolonial nationalist—nor that the landscape imagery of the *Cahier d'un retour au pays natal* is meant to resonate as national allegory (or, rather, protonational allegory, since Martinique never has acceded to the status of a nation). It achieves this national vision of the local place by superimposing the natural landscape of Martinique onto a verbal map of the island conceived as a unified homeland—an organic whole that has the indivisible integrity of a (feminine) body.

It seems equally clear that the Chamoiseau and Condé novels studied here illustrate the intersection of phase-two postcolonialism with the use of the neighborhood as an emblem of diversity within the nation. By emphasizing the complex internal social dynamics of the local community and the place of that community within the larger island space, these narratives deconstruct any presumption that the island can be conceived as a single unified whole. They stress instead the myriad competing interests out of which communities like neighborhoods and nations must be formed.

Finally, there can be no doubt that Glissant's *Tout-monde* represents postcolonial studies in its third (globalizing) phase. What, then, do we make of the image of the niche in Glissant's work? This is not a term that Glissant uses in any systematic way or that he theorizes explicitly, but I would like to suggest that the theory of cultural diversity that he develops in the last part of his career depends strongly, albeit implicitly, on a theory of the niche.

As we've already seen, the shift in focus that distinguishes Glissant's *Poetics of Relation* from his earlier cultural theory (esp. *Caribbean Discourse*) is a shift from the problematics of nationalism and regionalism to that of globalization. Chief among Glissant's concerns in this phase of his career is the problem of the survival of "minor" cultures in a global cultural and economic market dominated by hegemonic powers like the United States.[19] The fear is not only that smaller, weaker cultures will be diluted or destroyed as a result of economic competition with and cultural penetration by products from dominant cultures (although as a Martinican, that is clearly an issue of immediate concern for Glissant) but also that an excessive reduction in diversity would be harmful to the world system as a whole, leaving a small number of relatively homogenous megacultures that may not be agile enough to adapt to changing circumstances. If we think of how the concept of the niche has been used in evolutionary biology, the nature of his reasoning becomes clear. Niches play an important role in ensuring biodiversity within ecosystems, and biodiversity is crucial for the resiliency of those ecosystems when they are subjected to stresses of various kinds (drought, flood, fire, epidemics, etc.). Glissant simply applies the same logic to cultural systems: The diversity of small cultures occupying niches at various points along the cultural spectrum ensures that there will be a variety of different problem solving approaches available should unexpected cultural emergencies arise (resource depletion, technological change, etc.). Glissant often uses the Creole garden as a metaphor for the kind of mutually beneficial cultural promiscuity that is his ideal.[20]

This is a message of obvious relevance to "minor" cultures around the world, and it is one that is born out by niche theory in fields like biogeography, anthropology, and economics.[21] Among its implications for minor cultures (and the dominant cultures that interact with them) are the following: First, as we've seen, the survival of the minor cultures in the global cultural landscape is crucial, just as much for the dominant cultures as the minor ones; second, the concept of the niche suggests a number of useful survival strategies for minor cultures (which work by emphasizing the importance of occupying domains that have been left relatively unexploited by others rather than trying to compete head-to-head with the dominant players); third, it is reasonable and important to remain invested in local traditions and practices (since they grew up, adaptively, in response to local conditions) and to resist the pressure to bow to the authority or prestige of externally imposed values (e.g., that western products are superior to local products); and fourth, today's undervalued niche practice might become a dominant practice at some point in the future, as cultural attitudes and material conditions evolve.

Conceived in this way, niche theory can be a source of inspiration to minor cultures around the world, giving a sense of purpose and direction to the often demoralizing day-to-day struggles of individuals and communities searching to be productive and gain recognition for their efforts. It suggests that rather than focusing exclusively on the domains that are consecrated by the dominant cultures, it is equally important to remain open to exploring other possibilities—however marginal or lacking in prestige. As societies evolve, the zones of opportunity shift, and the successful niche players are the ones who identify those shifts in the early stages and are able to capitalize on them. For the niche player, moreover, success need not be defined in the all-or-nothing binary terms of triumph/death, dominance/submission, or stardom/obscurity. Between these extremes are many degrees of success and failure and, potentially at least, many routes to success.

In many cases, niche players may only stumble upon their niche by accident or might only choose to occupy it out of necessity or against their will (i.e., if they have been squeezed out of an established territory by the competition). But if they are able to adapt their various skillsets to the new situation, they may well find the new relation to be a creative one, leading them to innovate by, for example, providing a service that no one else offers, finding ways to make use of a resource that no one else is consuming, entering into alliances of various kinds, and so on. And although their new situation will not necessarily change much in the current balance of power, the ecological metaphor implies that this should not be the goal; many successful niches involve asymmetrical relationships between weaker and stronger players (consider the crocodile-plover couple or the relationship between a major manufacturer and its suppliers).

There is one last advantageous feature of the niche metaphor that must be stressed: niches have insides. Unlike the node in the node/network metaphor for globalization favored by Manuel Castells (which implies interchangeability and a lack of differentiation), the niche metaphor emphasizes the richly differentiated potentials that may be hidden away in even the smallest, most remote places. It suggests that every local place/culture has the potential to be an incubator or refuge of something that is both unique to that place/culture and contributes to the overall health of the system. The niche metaphor implies, in other words, that all cultural peculiarities have a kind of singularity and dignity that gets lost in the informational or mechanical model. In this way, the biological, evolutionary model helps to understand the inherent importance of diversity as a virtue in its own right. This is a crucial lesson for a world market subject to the homogenizing pressures of commodity capitalism.

Conclusion

Landscape, Map, and Vertical Integration

The "social-natural production of nature and man" . . . such is what we are asked to think at the dawn of the twenty-first century.

—Jean-Luc Nancy, "Banks, Edges, Limits (of Singularity)"

These are . . . new ways of explaining complex systems as only geographically-minded individuals, teetering on the balance of human and non-human, can achieve.

—Bonta and Protevi, *Deleuze and Geophilosophy*

We have been reminded at numerous points over the course of this study that there are, broadly speaking, two dominant methodological approaches to the study of place: from the inside and from the outside. The first approach is subjectivist or phenomenological in orientation; it is interested in place as an environing milieu—something experienced from within. The second approach is more properly objectivist and could be called scientific or cartographic; it emphasizes those aspects of place that can be extracted from phenomenological experience and considered in its absence. The first approach gives precedence to the density, complexity, and qualitative aspects of place experience and is associated with genres like landscape painting and first-person narrative. The second approach relies on the analytic abstraction and decentered perspective associated with maps; it appeals to the impersonal authority of science and emphasizes the search for structural regularities, quantifiable relationships, and other measurable characteristics, which can be represented in schematic or diagrammatic form—that is, as information.[1] The first, when pushed to its extreme limit, tends to a kind of fusional ecstasy—a disappearance of the self into the world—as in the Heideggerian account of dwelling. The second tends, in its extreme versions, to reduce human experience to a set of data points (as in quantitative geography) or an epiphenomenal product of deep structures (as in the antihumanist branch of poststructuralism).

It has become increasingly clear that one of the major methodological challenges facing any comprehensive theory of place is to bridge the gap between these two visions, bringing them together in a way that makes it possible to hold both perspectives in mind at the same time, as Entrikin attempts to do by promoting the in-between perspective of narrative and Malpas attempts to do in his effort to bring together Heidegger and analytic philosophy via the surveyor model of subjectivity. Without the effort to reconcile these two apparently opposed perspectives, we run the risk of ending up with either unsubstantiated impressions or empty abstractions. One of the central aims of this book has, accordingly, been to work toward a stereoscopic melding of theoretical and literary accounts of place, in the belief that the phenomenologically oriented perspective of the literary representations can both benefit from and contribute to theoretical discourses on place. Thus we looked at Beckett's work through the lens of Francisco Varela's attempt to bring together phenomenology and cognitive science; we then examined the rhetoric of community in banlieue narratives as a way to bridge the gap between the folk sociology of the literary and cinematic texts and formal sociological thought in the mode of Bourdieu, Wacquant, and Bidou-Zachariasen; and then we extended this debate into the French Caribbean, using postcolonial theory and Glissant's poetics of relation as a way to rethink place in light of the struggle of "minor" cultures for survival in the global cultural market place.

The question of how best to reconcile these two ways of knowing the world around us—experiential and informational—is one that Fredric Jameson has posed in terms of cognitive mapping. In his formulation, the problem is the sense of a growing chasm between phenomenological experience and what he calls the "structural conditions" of that experience, which are "often not even conceptualizable for most people." This is a problem whose origins he situates in the modern period and sees as reaching crisis proportions in the postmodern ("late capitalist") era:

> The problems of figuration that concern us . . . may be conveyed by way of a growing contradiction between lived experience and structure, or between a phenomenological description of the life of an individual and a more properly structural model of the conditions of existence of that experience . . . the phenomenological experience of the individual subject— traditionally the supreme raw materials of the work of art—becomes limited to a tiny corner of the social world . . . But the truth of that experience no longer coincides with the place in which it takes place . . . those structural co-ordinates are no longer accessible to immediate lived experience and

are often not even conceptualizable for most people. (Jameson, "Cognitive Mapping" 349; see also the reworking of this argument in Jameson, *Postmodernism* 50–54)

Jameson's use of the expression "cognitive mapping" is explicitly motivated by his interest in the geographical and spatial consequences of modernity and globalization. In fact, Jameson frames his use of the concept in a way that clearly meets up with the local-global dynamic discussed in the previous chapter. Thus he emphasizes that, already, in the early modern period, the daily experience of the Londoner was "bound up with the whole colonial system of the British Empire that determines the very quality of the individual's subjective life" (Jameson, "Cognitive Mapping" 349).[2]

More fundamentally, though, the question at the heart of Jameson's use of the cognitive mapping metaphor is that of defining "the truth" of our phenomenological experience of the world, which, according to Jameson, "no longer coincides with the place in which it takes place." On what level, then, is that truth to be situated? Jameson conceives of this (post)modern incommensurability of lived experience and structure in Marxist terms, as a consequence of changes in "the true economic and social form that governs that experience."[3] He concludes, following Althusser, "that the incapacity to map socially is as crippling to political experience as the analogous incapacity to map spatially is for urban experience. It follows that an aesthetic of cognitive mapping in this sense is an integral part of any socialist political project" (Jameson, "Cognitive Mapping" 353).

The basic premise of Jameson's argument is unassailable. Clearly, if we are unable to grasp the relationship between our "lived experience" and "the truth of that experience," then our decision making will be poor. If we do not understand how our phenomenological experience can be situated with respect to the "structural coordinates" that govern it, we will fail to understand the larger significance and consequences of our choices and will, as a result, lack the ability to orient our activities in meaningful directions. The epistemological problem, in other words, has profound ethical, existential, and political consequences.

It is possible, however, to agree with Jameson's general line of reasoning without accepting the precise terms in which it is formulated. What, after all, does the word "truth" mean in this context? Jameson, as a Marxian thinker, is convinced that the truth in question is socioeconomic in nature. But is the socioeconomic dimension of existence really the bedrock level of reference in the way that Jameson's formulation suggests? It is far from clear that the level of political economy provides the only legitimate point of reference against which all others—including, for example, the biophysical level of existence—must be judged. What I retain from Jameson's argument, then, is the idea of "cognitive mapping"—defined as the attempt to situate the subjective impressions of phenomenological experience with respect to an underlying ontological foundation or "truth"—without, however, requiring that that truth be defined in primarily social, political, or economic terms.

If we think of the works studied in the preceding chapters, it is clear that Jameson's preferred level of analysis works very well for the social novels studied in Chapter 4. Indeed, the *banlieue* protagonists provide a straightforward illustration of the epistemological gap between experience and structure that Jameson foregrounds and that the banlieue protagonists are able to bridge to a certain (limited) extent. In this sense, we might even want to think of these novels as dramatizations of the attempt to break out of a naïvely phenomenological perspective and enter into the more worldly "cartographic" perspective that Jameson promotes: after the *Bildungsroman*, the *Kartografroman*.

Jameson's sociopolitical approach also works, up to a point, with the Caribbean novels—most obviously those of Glissant, which explicitly situate the personal experiences of the Martinican protagonists with respect to larger global developments. Because the postcolonial experience makes the relationship between the metropolitan center and the colonial periphery a matter of central concern, even the most naïve protagonists of these novels are aware, in a way that the metropolitan protagonists are not, of the geopolitical framework that conditions their experience. That said, however, the insistent appeal to nature and the evolutionary model of cultural adaptation in these novels tends to short-circuit the Marxian mode of analysis deployed by Jameson. These novels tend to push straight on through the sociopolitical level and to ground their cultural analyses in nature itself— usually, as I argued, through the principle of adaptive evolution.

As for Beckett, his work demands an entirely different approach, since there is little overlap between his phenomenological framing of the epistemological problem and Jameson's socioeconomic framework. Certainly, it might be interesting and productive to ask how the work of a writer like Beckett can be situated with respect to a Marxian model of social and economic analysis, as Lukács has done (see Lukács, "Art and Objective Truth"), but it is also an approach that can lead to oversimplifications and misunderstandings (as it does for Lukács). Beckett's formulations of the ontological dimension of his quest are instead framed in terms of what he called the "subject object crisis" and are much closer to those of Heidegger in that both thinkers are involved in a search for an ontologically grounded refuge from the *entre-deux* of alienated consciousness.[4] It would be reductive, no doubt, to try to force Beckett's work into a Heideggerian mold, but there are enough points of contact between the two approaches to place to make a brief comparison instructive.

Like Beckett, Heidegger was engaged in a deconstructive project to conceive of human existence in postmetaphysical terms. But after the so-called *Kehre*, or turn, that took place after the publication of *Being and Time*, he took that project in a different direction. Whereas Beckett's characters are never able to overcome the sense of alienation that makes any definitive return home possible, Heidegger's "Building Dwelling Thinking" essay proposes a solution to the problem of alienation that culminates in a clear image of home as a place of rest and spiritual plenitude. For Heidegger, achievement of this enlightened state, which he calls dwelling, is possible provided that we recognize the fundamental truth of hermeneutic phenomenology—the unitary whole of *Dasein* that precedes any division into subject and object. Achieving this state involves a meditative awareness of man's oneness with the world that is embodied by the well-known image of the Black Forest farmhouse with which the essay ends: "Here [in the Black Forest farmhouse] the self-sufficiency of the power to let earth and heaven, divinities and mortals enter in simple oneness into things, ordered the house" (Heidegger 160). Awareness of *Dasein* enables the individual to transcend a merely subjective perspective and gain a more complete, decentered, understanding of his place in the totality of Being. Because this kind of awareness does a better job of accounting for the relationship between man and world, resisting the tendency to treat space as something that can exist independently of the places that populate it, it is, Heidegger argues, "closer to the nature of spaces and to the origin of the nature of 'space' than any geometry and mathematics" (158).[5]

However, as the pastoral cottage imagery already suggests, this solution seems to depend on a nostalgic longing for a way of life that no longer exists, if indeed it ever did. Achievement of this enlightened state is predicated on the resurrection of modes of thinking and doing ("building") that had, in Heidegger's opinion, fostered the awareness of *Dasein* before the advent of technological modernity. Heidegger knows full well that no such return is possible but does believe that it will be possible to reclaim this sense of oneness with the Earth through what he calls "originary thinking."[6] Still, however willing one might be to agree with Heidegger on the spiritual distractedness of modern man and on the need to reincorporate awareness of *Dasein* into our daily lives, this solution is striking for its neglect of contemporary social realities. One can't help but be troubled, for example, by Heidegger's oddly peremptory refusal to engage with the practical problem of Europe's housing shortage in the aftermath of World War II. This matter is explicitly brought up at both the beginning and end of the "Building Dwelling Thinking" essay—but only in order to be summarily dismissed as an epiphenomenal by-product of spiritual alienation: "as soon as man *gives thought* to his homelessness, it is a misery no longer" (Heidegger 181, emphasis in original). Such remarks remind us that the apparent timelessness of the Black Forest cottage implies a flight from history that might generously be construed as therapeutic (i.e., a form of momentary release from thinking about the suffering of World War II and its aftermath) but that a skeptic might interpret as nostalgia or evasion—or even, as some have suggested, a consequence of his susceptibility to the National Socialist ideology of the homeland. (See, on this last point, Pavel, esp. 888.) This is not to say that Heidegger is wrong to temporarily set aside social considerations to pursue his own line of philosophical inquiry. (As Mugerauer points out, Heidegger is concerned with "metaphysical homelessness," not homelessness per se [68]). But it does suggest that he is wrong to foreclose the social question so definitively as a false or non-philosophical question.

To the extent, then, that Heidegger's essay's account of dwelling suggests a theory of place, it can only be considered partial. Like Jameson's argument about cognitive mapping, which prioritizes the socioeconomic level of existence over all others, the Heideggerian theme of dwelling alerts us to an important dimension of place (the sense of being fully integrated into *Dasein* through our awareness of the landscape in which we find ourselves) that cannot, however, stand on its own as completely satisfying.[7] In order to construct a more complete, holistic sense of place, it is necessary to situate it with respect to the other dimensions of place. This brings us to the question of what I call vertical integration: What are the various levels of place, and how can they be brought together in support of a holistic theory of place? This question of vertical integration provides a somewhat more nuanced way to address the question of cognitive mapping raised by Jameson.

I would suggest that any holistic theory of place must be able to account for at least three layers of place—phenomenological, social, and natural/material—and be able to show how they fit together. This is, perhaps, a self-serving argument, since it is this tripartite division that dictated the organization of my study—Beckett prioritizes the phenomenological level (the interface between consciousness and place), the *banlieue* narratives focus on the social dimension of place, and the Caribbean writers put the question of place in a naturalistic, environmental context—but there is still a certain logic to this structure, since it entails an understanding of the relationship between the *inside* of consciousness, the *middle* ground of social existence, and the apparently inhuman *outside* of the material world and natural environment.

Of course, it is highly artificial to separate the layers of place in this way, since this layering is complex and shades into a potentially infinite number of overlapping strata. (Malpas and Lefebvre both emphasize this point, as we have seen.) Moreover, this is not the only possible way to order the various strata of place.[8] And, of course, none of the bodies of work studied in this book remains strictly confined to any one of these layers; they tend rather to give priority to one over the others. The primary utility of this tripartite division is to simplify the task of addressing the complexity of place by making it possible to deal with each of these levels of place in relative isolation.

Still the question remains: Is it possible to hold all these intersecting dimensions of place together within the space of a single representation—one that would show how the material, social, and psychological dimensions of place feed into each other and shape each other mutually? This is not something that has been easy to achieve in practice, but this goal seems necessary to any truly holistic theory of place. Indeed, it may be that one of the best tests of a comprehensive theory of place is its ability to mediate successfully between the different levels of analysis, showing how they are related to each other as well as the points at which they blend into one another.

Of all the theorists we have studied so far, it seems to be Lefebvre who has pushed this vertically integrated understanding of place the furthest. Malpas and the phenomenologists, as we have seen, make allowances for the social and material dimensions of place, but they tend to set those aspects of the question aside and instead focus on its phenomenological aspects. Meanwhile, most of the poststructuralists seem to push both nature and man off to the horizon and instead focus on space and social structures. But Lefebvre links the social production of space to the material underpinnings of spatial experience through the body and his notion of "reciprocal inherence," while also linking it to the psychological level, through the category of "perceived space." In this way, his work contributes powerfully to the Marxist theory of the base-superstructure relationship (i.e., the extent to which culture and subjectivity are expressions of economic relations) and strengthens Marxism's claim to be a thoroughgoing (historical or dialectical) materialism, with nature providing the ultimate referent for its analyses. But his is not the only attempt to achieve this feat of vertical integration—that of binding the various levels of place together within a single representational space.

Perhaps the most far-reaching attempt to develop a vertically integrated language of representation is that of Gilles Deleuze and Félix Guattari. In a statement that resonates strongly with the three-tiered understanding of place I have been describing, Guattari has called for the development of an "ecosophy," which would seek to achieve an "ethico-political articulation between the three ecological registers, that of the environment, that of social relations, and that of human subjectivity" (Guattari, *The Three Ecologies* back matter). We can see the implications of this desire to address the question of place in all of its dimensions in Guattari's collaborations with Gilles Deleuze, particularly in *A Thousand Plateaus* and *What Is Philosophy?*

What makes the collaborations of Deleuze and Guattari so useful for understanding the vertical integration of place is that, unlike Jameson or Heidegger, they refuse to pick a single level that would be "the real" of the phenomena in question. For them, the socioeconomic level of existence and the level of individual consciousness or subjectivity are but moments or strata or plateaus in a continuum that runs from the physical, chemical, and biological processes that govern all forms of life to the supraindividual forces that govern societies. All conceivable levels provide equally legitimate points of entry into the debates at hand. In their attempt to describe the world at the "molecular" level of particles interacting according to laws that are invisible at the "molar" level of analysis, they are able to relativize the phenomenological level of human subjectivity by breaking it into its component parts, so to speak, as something that arises from material processes and is, in turn, overdetermined by social structures. This shift in perspective leads them into a reflection on human subjectivity and its relation to the material world that cuts an always-surprising transversal path between the phenomenological approach to this question and to those questions employed in the social and biological sciences. As Mark Bonta and John Protevi explain, "Deleuze and Guattari's notion of the subject as product does not deny the agency of subjects, but does locate them as only an intermediate level of structure, the emergent effect of an assemblage of stratified organs constituting the focal point of an organism, but in turn 'subject to' . . . the constraints of social machines" (Bonta and Protevi 155). Or, as Deleuze and Guattari put it in *What is Philosophy?*, from the perspective of empiricism (or at least the kind of "radical empiricism" they practice), "the subject [is] a *habitus*, a habit, nothing but a habit in a field of immanence, the habit of saying I" (48). Human consciousness is but one level in the field of immanence of a self-differentiating nature.

This "molecular" outlook enables them to provide an equally novel approach to the study of place—one that subverts the very distinction between the inside of the landscape and the outside of the map while also taking into account the material, social, and psychological levels of place. Central to their project are the geographically overdetermined principles of nomadism and deterritorialization, and many of their arguments are laid out in terms that shift from the zoological (the territorial behavior of animals) to the anthropological (the complex forms of territoriality found in nomadic cultures) to the geopolitical (geophilosophy as the study of how national philosophical "styles" are shaped by economic and social formations that are themselves shaped by geography and environment). Their emphasis on deterritorialization leads them to treat the Heideggerian attachment to place in much the same way as Certeau and Blanchot, as a kind of atavistic nostalgia. Whereas Heidegger had shown nostalgia for a lost past that is associated with dwelling in place in a rooted manner, Deleuze and Guattari move in the exact opposite direction, arguing instead for the need to be nomadic and mobile and to get used to being exposed to the elements of a postfoundational world in which the Nietzschean death of the gods has made borders of all kinds (territorial, philosophical, disciplinary) more permeable than ever before. Thus, for them, the landscape is, like the human face, a "'black hole' of subjectivity"—a "trap of the signifying and postsignifying regimes."[9] And the all-encompassing totality of *Dasein* is something they shatter in their molecular explorations of the different planes of existence.

Their insistent demand to relativize the phenomenological plane of experience would seem to put them squarely on the side of the cartographic tradition described above. And indeed, they argue vehemently for the importance of adopting a cartographic outlook—one able to take the objects that appear on the molar plane (which is, in this sense, akin to the phenomenological plane) and plot them onto other planes of analysis. And although this outlook is only cartographic in a metaphorical sense, involving "mapping" from the level of phenomenological experience to the more abstract level of "structural" conditions, it has, as Bonta and Protevi have amply shown, important implications for the study of place.

As is often the case with Deleuze and Guattari, however, there is a certain amount of terminological gamesmanship that needs to be taken into account here. Their definition of the map, for example, would mystify any conventional geographer. Rather than defining it as a form of abstract spatial representation, the map is, as they see it, "entirely oriented toward an experimentation in contact with the real." It does not "reproduce" or "represent" a territory but "constructs" the territory; it "has to do with performance" (Deleuze and Guattari, *A Thousand Plateaus* 12–13). For them, in other words, mapping is a form of direct *experience* ("contact with the real"). It is not a form of (abstract) representation but a mode of experience and expression that interacts directly with the real. In what sense can we say that mapping transcends mere representation in order to interact with the real? We can do so in somewhat the same sense that Lefebvre's third phase of space (spaces of representation) is considered to be more "lived" than the mode of representation he calls "conceived space." What interests Deleuze and Guattari is the problem of mapping the territory *from within*—from the limited perspective of nomads and molecules, who have no privileged vantage point to help them and whose activities modify the milieu through which they move (laying down tracks and markers) even as they attempt to map it. In this, their account of cartography meshes not only with Lefebvre's "lived space" but also with Malpas's surveyor model of human subjectivity.

This phase of mapmaking (surveying and correlating) is especially important for Deleuze and Guattari because of their emphasis on the molecular level of analysis. Once we understand this important point—that their account of the map is considered from the angle of map-*making*—then the cartographic (and existential) relevance of their preference for the map becomes clear: they are interested in mapping those areas of human experience that have remained resistant to the theories of "royal science"—those areas about which established science has little or nothing to tell us. Thus rather than distances, areas, angles, borders, routes, and other spatial features, they seek to map such things as "lines of flight" and "becomings" (which involve changes of state rather than location) and "intensities" (which measure the amount of energy per unit of space/time). Moreover, they define the concept of territory in terms of "a 'becoming' or 'emergence' of the interaction of functions and expressive markers" and conceive of matter in terms of energy and force that has entered into a state of relative (and temporary) equilibrium (Bonta and Protevi 111, 158). Objects, in this view, may be mapped spatially but must also be mapped onto the virtual realm of becomings and lines of flight. And it is this latter task that they see as paramount.

I have presented Deleuze and Guattari's geophilosophy as representing an important advance in the search for better ways to account for the vertical integration of the various levels of place. It is also important to recognize, however, that for as evocative as the Deleuzoguattarian idiom may be as a way to think about the relations between the phenomenological, sociological, and biophysical levels of existence, it remains speculative, utopian, and (despite their many protestations to the contrary) largely metaphorical, using the language of nomadism and deterritorialization as a way to think about *conceptual* mobility and the deconstruction of received wisdom. It is interesting and instructive to see how they use biological analogies to explain their ideas (as in their critique of imitative theories of representation through the wasp-orchid symbion), and they are quite effective at getting us to think about human experience from an infrahuman and supraindividual perspective, but they tend to play fast and loose with the scientific ideas they borrow, using them in speculative ways that would fail most tests of scientific accountability. All this makes it difficult to know how one might build upon their insights into the nature of place and makes their work vulnerable to the kind of polemics against French theory that have become commonplace in Anglo-American philosophical and scientific communities.[10]

What is needed in order to bring this vision of things to fruition, it seems, is a project that would take the kind of vertical integration exemplified by their work but reterritorialize it in a way that is compatible with the scientific (data driven, empirical, and falsifiable) understanding of these three major orders of place experience. Indeed, this eventual reterritorialization of nomadic science onto royal science is something Deleuze and Guattari explicitly recognize and, in a sense, call for:

> However refined or rigorous, [the] "approximate knowledge" [of nomadic science] is still dependent upon sensitive and sensible evaluations that pose more problems than they solve: problematics is still its only mode. In contrast, what is proper to royal science, to its theorematic or axiomatic power, is to isolate all operations from the conditions of intuition, making them true intrinsic concepts, or "categories." That is precisely why deterritorialization, in this kind of science, implies a reterritorialization in the conceptual apparatus. (*A Thousand Plateaus* 373)

What would such a reterritorialized science look like? We have already seen one possible answer to this question in the work of Varela, Thompson, and Rosch, who use cognitive science as a way to bring together phenomenological philosophy and Buddhist spirituality with scientific theories of the mind and evolutionary biology, using them to enrich and complete each other without subordinating one to the other.

More generally, we could adduce most recent work in cognitive science as seeking to build bridges between the natural sciences, the philosophy of mind, and observable human practices (including social behavior and cultural institutions like literature). Similarly, evolutionary psychology in the mode of Tooby and Cosmides also seeks to explain human social behavior and cultural production in terms of human evolutionary history, though it tends to emphasize the tensions that arise from the slow tempo of evolutionary adaptation and the rapidly changing environments of the modern and postmodern world. In fields such as ethics, too, apparent conflicts between the Kantian demand for a universal morality and the presumably "selfish" instinct for self-preservation ingrained in us by the pressures of natural selection have given rise to interesting work on topics such as altruism and social solidarity—work that seeks to revise our understanding of both evolutionary processes and observable human behaviors.

Another interesting example of a reformed or reterritorialized approach to the sciences built around the principle of vertical integration is that of Bruno Latour. What makes Latour's case interesting, for our purposes, is that he began his career in the poststructuralist camp, staking out a strong social constructionist position that tended to undermine the authority habitually attributed to scientific research. Since turning to the development of Actor-Network Theory (ANT), however, he has begun arguing for the "cultivation of a stubbornly realist attitude" and emphasizing the importance of reconciling social critique in the poststructuralist vein with the scientific emphasis on empirical evidence and testable results. (See, in particular, Latour, "Why Has Critique Run out of Steam?".) This has had important consequences for the way he views the relationship between culture, society, and nature. In his recent "Attempt at a Compositionist Manifesto" (2010), Latour argues for the need to "recompose" the idea of nature in a way that incorporates human culture and politics while also considering nature not as something built out of inert matter but as something that has its own kinds of agency, from the molecular level on up.

Such approaches strive for what E. O. Wilson has called consilience (in his eponymous 1998 book). Wilson, best known for his role in founding the discipline of sociobiology, defines consilience as the search for a grand unifying theory able to bring together the humanities, the social sciences, and the hard sciences. What is at stake in the search for consilience is the possibility of a thoroughgoing materialism—one able to explain cultural and social phenomena with respect to their material infrastructure (as opposed to presenting human cultures as somehow outside of or above nature), and that is able to do so without adopting a reductive or deterministic outlook (i.e., that would reduce all cultural and social phenomena to the status of epiphenomenal or incidental effects of deeper biological or physical processes). There are good reasons to doubt that sociobiology has been able to achieve the latter objective, but the notion of consilience remains a valuable one.[11]

Place, it seems to me, provides a prime candidate for the application of such an approach, because it has a built-in interdisciplinary component. If we agree that a truly holistic account of place must be prepared to take into account all the various levels of place (even if, for practical reasons, it will tend to emphasize one of them over the others), then it provides a particularly potent laboratory for the development of consilient modes of inquiry. This has certainly been the case for me. My inquiry began as a fairly conventional study of the literary representation of place, motivated by my experiences living and working in the kinds of places studied here. But the limitations of a strictly literary or autobiographical approach to the subject soon became apparent, and they had the effect of pushing me ever further afield, into disciplines I had never expected to encounter at the outset. Although my approach no doubt shows all the limitations of such a home-grown mode of interdisciplinarity, I hope to have been able to deploy my insights in a way that fulfills the traditional functions of literary criticism (furthering our understanding of the works and showing what makes them significant), while also furthering our understanding of the places in question, all without violating the spirit of the scientific disciplines brought into play. I believe that this approach to the study of literature and place is of value to anyone interested in building bridges between the humanities and sciences, both social and natural. And in a historical moment marked by declining public confidence in (and respect for) the humanities, the ability to demonstrate such links is of the utmost importance—if, that is, the humanities is not to disappear from the consilient equation.

It would be unrealistic of me to claim that my analyses of these works have made any groundbreaking contributions to the scientific fields in question. At best, I have been able to corroborate or contest certain theses while providing more data to crunch. But I do believe that the works studied here have themselves been able to play such a role, even if the paths of those contributions are circuitous and hard to detect. Beckett, the *Beur* and *banlieue* writers, and the Caribbean writers grouped around Glissant are notable precisely because they have been able to draw attention to problems in the lived experience of place that are difficult to address from a scientific or institutional standpoint. Thus we saw in Chapter 1 how closely the terms of the Beckettian quest are mirrored by Varela, Thompson, and Rosch. There is no doubt that works like those of Beckett helped to clear a space for scientists interested in the philosophy of mind, making available a language of interstitiality that has shaped public perception and, by extension, the preoccupations of the scientists themselves. In a more direct way, Azouz Begag's voice as a sociologist of France's *banlieues* was both shaped by and amplified by his literary texts. His fictions helped him to formulate his ideas in a way that has certainly fed into his scientific research while also helping that research and those ideas to reach a much broader audience than they would have otherwise. Much the same thing could be said about Chamoiseau and his role in shaping and disseminating the mode of urbanism promoted by Serge Letchimy—or Glissant, whose work lives on and now has an institutional reality in the *Institut du Tout-monde* that he founded in Paris.

The work of these writers has contributed to the emergence of new conceptions of place, changing the ways we understand our relation to place and also shaping our expectations of what a place is, should, or can be. In so doing, it has exercised a no doubt subtle but nonetheless important influence on the kinds of places that may emerge in the future, nudging in new directions public consciousness of the issues they address and alerting it to considerations that might otherwise have been ignored. Given the ongoing evolution of human societies and the forms of community and dwelling they generate, this kind of work is of the utmost importance. There will always be people who find themselves caught in the *entre-deux*, inhabiting social positions and geographical identities that no longer fit the old categories but that have not yet found new categories adequate to them. It is in this space that literature can insert itself with the greatest efficacy, participating in the creation of those new categories. Given this, I can think of no better way to close than with an important Glissantian exhortation on the vital role played by such interstitial communities. Although addressed specifically to the identitarian malaise of Antilleans living in France's working-class suburbs, it applies to all who find themselves inhabiting the *entre-deux* in any of its many forms:

> When I give talks in the suburbs of Paris, they tell me:—So what are we? When we go to the Antilles, people tell us "You're nothing but little French shits [merdeux]," and when we are in France, they tell us "You're just Caribbean shits." What I tell them is: "Never mind about all that! You are above all of that, you are in advance of all that, you are the future of the world. You are bringing about something that is beyond everything that they can tell you, be it in the Antilles or in France." And when I tell them that, their eyes sparkle, because they say to themselves "Alright, we aren't useless, we have a task to accomplish, we are not worn down, lost at sea." I tell them, "Put into play your poetics of relation and you will see that you will be of service to everyone." (Glissant, "Métissage et créolisation" 53, my translation)

It is never easy to dwell in the *entre-deux*, but it is there that the most important work is to be done.

Notes

Introduction

1. I borrow the term geocriticism from Bertrand Westphal. See his *Géocritique; réel, fiction, espace*. Although my approach differs from Westphal's in many respects, we share an emphasis on the encounter between literature and the social sciences, a belief in the performative efficacy of literary discourse, and an insistent focus on interstitial areas of human experience. Robert Tally's recent translation of Westphal's book, *Geocriticism: Real and Fictional Spaces*, will help to make Westphal's important contribution to the spatial study of literature more readily accessible to English speakers, as will Tally's edited volume of geocritical essays, titled *Geocritical Explorations: Space, Place, and Mapping in Literary and Cultural Studies*.

2. As Wittgenstein pointed out, scientists play language games, too. The advantage of literature, in this context, is that it has, so to speak, specialized in the exploration and development of new modes of representation. It is in this sense that Pound characterized artists as the "antennae of the race."

3. "Isn't it the role of literature to help us in naming the unnamable, or more precisely that which had not up till then had a name in the accumulation of clichés that constitutes a large part of everyday language?" (Bonn 38–39).

4. This rendering of Baudelaire's justly celebrated line is used by Keith and Rosmarie Waldrop as the title for their translation of Jacques Roubaud's *La forme d'une ville*.

5. Marshall Berman emphasizes this tension in Baudelaire between regret and exhilaration in *All That Is Solid Melts into Air* 131–71.

6. See Richard Sennett's *The Conscience of the Eye*, among others, and Jane Jacob's classic *The Death and Life of Great American Cities*.

7. See Raymond Williams, *The Country and the City*.

8. Fredric Jameson and David Harvey have given the classic analyses of these phenomena. See Jameson's *Postmodernism, or, The Cultural Logic of Late Capitalism* and Harvey's *The Condition of Postmodernity*.

9. See Howard Kunstler, *The Geography of Nowhere*. Kunstler, who *hates* suburbia, is a proponent of the New Urbanism movement, which promotes a return to traditional neighborhood design standards. Although the New Urbanism has promoted many useful ideas for zoning reform that would encourage walking neighborhoods of relatively high density and mixed residential/business zoning, it shows a perhaps utopian nostalgia for the preautomobile era that has

risks of its own. (See the Disney-sponsored Celebration, Florida, a master-planned community that was inspired by New Urbanist principles but that has a distinctly backward-looking feel).

10. Compare, for example, the way the politics of urban renewal have worked in the United States since the 1950s, with the phenomenon of white flight leaving poor and minority populations concentrated in the city center. Although they are spatial antonyms, the American "inner city" has become sociologically synonymous with the French "urban periphery."

11. David Harvey has written insightfully on the cost-benefit analysis that must be undertaken before judging Haussmann and Napoléon III one way or the other. See his *Paris, Capital of Modernity*.

12. Moses's reputation as a socially insensitive tyrant was established by Jacobs's public campaign against his projects and her book *The Death and Life of Great American Cities*. It was then cemented in place by Robert Caro's authoritative biography of Moses, *The Power Broker: Robert Moses and the Fall of New York*.

13. On recent attempts to rehabilitate Moses's reputation, see *Wrestling with Moses* by Anthony Flint and "What a City Needs" by Edward Glaeser. And in rebuttal to such gestures, see Robert Caro's "The City-Shaper" and Nicholas Von Hoffman's "Beware of the Robert Moses Revisionists." This debate is by no means over.

14. This is a debate of particular importance in the contemporary French context, as Nicolas Sarkozy's Haussmannesque vision for *Le Grand Paris*, which was initially sold as a way to better integrate the ring of suburbs around Paris into the social and economic life of the city, wends its way through the political process

15. Thus, for example, the humanistic approach of Tuan is justly criticized by Derek Gregory for its lack of interest in the kind of theoretical apparatus favored by radical geographers in the tradition of Lefebvre and Foucault, which might have allowed him to test the limits of the "common-sense" presuppositions that shape his arguments (see Gregory 78-80). Conversely, Peta Mitchell's *Cartographic Strategies of Postmodernity* does an excellent job laying out the poststructuralist, postmodern use of cartographic models and metaphors, but leaves aside consideration of phenomenological questions that might have enabled her to bridge the gap between the humanist and poststructuralist camps.

16. See, on this subject, Milne, *The Extreme In-Between*.

17. Ingrid Leman Stefanovic makes this remark in "Speaking of Place" (6).

18. The geographer Jacques Lévy makes a similar point: "The characterization of a space as a place is the result of a construction. The same reality can be treated as a region (*aire*), a collection of places, if one activates its internal distances." Rather than speaking of placefulness as an ontologically stable attribute, he emphasizes "*the extent to which* a space can be considered as a place" and argues that "in identifying it as a place, one privileges the proximity of the interactions within, and its distant relations with other spaces" ("Lieu," in Lévy and Lussault 560-61).

19. Said cites two clear examples of the forcible imposition of meaning onto a landscape: the medieval Crusaders' fantasy of Jerusalem as a Capital of Christendom in need of liberation and the Zionist belief that "Palestine had stood still in time and was theirs, again despite millennia of history and the presence of actual inhabitants" ("Invention, Memory, and Place" 180).

Chapter 1

1. See the brief history given in Barnes.
2. Tuan's "Space and Place: Humanistic Perspective" (1974), his "Humanistic Geography" (1976), and Relph's *Place and Placelessness* (1976) are usually cited as the catalytic moments of this movement. See Cresswell, 18–24 for a brief overview of this history.
3. David Seamon publishes an excellent "Environmental & Architectural Phenomenology Newsletter," which has a strong online presence at http://www.arch.ksu.edu/seamon/EAP.html.
4. On the *Chora* in Derrida and Kristeva, see Rickert.
5. Casey, on the other hand, fits squarely within the continental tradition. The only Anglophone philosophers to capture his attention in *The Fate of Place* are Locke and Whitehead. He is aware of the existence of humanist geography and its significance for his overarching argument (about the need to revitalize the study of place) but devotes no space to the study of the field or its thinkers. (Relph, Tuan, and Entrikin are named in passing in a list of North American thinkers who have sought "to face up to place" [286], but receive no further attention.)
6. Edouard Glissant, as we will see in Chapter 6, emphasizes this extension of the local place into the environing *Tout-monde*. The principle of interconnectedness is crucial for his conception of place.
7. At one point, Malpas takes Entrikin to task, arguing that although Entrikin claims to want to walk the line between the subjective and objective poles, his choice of narrative as the mediating term leads him too far in the direction of the subjective (Malpas 31fn35).
8. This kind of chiasmatic formulation is a recurrent figure in *Place and Experience* and is important for what it reveals about the perspectival shift that Malpas is trying to effect.
9. This should not be construed to imply that Malpas has fallen into the trap of the mimetic fallacy—that is, that if we knew where to look in the brain, we would find a kind of miniature imprint of the world. The point Malpas is making is more subtle: Given that the structures of the brain have grown up in response to environmental stimuli that shape and constrain their development, they must have some necessary relation to those conditions.
10. Edouard Glissant proposes a response to such questions in his theory of *Tout-monde*. See the last section of Chapter 6 for my analysis of Glissant's contribution to this question.
11. See also pages 7 and 9fn23, which work the same point from various angles.

12. Richard J. Bernstein popularized this term in *Beyond Objectivism and Relativism: Science, Hermeneutics, and Praxis* (1983).

Chapter 2

1. O'Brien provides ample photographic confirmation of the Irish character of many of the landscapes in texts like *Molloy*, *Cascando*, and *Ill Seen Ill Said*. But Junker surely goes too far when she suggests that we can best "understand Beckett by going back to his Irish roots, the soil that nourished them, and the landscape in its varied and violent beauty his mature writing assumes" (11). Seán Kennedy seems much closer to the mark in his editorial introduction to *Beckett and Ireland* (2010) when he writes (quoting Peter Boxall) of "the systole-diastole of his rhythmic movement between resistance to and longing for a homeland" (10), adding, "It is not that the drive toward negation is not there. It is just that it is not absolute" (11).

2. The publication history of Beckett's bilingual *oeuvre* is complicated. In order to streamline my references, I give the date of first publication (where relevant to my argument) and list all titles in English, whether they were first published in English or in French. When quoting, I refer to the versions of these works that appear in the main English-language collections: *Complete Short Prose* (hereafter *CSP*), *Complete Dramatic Works*, *Disjecta*, *Nohow On* (for *Company*, *Ill Seen Ill Said*, and *Worstward Ho*), and *Three Novels* (for *Molloy*, *Malone Dies*, and *The Unnamable*).

3. This idea of the middle voice as a tympanum gets developed in the work of other writers of the *entre-deux*, including Michel Leiris and Jacques Derrida, both of whom have written eloquently about consciousness as a tympanum. On the middle voice as a grammatical construct (neither active nor passive), see Barry; Abbott, *Beckett Writing Beckett*; and Riquelme.

4. Derrida's critique of the metaphysics of presence is first set forth in his three major works published in 1967: *De la grammatologie*, *La voix et le phénomène*, and *L'écriture et la différence*.

5. Eyal Amiran's *Wandering and Home* (1993) covers some of the same territory that I do here, though he seems to underestimate the importance of the effort to return to place and the outside in Beckett's second phase.

6. I'm reminded of the story Hamm tells in *Endgame* about the madman who saw only blight and destruction where others saw the world as we know it: "Look! There! All that rising corn! And there! Look! The sails of the herring fleet! All that loveliness! [*Pause.*] He'd snatch away his hand and go back into his corner. Appalled. All he had seen was ashes . . . It appears the case is . . . was not so . . . so unusual" (*Complete Dramatic Works* 113).

7. Lukács, arguing that modernist art "rests on the assumption that the objective world is inherently inexplicable," cites Beckett's *Molloy* as a particularly egregious example of this tendency (Lukács, "The Ideology of Modernism" 147, 162). Although Lukács's primary focus is on modernism in the tradition of Joyce, Musil, Faulkner, and Kafka, his treatment of Beckett makes it clear

that he considers Beckett's work to represent a radicalization of modernist tendencies that has today come to be called postmodern. See also Lukács's "Art and Objective Truth" and *The Meaning of Contemporary Realism* for further elaborations of this argument, as well as Theodor Adorno's rebuttal to Lukács's critique of Beckett in "Trying to Understand *Endgame*."

8. It is important to distinguish between this minimal or "weak" definition of representation and the more baggage-laden definitions (i.e., that states of mind resemble, imitate, or reproduce states of the world in some sense). Varela, Thompson, and Rosch accept the former but spend much of their book militating against all "strong" definitions of representation—to the extent that they present their enactivist model of mind as being *anti*representational.

9. Gilles Deleuze has written powerfully, in "L'épuisé," on the injunction to do the image ("faire l'image").

10. I have given a more extensive analysis of these rituals in *Listening In*, 218–47.

11. This aspect of Beckett's relationship with his father is documented in both the Bair and Knowlson biographies of Beckett.

12. Theodor Adorno pursues a related argument in *Negative Dialectics:* "The need to let suffering speak is a condition of all truth. For suffering is objectivity that weighs upon the subject" (*Negative Dialectics* 17–18).

13. This translation is slightly modified in order to highlight how this expression prefigures the title of *Comment c'est/How It Is*.

Chapter 3

1. Another important text, Foucault's "Des espaces autres," which I alluded to previously, originated as a paper given in 1967, though it wasn't authorized for publication until 1984.

2. François Dosse quotes Foucault on this point: "Our Middle Ages in the modern era is humanism" (*Histoire du Structuralisme* 389). This critique meets up with that of Adorno and Horkheimer in *Dialectic of Enlightenment*.

3. This text has an odd publication history. Written in 1961, "it was meant," according to the website Atopia, "to be published in all the different languages of the planned *Revue internationale*." Ultimately, though, it "only appeared in the Italian literary magazine *Gulliver/Il Menabò* directed by Elio Vittorini and Italo Calvino in 1964 (trans. Guido Neri). The original manuscript is considered to be lost. Christopher Stevens has retranslated the text from Neri's version for Mike Holland's *Blanchot Reader*." For further information, see: http://www.atopia.tk/. My references are to the version in the *Blanchot Reader*.

4. Ann Smock has written elegantly of this dimension of Blanchot's work, in *What Is There To Say?*

5. Frank's much anthologized essay "Spatial Form in Modern Literature" calls spatial just about anything that slows down the linear flow of narrative sequentiality, including the organization of a text around a geographical site (as in Joyce's *Ulysses*) but also the representation of polyphonic simultaneity (as in the "Comices Agricoles" scene in Flaubert's *Madame Bovary*)

and the abstract ordering of binary oppositions, as in structuralism. It is not at all clear that there is anything inherently spatial about either of these last two examples. On the contrary, the first simply intertwines two chronological sequences, while the second involves the dimensionless processes of logical categorization.

6. Henri Lefebvre takes care to distance himself from this metaphorical use of space at the beginning of *The Production of Space*: "We are forever hearing about the space of this and/or the space of that; about literary space, ideological space, the space of the dream, psychoanalytic topologies, and so on and so forth. Conspicuous by its absence from supposedly fundamental epistemological studies is not only the idea of 'man' but also that of space—the fact that 'space' is mentioned on every page notwithstanding" (3).

7. In the original French article, Foucault uses the term "*localisation.*" The fact that it is translated here as "emplacement" could lead to confusion, as Foucault goes on later in the essay to use the French term *emplacement* to designate an entirely different mode of spatiality (which is translated as "site" in the English version). Although we might be tempted to dismiss this as a flawed translation, it actually makes good sense, if we consider that the word "emplacement" contains the word "place." In this way, the translator found a way to emphasize Foucault's insistence on the importance of place in the medieval period and its subsequent decline. For this reason, I will retain the translator's terminology here, which provides, in a sense, an improvement on Foucault's terminology.

8. Curiously, Casey completely overlooks the structuralist characteristic of Foucault's third epoch and instead emphasizes the concept of *sites*, a term that he seizes, somewhat carelessly, in order to coopt Foucault for his own argument on the importance of getting back into place. Although this choice implies a fundamental misreading of Foucault, it is a move that has been repeated by many other critics.

9. He is not, however, the very first. Indeed, although he does not mention them by name, many of the examples he gives are clearly inspired by the work of the anthropologists Arnold Van Gennep and Victor Turner, who promoted the concept of liminality in relation to ritual practices (see Van Gennep, *Les rites de passage*, and Turner, *The Ritual Process*).

10. This is a recurrent analogy in Lefebvre's work: "A living creature has slowly secreted a structure . . . it is precisely this link, between the animal and its shell, that one must try to understand . . . This community has shaped its shell, building and rebuilding it, modifying it again and again according to its needs" (cited in Fraser 369). See also the spider web metaphor in *The Production of Space* (Lefebvre 173).

11. For a different perspective on this question, see Derek Gregory, who emphasizes Lefebvre's attempts to rehabilitate the image of a Hegelian Marx (see Gregory 353–68).

12. This research is presented in volume two of *L'invention du quotidien*, cowritten with Luce Giard and Pierre Mayol.

13. One of the most interesting things about this essay is that it does not present us with a carefully composed argument that proceeds in linear fashion but instead shows Certeau in the process of thinking through an intractable problem—the problem of urban alienation.

Chapter 4

1. Any attempt to fully understand patterns of racial segregation is hampered by the fact that the French government does not keep official statistics on ethnicity or religion.

2. For Wacquant, unlike the American ghetto, "the French urban periphery is typified . . . by a fundamentally *heterogeneous* population according to ethnonational provenance" (*Urban Outcasts* 5), one that is, moreover, becoming "*increasingly* heterogeneous" in his view (118). See, however, Pan Ké Shon and also Levy-Vroelant and Tutin, which interpret the demographic data differently. See also Lapeyronnie and Courtois, *Ghetto urbain*, which seeks to contest Wacquant's argument by putting the emphasis on "systems of social conduct" and the "social imagination" of the ghetto. Wacquant is so heavily invested in an argument relying on a stark contrast between the racialized American ghetto and the less exclusionary French "antighetto" that he may overplay his hand. Lapeyronnie's emphasis on the social imagination supports my contention that literary and filmic representations of such communities can play an important role in addressing their problems.

3. Probably the best and most comprehensive introduction to these matters, at least in English, is Alec Hargreaves's *Immigration, 'Race' and Ethnicity in Contemporary France*. The influence of Hargreaves's work, which was instrumental in drawing attention to Beur writing in the 1990s (see Hargreaves, *Voices*), is evident throughout this chapter.

4. For a somewhat different interpretation of this plot-line, see Michel Laronde's "La Fontaine et *Salut cousin!*"

5. Allouache, it should be noted, is not himself a *Beur*. Born in Algeria, his films take their subject matter from both sides of the Mediterranean. To what extent this fact accounts for his skepticism with regard to *métissage* is a matter of speculation.

6. In *Frenchness and the African Diaspora* (Tshimanga, Gondola, and Bloom), the editors characterize this violence in terms of insurrection and uprisings. Murphy, "Baguettes, Berets and Burning Cars," offers one of many readings of the violence that emphasize its compatibility with republican values. Kenan Malik, "Multiculturalism at its Limits" provides a cogent critique of French arguments in favor of "color blindness" as in fact promoting "racism blindness."

7. As an aside: the plot of the novel revolves around the protagonist's involvement in a series of events that was clearly inspired by a media cause célèbre from 1996, when undocumented immigrants occupied the Saint-Bernard church in Paris in order to draw attention to the plight of undocumented

workers. The real-life occupation ended with the defeat of the protesters (a forcible eviction), but Tadjer's novel ends with success.

8. This stunting quality of ghetto life may help to explain why Annie Ricks (whose case was mentioned in the introduction to this book) was so reluctant to leave Cabrini Green—even on the eve of its destruction.

9. On geographical determinism in *Beur* literature, see Jaccomard's "Harem ou galère: le déterminisme géographique dans deux écrits beurs" and Samia Mehrez's excellent "Azouz Begag . . . A question of Territory."

10. Samia Mehrez's article, cited previously, makes a closely related point with regard to Deleuze and Guattari.

11. The plan was criticized, however, for favoring business interests over the needs of the population, for taking power away from existing local authorities, and for relaxing construction regulations in order to speed the project along. (See John Litchfield's article for *The Independent*, "Sarko's 35bn rail plan for a 'Greater Paris.'") As of this writing, the project has been vastly scaled back, and it seems unlikely to promote the goals enunciated by Begag.

12. Mahmoud Zemmouri's 1997 film *100% Arabica* addresses this issue with comic panache. In a plot pitting the appeal of a fundamentalist Imam (himself a fraud in cahoots with the local mayor) against that of a local Raï group, the music wins, hands down.

13. On the supposed failure of European multiculturalism postulated by Sarkozy, Cameron, and Merkel, see Kenan Malik's analysis in "A Merkel attack on multiculturalism."

14. It is, in particular, the police—which is perceived as acting with impunity against the *banlieusards* via such practices as intrusive ID checks, racial profiling (*le délit de faciès*), targeted violence (station house beatings, unprovoked harassment on the street, and the occasional *bavure*), and the overtly racist attitude of some police officers—that both provokes and is the targeted audience of this kind of violence.

Chapter 5

1. W. J. T. Mitchell makes a related point about landscape painting, which has been used by colonial powers to "naturalize" their rule by inscribing ideologically determined messages into images of nature ("Imperial Landscape" 5).

2. Of the six essays they include under the heading of place, all but one posit place as an ultimately inaccessible entity, only knowable indirectly, through, for example, naming and mapping conventions. Of these, Paul Carter's "Naming Place" and Graham Huggan's "Decolonizing the Map" are representative. The one exception is Alfred Crosby's "Ecological Imperialism," which treats the spread of Europeans throughout the globe as an ecological event and explores its consequences for the planetary food supply. From a phenomenological perspective, the most interesting selection is Dennis Lee's "Writing in Colonial Space," which is notable for its insistence on the experiential

dimension of place as he tries to tease out the ways in which attentiveness to one's environment shapes the rhythms of poetic invention.

3. This chronology meshes with that provided by Mbembe in "What Is Postcolonial Thinking?" Gayatri Spivak gives a comparable three-stage chronology in *Critique of Postcolonial Reason* 358–62. The evolution of Edouard Glissant's career—from *La Lézarde* to *Discours Antillais* and to the *Poétique de la relation/Tout–monde* period—confirms this tripartite division. In short, the applicability of the sequence has been well established and seems to apply across the geographical and disciplinary range of the field—from Africa, to India, to the Caribbean and from political science to subaltern studies to cultural theory.

4. See Arif Dirlik, "The Postcolonial Aura." Spivak picks up this critique in *Critique of Postcolonial Reason*, and Richard Serrano has promoted this point of view in his *Against the Postcolonial*.

5. See also Reiss's *Against Autonomy*.

Chapter 6

1. "S'cuse me?!" is Linda Coverdale's translation of "*Eti?!*" (Chamoiseau, *School Days* 30).

2. See also Glissant's *Tout-monde*: "Places were people for him, some like men some like women . . . If you don't understand the relationships between all these landscapes you don't understand the country" (476–7); and Maximin's recent *Les fruits du cyclone: Une géopoétique de la Caraïbe* (2006), which carries on with this environmental tradition: "Nature in the Caribbean is not a décor, it is a central character of its history" (81).

3. This chapter has its origins in an earlier article (Prieto, "Landscaping Identity"). Although some of the textual analyses of that article have been incorporated into this chapter, the principal thrust of my argument has changed considerably.

4. The major exception to this rule is Aimé Césaire—at least in the early phase of his career. But as we will see later, despite the heroic, revolutionary rhetoric of Césaire's *Cahier d'un retour au pays natal*, he was to play an important role in shaping the more properly evolutionary outlook of his successors.

5. For a revisionist view of the respective roles of Marxism and negritude in Césaire's work that overlaps in some ways with my own, see Miller, "The (Revised) Birth of Negritude."

6. In an intriguing article titled "Fouiller le paysage: the Geo-Poetics of Édouard Glissant," Christina Kullberg argues that the landscape literally shapes the thoughts and movements of the protagonists of the novel, concluding that Glissant's goal is to invent "a kind of *geo-poetics* close to Deleuze and Guattari's idea of geo-philosophy, in which geography, the land, invades thinking and has implications for the conception of the subject" (Kullberg 189).

7. The urban mangrove metaphor is borrowed from Serge Letchimy's treatise on urban development, *De l'habitat précaire à la ville*. Letchimy, who was trained

as a sociologist and urban planner, has since become one of the major figures of Martinican politics. Handpicked by Aimé Césaire to succeed him as mayor of Fort-de-France, he is also, as of this writing, a legislator representing Martinique in the French National Assembly, President of the *Conseil Régional* of Martinique, leader of the *Parti Progressiste Martiniquais* (PPM), and author of *Discours sur l'Autonomie*, which proposes a path toward political autonomy for the island that stops short of a demand for formal independence.

8. See the preceding note for information on Letchimy's career.

9. Other examples include *Désirada* and *Le cœur à rire et à pleurer*.

10. Each of these figures appears over and over in West Indian literature—not only in Césaire, Glissant, and Chamoiseau but also in Roumain, Zobel, Confiant, Schwarz-Bart, and many others.

11. In fact, *Tout-monde* seems to have brought this cycle to a close with the death of Mathieu Béluse at the end of the novel. Glissant published two novels after *Tout-monde*—*Sartorius* and *Ormerod*—and they are his first to set aside the cast of characters and *mythos* that is set into motion with *La Lézarde*.

12. *La case du commandeur* was organized around Marie Celat's mental breakdown and subsequent stay in a mental hospital—a trajectory that seems meant as an emblem of the identitarian plight of contemporary Martinique. Significantly, the novel culminates with Marie Celat's escape from the mental hospital, which leads her to take refuge in a highly overdetermined site: a hut that appears to be the overseer's shack named in the novel's title. (*La case du commandeur* could be translated as "the overseer's hut.")

13. The term is fairly close to untranslatable. Literal approximations like "whole world" or "one world" fail to catch its full complexity. A closer approximation is suggested by the term "cosmos," which connotes an ordered totality. Perhaps, then, something on the order of "Cosmos-world" would serve as a viable translation. Having said that, I will retain the original French in what follows.

14. For more detailed explorations of the core concepts of Glissant's poetics, see Britton, *Edouard Glissant and Postcolonial Theory* (1999) and Dash, *Edouard Glissant* (1995).

15. Many other variations on this theme are sprinkled throughout *Tout-monde* and *Traité du Tout-monde*.

16. This, for example, is how Nick Coates reads this refrain in his otherwise excellent doctoral dissertation: "Postcolonial criticism . . . restores the emphasis on the particular, 'le lieu est incontournable' as Glissant" insists (Coates 16). Or again, "'Le lieu est incontournable', a statement which echoes Lefebvre's observation that 'le local . . . ne disparaît pas, absorbé par le régional, le national, le mondial lui-même'" (Coates 33). Or yet again: "The universality of space . . . is resisted by Glissant's insistence that 'le lieu est incontournable'" (Coates 60).

17. This is the first sense of the term listed in the *Trésor de la langue française*: "To give form (to something) by tracing or by establishing its contours."

18. Mathieu Béluse, the reader will recall, is writing his own *Traité du Tout-monde*. Many passages of this (fictional) treatise are "quoted" in *Tout-monde*. To further complicate the self-referential play of this technique, Glissant will

incorporate many of the passages attributed to Béluse's *Traité* in the novel into the *Traité du tout-monde* published under his own name.

19. I use the term "minor" to designate minority or minoritarian status—not relative importance. This is the sense Deleuze and Guattari give to the term in their *Kafka* (see esp. 16–27).

20. "But look at the Creole garden, you put all the crops on such a little lick of land, the avocados, the lemons, the yams, the sugarcane ... plus thirty or forty other species on this bit of land that doesn't go more then fifty feet up the side of the hill, they protect each other. In the great Circle, everything is in everything else" (Glissant, *Tout-monde* 555).

21. See the following works, which were helpful to me as I prepared these remarks: *Animal Ecology* by Charles Sutherland Elton (1927), a foundational text for the field of biogeography; *Biocultural Diversity Conservation* by Maffi and Woodley, for an anthropological study of cultural diversity as a function of biological diversity ; and "Niches and Economic Competition" by Tisdell and Seidl, for the economic aspect.

Conclusion

1. Justin Read articulates this relationship in terms of an opposition between planetary space and global space, the first being experiential and the second informational: "There is planetary space, that which we know of primarily through our senses, and there is global space, the informational environment through which we know how the world works (measurement). We reside in or inhabit planetary space; we locate ourselves in global space" (Read 116–17).

2. Franco Moretti takes steps towards responding to Jameson's challenge by mapping out (literally) the colonial context for the emplotment of British novels in chapter one, part three of his *Atlas of the European Novel 1800-1900*.

3. David Harvey emphasizes this problem as well, framing the postmodern sense of disorientation in terms of "space-time compression" in *The Condition of Postmodernity*.

4. Among the many Heideggerian-tinged statements in Beckett, I will cite just one: "Being has a form. Someone will find it someday. Perhaps I won't but someone will. It is a form that has been abandoned, left behind, a proxy in its place" (qtd. in Lawrence Harvey 249). It is not just the term "Being" that resonates with Heidegger's thinking but the idea that Being is an underlying structure that, lost in the modern era, could be retrieved once a suitably enlightened outlook is achieved.

5. Casey and Malpas strongly emphasize this aspect of Heidegger's argument, as we saw in Chapter 1.

6. For a more favorable account of Heidegger's argument, see Mugerauer 67–76.

7. Jean-Luc Nancy has attempted to make up for this gap in Heidegger's thought by foregrounding the role of *Mitsein* (Being-in-common) in Heidegger's writings. (Nancy seeks to show how the social dimension of being [*Mitsein*] is

always already present in *Dasein*: Because individuals are born into a society that predates them, they are, ontologically speaking, social beings before they are individuals.) The point is well taken. However, after establishing this fundamental insight into the social implications of Heidegger's thinking, Nancy has trouble pushing it much further. I would argue that the gauziness of much of Nancy's thinking on community and globalization shows how difficult it is to adapt the Heideggerian approach to philosophy, which Nancy has always maintained, to questions of social justice (see Nancy, *La Communauté Désœuvrée*, *The Sense of the World*, and *The Creation of the World*).

8. A biologist or anthropologist might prefer to change this order, emphasizing instead, for example, a progression from nature to man (product of nature) to society (product of man). Then again, Jean-Luc Nancy, in *La communauté désœuvrée*, argues that social existence (*Mitsein*) precedes individual consciousness, as discussed in the previous footnote. This account of the structure of Being implies that the true progression is from nature to society to the individual.

9. From Bonta and Protevi's entries on the term "landscape" and its derivates (103–4); see also the entry on "place" (123–24) and those related to the term "face" (84–85).

10. See, for example, Sokal and Bricmont's *Fashionable Nonsense*, especially the chapter on Deleuze (154–68), although it must be said that the analyses of Sokal and Bricmont should be taken with a large grain of salt. However valid the underlying argument against the casual or metaphorical use of scientific concepts may be, their chapter on Deleuze amounts to little more than a hatchet job—cherry picking its examples and declaring them, out of context and with minimal supporting analysis, to be nonsense. What is missing is an attempt to read *with*, as well as against, their targets.

11. On this point, see Tanaka.

Works Cited

Abbott, H. Porter. *Beckett Writing Beckett: The Author in the Autograph*. Ithaca: Cornell University Press, 1996. Print.
———. "I Am Not a Philosopher." *Beckett at 100: Revolving It All*. Ed. Linda Ben-Zvi and Angela Moorjani. Oxford: Oxford University Press, 2008. 81–92. Print.
Adorno, Theodor. *Negative Dialectics*. Trans. E. B. Ashton. New York: Seabury Press, 1973. Print.
———. "Trying to understand Endgame." *Samuel Beckett's Endgame*. Ed. Harold Bloom. New York: Chelsea House, 1988. 9–40. Print.
Ahmad, Aijaz. *In Theory: Classes, Nations, Literatures*. London: Verso, 1992. Print.
Allouache, Merzak, dir. *Salut cousin!* Leo Films, 1996. Film.
Altman, Erwin, and Setha M. Low. *Place Attachment*. New York: Springer, 1992. Print.
Amiran, Eyal. *Wandering and Home: Beckett's Metaphysical Narrative*. University Park: Pennsylvania State University Press, 1993. Print.
Amselle, Jean-Loup. "Black, blanc, beur: Ou le fantasme du métissage." *Discours sur le métissage, identités métisses: En quête d'Ariel*. Ed. Sylvie Kandé. Paris: l'Harmattan, 1999. 35–53. Print.
———. *Logiques métisses*. Paris: Payot, 1990. Print.
. *Vers un multiculturalisme français*. Paris: Aubier, 1996. Print.
Anderson, Benedict. *Imagined Communities: Reflections on the Origin and Spread of Nationalism*. London: Verso, 2000. Print.
Anzaldúa, Gloria. *Borderlands: The New Mestiza/La Frontera*. San Francisco: Spinsters/Aunt Lute, 1987. Print.
Appiah, Kwame Anthony. *Cosmopolitanism: Ethics in a World of Strangers*. New York: Norton, 2006. Print.
———. *In My Father's House*. New York: Oxford University Press, 1993. Print.
———. "The Multiculturalist Misunderstanding." *The New York Review of Books*, 9 Oct. 1997. Web. 5 Sept. 2012 http://www.nybooks.com/articles/archives/1997/oct/09/the-multiculturalist-misunderstanding/?pagination=false.
Ashcroft, Bill, Gareth Griffiths, and Helen Tiffin, ed. *The Post-colonial Studies Reader*. London: Routledge, 1995. Print.
Augé, Marc. *Non-Places: Introduction to an Anthropology of Supermodernity*. London: Verso, 1995. Print.
Bachelard, Gaston. *The Poetics of Space*. With a new foreword by John R. Stilgoe. Boston: Beacon, 1994. Print.
Badiou, Alain. *On Beckett*. Manchester: Clinamen, 2003. Print.

Baetens, Jan. "Le lieu et l'espace: expérience et théorie." *Image and Narrative: Online Magazine of the Visual Narrative* 4 (2002): n. pg. Web. 9 Oct. 2009.

Bair, Deirdre. *Samuel Beckett: A Biography*. New York: Harcourt Brace Jovanovich, 1978. Print.

Barnes, Trevor J. "Retheorizing Economic Geography: From the Quantitative Revolution to the Cultural Turn." *Annals of the Association of American Geographers* 91.3 (2001): 546–65. Print.

Barry, Elizabeth. "One's Own Company: Agency, Identity and the Middle Voice in the Work of Samuel Beckett." *Journal of Modern Literature* 31.2 (2008): 115–32. Print.

Barthes, Roland. *The Rustle of Language*. Trans. Richard Howard. New York: Farrar, Strauss, & Giroux, 1986. Print.

Baudelaire, Charles. *The Poems in Prose, Volume II*. Ed. Francis Scarfe. London: Anvil Press Poetry, 2003. Print.

Baudrillard, Jean. *Simulacra and Simulation*. Ann Arbor: University of Michigan Press, 1994. Print.

Beckett, Samuel. *Complete Dramatic Works of Samuel Beckett*. London: Faber & Faber, 1986. Print.

———. *The Complete Short Prose*. Ed. S. E. Gontarski. New York: Grove, 1995. Print.

———. *Disjecta*. London: Calder, 1983. Print.

———. *Dream of Fair to Middling Women*. London: Calder, 1993. Print

———. *More Pricks than Kicks*. London: Calder, 1993. Print.

———. *Murphy*. London: Calder, 1957. Print.

———. *Nohow On: Company, Ill Seen Ill Said, Worstward Ho*. Ed. S. E. Gontarski. New York: Grove, 1996. Print.

———. *Quad et autres pièces pour la télévision*. Paris: Minuit, 1992. Print.

———. *Three Novels: Molloy, Malone Dies, The Unnamable*. New York: Grove, 1995. Print.

———. *Watt*. London: Calder, 1963. Print.

Begag, Azouz. *Les dérouilleurs: Ces français de banlieue qui ont réussi*. Paris: Mille et une nuits, 2002. Print.

———. *Le gone du Chaâba*. Paris: Seuil, 1986. Print.

Béland, Daniel. "Identity Politics and French Republicanism." *Society* 40.5 (2003): 66–71. Print.

Benguigui, Yamina, dir. *Inch'Allah Dimanche*. Gaumont, 2001. Film.

Benítez-Rojo, Antonio. *The Repeating Island: The Caribbean and the Postmodern Perspective*. Durham: Duke University Press, 1992. Print.

Berman, Marshall. *All That is Solid Melts into Air*. New York: Penguin, 1988. Print.

Bernstein, Richard J. *Beyond Objectivism and Relativism: Science, Hermeneutics, and Praxis*. Philadelphia: University of Pennsylvania Press, 1983. Print.

Bersani, Leo, and Ulysses Dutoit. "Beckett's Sociability." *Raritan* 12.1 (1992): 1–19. Print.

Bhabha, Homi. "DissemiNation." *Nation and Narration*. New York: Routledge, 1990. 291–322. Print.

———. *The Location of Culture*. London: Routledge, 1994. Print.

Bidou-Zachariasen, Catherine. "La prise en compte de l'"effet de territoire' dans l'analyse des quartiers urbains." *Revue française de sociologie* 38.1 (1997): 97–117. Print.

Blanchot, Maurice. "The Conquest of Space." Trans. Christopher Stevens. *Blanchot Reader*. Ed. Mike Holland. Oxford: Blackwell, 1995. 269–71. Print.

Bongie, Chris. *Islands and Exiles: The Creole Identities of Post/Colonial Literature.* Stanford: Stanford University Press, 1998. Print.

Bonn, Charles. "L'exil et la quête de l'identité, fausses portes pour une approche des littératures de l'immigration?" *Cultures transnationales de France: des "Beurs" aux . . . ?* Ed. Hafid Gafaïti. Paris: *L'Harmattan*, 2001. 37–53. Print.

Bonta, Mark, and John Protevi. *Deleuze and Geophilosophy.* Edinburgh: Edinburgh University Press, 2004. Print.

Bosteels, Bruno. "Nonplaces: an Anecdoted Topography of Contemporary French Theory." *Diacritics* 33.3–4 (2003): 117–39. Print.

Bourdieu, Pierre, ed. *La Misère Du Monde.* Paris: Seuil, 2007. Print.

Brand, Stewart. *Whole Earth Discipline.* New York: Viking, 2009. Print.

Brathwaite, Edward. "Timehri." *Is Massa Day Dead? Black Moods in the Caribbean.* Ed. Orde Coombs. New York: Anchor, 1974. 29–30. Print.

Britton, Celia. *Edouard Glissant and Postcolonial Theory: Strategies of Language and Resistance.* Charlottesville: University Press of Virginia, 1999. Print.

———. *The Sense of Community in French Caribbean Fiction.* Liverpool: Liverpool University Press, 2008. Print.

Brosseau, Marc. *Des romans géographes.* Paris: L'Harmattan, 1996. Print.

Caldwell, Christopher. *Reflections on the Revolution in Europe: Immigration, Islam, and the West.* New York: Doubleday, 2009. Print.

Caro, Robert. "The City-Shaper." *The New Yorker* 5 Jan. 1998: 38–49. Print.

———. *The Power Broker: Robert Moses and the Fall of New York.* New York: Knopf, 1974. Print.

Casey, Edward. *The Fate of Place.* Berkeley: University of California Press, 1997. Print.

———. *Getting Back into Place.* Bloomington: Indiana University Press, 1993. Print.

Castells, Manual. *The Power of Identity, The Information Age: Economy, Society and Culture Vol. II.* London: Blackwell, 1997. Print.

———. *The Rise of the Network Society: The Information Age: Economy, Society and Culture Vol. I.* London: Blackwell, 1996. Print.

Céline, Louis-Ferdinand. "Chanter Bezons, voici l'épreuve!" *Le Style Contre Les Idées: Rabelais, Zola, Sartre Et Les Autres.* Bruxelles: Editions Complexe, 1987. 127–34. Print.

Certeau, Michel de. *The Practice of Everyday Life.* Berkeley: University of California Press, 1988. Print.

Certeau, Michel de, Luce Giard, and Pierre Mayol. *The Practice of Everyday Life. Vol. 2, Living and Cooking.* Trans. Timothy J. Tomasik. Minneapolis: University of Minnesota Press, 1998. Print.

Césaire, Aimé. *The Collected Poetry.* Trans. Clayton Eshleman and Annette Smith. Berkeley: University of California Press, 1983. Print.

Césaire, Suzanne. "Le grand camouflage." *Tropiques* 14 (1945): 267–73. Paris: Jean-Michel Place, 1978. Print.

Chamoiseau, Patrick. *Les Neuf Consciences du Malfini.* Paris: Gallimard, 2009. Print.

———. *School Days.* Trans. Linda Coverdale. Lincoln: University of Nebraska Press, 1997. Print.

———. *Texaco.* Paris: Gallimard, 1992. Print.

Chamoiseau, Patrick, Jean Bernabé, and Raphaël Confiant. *Eloge de la créolité/In Praise of Creoleness.* Trans. M. B. Taleb-Khyar. Paris: Gallimard, 1997. Print.

Charef, Mehdi. *Le thé au harem d'Archi Ahmed.* Paris: Gallimard, 1988. Print.

Chibane, Malik, dir. *Douce France.* Alhambra Films avec le concours du Centre national de la cinématographie et la participation de Canal Plus, 1995. Film.

Coates, Nick. "Gardens in the Sands: the notion of space in recent critical theory and contemporary writing from the French Antilles." Diss. University College London, 2001. Print.

Condé, Maryse. *Le cœur à rire et à pleurer: Souvenirs de mon enfance.* Paris: Laffont, 1998. Print.

———. *Crossing the Mangrove.* Trans. Richard Philcox. New York: Anchor/Doubleday, 1995. Print.

———. *Désirada.* Paris: Laffont, 1997. Print.

———. "Order, Disorder, Freedom, and the West Indian Writer." *Yale French Studies* 83 (1993): 121–35. Print.

Confiant, Raphaël. *Aimé Césaire: Une traversée paradoxale du siècle.* Paris: Stock, 1993. Print.

———. *Ravines du devant jour.* Paris: Gallimard, 1993. Print.

Cresswell, Tim. *Place: A Short Introduction.* Malden, MA: Blackwell, 2004. Print.

Dainotto, Roberto. *Place in Literature: Regions, Cultures, Communities.* Ithaca: Cornell University Press, 2000. Print.

Dash, J. Michael. *Edouard Glissant.* Cambridge: Cambridge University Press, 1995. Print.

———. Introduction. *The Ripening.* By Edouard Glissant. Trans. Dash. Portsmouth, NH: Heinemann, 1985. 1–17. Print.

De Soto, Hernando. *The Mystery of Capital: Why Capitalism Triumphs in the West and Fails Everywhere Else.* New York: Basic Books, 2000. Print.

Deleuze, Gilles. *Différence et répétition.* Paris: PUF, 1968. Print.

———. "L'épuisé." *Quad et autres pièces pour la télévision.* By Samuel Beckett. Paris: Minuit, 1992. 57–106. Print.

Deleuze, Gilles and Félix Guattari. *Kafka: Toward a Minor Literature.* Minneapolis: University of Minnesota Press, 1986. Print.

———. *A Thousand Plateaus.* Minneapolis: University of Minnesota Press, 1987. Print.

———. *What Is Philosophy?* New York: Columbia University Press, 1996. Print.

Dell'Oca, Claudio. *Les enjeux des rencontres performatives dans les représentations des banlieues: Du détournement à la contamination des genres.* Diss. University Of California, Santa Barbara, 2011. Ann Arbor: UMI, 2011. Print.

Dennett, Daniel C. "Review of F. Varela, E. Thompson and E. Rosch: *The Embodied Mind.*" *American Journal of Psychology* 106 (1993): 121–26. Print.

Derrida, Jacques. *De la grammatologie.* Paris: Minuit, 1967. Print.

———. *La voix et le phénomène.* Paris: PUF, 1967. Print.

———. *L'écriture et la différence.* Paris: Éditions du Seuil, 1967. Print.

Diamond, Jared M. *Guns, Germs, and Steel: The Fates of Human Societies.* New York: W. W. Norton & Co, 1998. Print.

Dirlik, Arif. "The Postcolonial Aura: Third World Criticism in the Age of Global Capitalism." *Critical Inquiry* 20 (1994): 328–56. Print.

Dosse, François. *Histoire du Structuralisme, Vol I.* Paris: La Découverte, 1992. Print.

Entrikin, Nicholas. *The Betweenness of Place.* Baltimore: Johns Hopkins, 1991. Print.

Farah, Nuruddin. *Maps.* New York: Arcade Pub, 1999. Print.

Flint, Anthony. *Wrestling with Moses.* New York: Random House, 2009. Print.

Foucault, Michel. "Des espaces autres." *Architecture, Mouvement, Continuité* 5 (1984): 46–49. Print.

———. *Discipline and Punish.* New York: Pantheon, 1977. Print.

———. *The Order of Things.* London: Routledge, 1989. Print.

———. "Of Other Spaces." *Diacritics* 16.1 (Spring 1986): 22–27. Print.

"France's ethnic minorities: To count or not to count." *The Economist*, 28 Mar. 2009. Web. 1 Dec. 2010.

Frank, Joseph. "Spatial Form in Modern Literature." *Sewanee Review* 53 (1955): 221–40. Print.

Fraser, Benjamin. "Narrating the Organic City: A Lefebvrian Approach to City Planning, the Novel, and Urban Theory in Spain." *Journal of Narrative Theory* 39.3 (2009): 369–90. Print.

Frichot, Hélène. "Nathalie's Rotunda: Breaching the Threshold of Maurice Blanchot's *L'Arrêt de mort.*" *COLLOQUY text theory critique* 10 (2005): 171–80. Print.

Garreau, Joel. *Edge City: Life on the New Frontier.* New York: Doubleday, 1991. Print.

Gikandi, Simon. "Theory, Literature, and Moral Considerations." *Research in African Literature* 32.4 (2001): 1–18. Print.

Glaeser, Edward L. "What a City Needs." Review of *Wrestling With Moses: How Jane Jacobs Took on New York's Master Builder and Transformed the American City*, by Anthony Flint. *New Republic*, 240.16 (2009): 42–45. Print.

Glissant, Edouard. *Caribbean Discourse.* Charlottesville: CARAF University Press of Virginia, 1989. Print.

———. *La case du commandeur.* Paris: Seuil, 1981. Print.

———. *La Lézarde.* Paris: Seuil, 1958. Print.

———. *Malemort.* Paris: Seuil, 1975. Print.

———. "Métissage et créolisation." *Discours sur le métissage, identités métisses: En quête d'Ariel.* Ed. Sylvie Kandé. Paris: l'Harmattan, 1999. Print.

———. *Poetics of Relation.* Trans. Betsy Wing. Ann Arbor: University of Michigan Press, 1997. Print.

———. *The Ripening.* Trans. Michael Dash. Portsmouth, NH: Heinemann, 1985. Print.

———. "Solitaire et solidaire." Ed. Michel Le Bris and Jean Rouad. *Pour une littérature-monde*. Paris: Gallimard, 2007. 77–86. Print.

———. *Tout-monde*. Paris: Gallimard, 1993. Print.

———. *Traité du Tout-monde*. Paris: Gallimard, 1997. Print.

Gregory, Derek. *Geographical Imaginations*. Cambridge, MA: Blackwell, 1994. Print.

Guattari, Félix. *The Three Ecologies*. London: Athlone Press, 2000. Print.

Hallward, Peter. *Absolutely Postcolonial*. Manchester: Manchester University Press, 2002. Print.

Hardt, Michael and Antonio Negri. *Empire*. Cambridge: Harvard University Press, 2001. Print.

Hargreaves, Alec. *Immigration, 'Race' and Ethnicity in Contemporary France*. London: Routledge, 1995. Print.

———. *Voices from the North African immigrant community in France: Immigration and identity in Beur fiction*. Oxford: Berg, 1991. Print.

Harvey, David. *The Condition of Postmodernity: An Enquiry into the Origins of Cultural Change*. Cambridge, MA: Blackwell, 1990. Print.

———. *Justice, Nature and the Geography of Difference*. London: Blackwell, 1996. Print.

———. *Paris, Capital of Modernity*. New York: Routledge, 2003. Print.

Harvey, Lawrence. *Samuel Beckett: Poet and Critic*. Princeton: Princeton University Press, 1970. Print.

Heidegger, Martin. "Building, Dwelling, Thinking." *Poetry, Language, Thought*. Trans. Albert Hofstadter. New York: Harper & Row, 1975. 141–60. Print.

Hirshfield, Jane. "These Also Once Under Moonlight." *American Poetry Review* 38.5 (2009): 38. Print.

Jaccomard, Hélène. "Harem ou galère: le déterminisme géographique dans deux écrits beurs." *The Australian Journal of French Studies* 37.1 (2000): 105–115. Print.

Jacobs, Jane. *The Death and Life of Great American Cities*. New York: Random House, 1961. Print.

Jameson, Fredric. "Cognitive Mapping." *Marxism and the interpretation of culture*. Ed. Cary Nelson and Lawrence Grossberg. Urbana: University of Illinois Press, 1988. 347–60. Print.

———. *Postmodernism, or, The Cultural Logic of Late Capitalism*. Durham, NC: Duke University Press, 1991. Print.

———. "Third World Literature in the Era of Multinational Capitalism." *Social Text* 15 (1986): 65–88. Print.

Janvier, Ludovic. "Place of Narration/Narration of Place." *Samuel Beckett: A collection of Criticism*. Ed. Ruby Cohn. New York: McGraw-Hill, 1975. 96–110. Print.

———. "Lieu dire." *Cahier de L'Herne: Samuel Beckett*. Ed. Tom Bishop and Raymond Federman. Paris: Editions de L'Herne, 1976. 167–89. Print.

Junker, Mary. *Beckett: The Irish Dimension*. Dublin: Wolfhound Press, 1995. Print.

Kassovitz, Mathieu, dir. *La haine*. MKL/Lazennec Diffusion, 1995. Film.

Kandé, Sylvie. *Discours sur le métissage, identités métisses: En quête d'Ariel*. Paris: l'Harmattan, 1999. Print.

Kechiche, Abdellatif, dir. *L'esquive*. Noé productions, 2003. Film.

Kennedy, Sean, ed. *Beckett and Ireland*. Cambridge, UK: Cambridge University Press, 2010. Print.

Knowlson, James. *Damned to Fame: The Life of Samuel Beckett*. New York: Simon & Schuster, 1996. Print.

Koltès, Bernard-Marie. *Le retour au désert*. Paris: Éditions de Minuit, 1988. Print.

Kourouma, Ahmadou. *Les soleils des indépendances*. Paris: Editions du Seuil, 1970. Print.

Kullberg, Christina. "Fouiller le paysage: the Geo-Poetics of Édouard Glissant." *Literature, Geography, Translation*. Ed. Cecilia Alvstad, Stefan Helgesson, and David Watson. Newcastle upon Tyne, UK: Cambridge Scholars, 2011. 187–97. Print.

Kunstler, Howard. *The Geography of Nowhere*. New York: Simon & Schuster, 1994. Print.

Lapeyronnie, Didier. "Primitive Rebellion in the French *Banlieues*." *Frenchness and the African Diaspora*. Ed. Charles Tshimanga, Didier Gondola, and Peter J. Bloom. Bloomington: Indiana University Press, 2009. Print.

Lapeyronnie, Didier, and Laurent Courtois. *Ghetto urbain: Ségrégation, violence, pauvreté en France aujourd'hui*. Paris: Laffont, 2008. Print.

Laronde, Michel. "La Fontaine et *Salut cousin!* Le stéréotype scolaire comme sociocritique dans le cinéma arabo-français." *Discursive Geographies: Writing Space and Place in French*. Ed. Jeanne Garanne. Amsterdam: Rodopi, 2005. 207–21. Print.

Latour, Bruno. "An Attempt at a Compositionist Manifesto." *New Literary History* 41 (2010): 471–90. Print.

———. "Why Has Critique Run out of Steam? From Matters of Fact to Matters of Concern." *Critical Inquiry* 30.2 (2004): 225–48. Print.

Lefebvre, Henri. *The Production of Space*. Oxford: Wiley-Blackwell, 1992. Print.

Le Bris, Michel. "Pour une littérature-monde en français." *Le monde des livres*, 16 Mar. 2007. Web. 10 Sept. 2012. http://www.lemonde.fr/livres/article/2007/03/15/des-ecrivains-plaident-pour-un-roman-en-francais-ouvert-sur-le-monde_883572_3260.html.

Le Bris, Michel, and Jean Rouad, eds. *Pour une littérature-monde*. Paris: Gallimard, 2007. Print.

Leman Stefanovic, Ingrid. "Speaking of Place: In Dialogue with Malpas." *Environmental & Architectural Phenomenology Newsletter* 15.2 (2004): 6–8. Print.

Letchimy, Serge. *De l'habitat précaire à la ville*. Paris: L'harmattan, 1992. Print.

———. "Tradition et créativité: les mangrove urbaines de Fort-de-France." *Carbet: Revue martiniquaise de sciences humaines et de littérature* 2 (1984): 83–110. Print.

———. "Urbanisme et urbanisation en Martinique: le cas de Fort-de-France." Diss. Sorbonne, Paris IV, 1984. Print.

Lévy, Jacques, and Michel Lussault, eds. *Dictionnaire de la géographie*. Paris: Belin, 2003. Print.

Levy-Vroelant, Claire and Christian Tutin, "Social Housing in France." *Social Housing in Europe*. Ed. Christine Whitehead and Kathleen Scanlon. London: London School of Economics, 2007. 70–89. Print.

Lippard, Lucy. *The Lure of the Local*. New York: Norton, 1997. Print.

Litchfield, John. "Sarko's 35bn rail plan for a 'Greater Paris.'" *The Independent*, 29 Apr. 2009. Web. 16 Sept. 2011. http://www.independent.co.uk/news/world/europe/sarkos-euro35bn-rail-plan-for-a-greater-paris-1676196.html.

Lukács, György. "Art and Objective Truth." *Writer and Critic, and Other Essays*. Ed. Arthur D. Kahn. New York: Grosset & Dunlap, 1971. Print.

———. "The Ideology of Modernism." *Marxist Literary Theory*. Ed. Terry Eagleton and Drew Milne. Oxford: Blackwell, 1996. 141–62. Print.

———. *The Meaning of Contemporary Realism*. London: Merlin, 1962. Print.

Lynch, Kevin. *The Image of the City*. Cambridge, MA: Technology Press, 1960. Print.

Lyotard, Jean-François. *The Postmodern Condition: A Report on Knowledge*. Minneapolis: University of Minnesota Press, 1984. Print.

Malik, Kenan. "Assimilation's Failure, Terrorism's Rise." *New York Times*, 7 July, 2011. Web. 7 July 2011. http://www.nytimes.com/2011/07/07/opinion/07malik.html.

———. "A Merkel attack on multiculturalism." *Expressen*, 27 Oct. 2010. (Eurozine 21 Feb. 2011 for English translation.) Web. 1 Sept. 2011. http://www.eurozine.com/articles/2011-02-21-malik-en.html.

———. "Multiculturalism at its limits." *Eurozine*, 18 Jan. 2011. Web. 17 Sept. 2011. http://www.eurozine.com/articles/2011-01-18-debate-en.html.

Malpas, Jeff. *Place and Experience*. Cambridge: Cambridge University Press, 1999. Print.

Maspero, François. *Les passagers du Roissy-Express*. Paris: Seuil, 1990. Print.

Massey, Doreen B. *Space, Place, and Gender*. Minneapolis: University of Minnesota Press, 1994. Print.

Maude, Ulrika. "On Beckett's Landscapes: The Trilogy." *Anglicana Turkuensia* 15 (1996): 63–72. Print.

Maximin, Daniel. *Lone Sun*. Charlottesville: University Press of Virginia, 1989. Print.

———. *Les fruits du cyclone: Une géopoétique de la Caraïbe*. Paris: Seuil, 2006. Print.

Mbembe, Achille. "At the Edge of the World: Boundaries, Territoriality, and Sovereignty in Africa." *Public Culture* 12.1 (2000): 259–84. Print.

———. "Décoloniser les structures psychiques du pouvoir." *Mouvements* 51, Sept.–Oct. 2007. Web. 18 June 2012. http://www.mouvements.info/Decoloniser-les-structures.html.

———. *On the Postcolony*. Berkeley: University of California Press, 2001. Print.

———. "Pour l'abolition des frontières héritées de la colonisation." *MEDIAFRERES*, 6 Oct. 2010. Web. 26 Oct. 2010. http://www.mediasfreres.org/interview.shtml.

———. "Provisional Notes on the Postcolony." *Africa* 62.1 (1992): 3–37. Print.

———. "What Is Postcolonial Thinking? An Interview with Achille Mbembe." Trans. John Fletcher. *Eurozine*, 9 Jan. 2008. Web. 1 Dec. 2010. http://www.eurozine.com/articles/2008-01-09-mbembe-en.html.

Mehrez, Samia. "Azouz Begag: *Un di zafas di bidoufile* or The Beur Writer: A Question of Territory." *Yale French Studies* 82 (1993): 25–42. Print.

Miller, Christopher. *Nationalists and Nomads*. Chicago: University of Chicago Press, 1999. Print.

———. "The (Revised) Birth of Negritude: Communist Revolution and 'the Immanent Negro' in 1935." *PMLA* 125.3 (2010): 743–49. Print.

Milne, Anna-Louise. *The Extreme In-Between: Jean Paulhan's Place in the Twentieth Century*. Oxford: Legenda, 2006. Print.

———. "The Singular Banlieue," *L'Esprit Créateur* 50.3 (2010): 53–69. Print.

Mitchell, Peta. *Cartographic Strategies of Postmodernity*. New York: Routledge, 2008. Print.

Mitchell, W. J. T. "Imperial Landscape." *Landscape and Power*. Ed. Mitchell. Chicago: University of Chicago Press, 1994. 5–34. Print.

Moï, Anna. *L'echo des rizières*. La Tour d'Aigues: éditions de l'Aube, 2001. Print.

Moretti, Franco. *Atlas of the European Novel 1800–1900*. London: Verso, 1998. Print.

Morrison, Toni. *Beloved: A Novel*. New York: Knopf, 1987. Print.

Mugerauer, Robert. *Interpretations on Behalf of Place: Environmental Displacements and Alternative Responses*. Albany: State University of New York Press, 1994. Print.

Murphy, John P. "Baguettes, Berets and Burning Cars: The 2005 Riots and the Question of Race in Contemporary France." *French Cultural Studies* 22.1 (2011): 33–49. Print.

Nagel, Thomas. *The View from Nowhere*. New York: Oxford University Press, 1986. Print.

Nancy, Jean-Luc. "Banks, Edges, Limits (of Singularity)." *Angelaki* 9.2 (2004): 41–53. Print.

———. *The Creation of the World or Globalization*. SUNY series in contemporary French thought. Albany: State University of New York Press, 2007. Print.

———. *La Communauté Désœuvrée*. Paris: C. Bourgois, 1986. Print.

———. *The Sense of the World*. Minneapolis: University of Minnesota Press, 1998. Print.

Neuwirth, Robert. *Shadow Cities: A Billion Squatters, a New Urban World*. New York: Routledge, 2006. Print.

O'Brien, Eoin. *The Beckett Country*. Dublin: Black Cat, 1986. Print.

Pan Ké Shon, Jean-Louis. "The Ambivalent Nature of Ethnic Segregation in France's Disadvantaged Neighbourhoods." *Urban Studies* 47 (July 2010): 1603–1623,

Pavel, Thomas. "The Heidegger Affair." *MLN* 103.4 (1998): 887–901. Print.

Perlman, Janice E. *Favela: Four Decades of Living on the Edge in Rio de Janeiro*. Oxford: Oxford University Press, 2010. Print.

———. *The Myth of Marginality: Urban Poverty and Politics in Rio de Janeiro*. Berkeley: University of California Press, 1980. Print.

Pinker, Steven. *How the Mind Works*. New York: Norton, 1997. Print.

Portier, Pascale Duparc. "Labor Law Protests in France: 1968 Encore?" *Jurist: Legal News and Research*, Mar. 28, 2006. Web. 17 Sept. 2011. http://jurist.law.pitt.edu/forumy/2006/03/labor-law-protests-in-france-1968.php.

Prieto, Eric. "Edouard Glissant, *Littérature-monde*, and *Tout-monde*." *Small Axe* 33 (2010): 111–120. Print.

———. "Landscaping Identity in Contemporary Caribbean Literature." *Francophone Post-Colonial Cultures: Critical Essays*. Ed. Kamal Salhi. Lanham, MD: Lexington Books, 2003. 141–52. Print.

———. *Listening In: Music, Mind, and the Modernist Narrative*. Lincoln: University of Nebraska Press, 2002. Print.

Read, Justin. "Speculations on Unicity: Rearticulations of Urban Space and Theory during Global Crisis." *CR: The New Centennial Review* 9.2 (2009): 109–137. Print.

Reiss, Timothy. *Against Autonomy*. Stanford: Stanford University Press, 2002. Print.

———. "Mapping Identities: Literature, Nationalism, Colonialism." *Debating World Literature*. Ed. Christopher Prendergast. London: Verso, 2004. 110–47. Print.

Relph, Edward. "Disclosing the Ontological Depth of Place: a review of *Heidegger's Topology* by Jeff Malpas." *Environmental & Architectural Phenomenology Newsletter* 19.1 (2008): 5–8. Print.

———. *Place and Placelessness*. London: Pion, 1976. Print.

Rickert, Thomas. "Toward the *Chora*: Kristeva, Derrida, and Ulmer on Emplaced Invention." *Philosophy and Rhetoric* 40.3 (2007): 251–73. Print.

Ricoeur, Paul. *The Rule of Metaphor*. London: Routledge, 1978. Print.

———. *Time and Narrative Vol. I*. Chicago: University of Chicago Press, 1984. Print.

Riquelme, J. P. "Location and Home in Beckett, Bhabha, Fanon, and Heidegger." *Centennial Review* 42 (1998): 541–68. Print.

Rolin, Jean. *Zones*. Paris: Gallimard, 1995. Print.

Ropars-Wuilleumier, Marie-Claire. *Ecrire l'espace*. Paris: Presses Universitaires de Vincennes, Collection Hors-cadre, 2002. Print.

Rosello, Mireille. "The 'Beur Nation': Toward a Theory of 'Départenance.'" *Research in African Literatures* 24.3 (1993): 13–24. Print.

———. *Declining the Stereotype*. Hanover: University Press of New England, 1998. Print.

Roumain, Jacques. *Masters of the Dew*. London: Heinemann, 1978. Print.

Said, Edward. "Invention, Memory, and Place." *Critical Inquiry* 26.2 (2000): 175–92. Print.

———. *Nationalism, Colonialism and Literature*. Minneapolis: University of Minnesota Press, 1988. Print.

———. *Orientalism*. New York: Pantheon, 1978. Print.

Schama, Simon. *Landsape and Memory*. New York: Vintage, 1996. Print.

Sennett, Richard. *The Conscience of the Eye*. New York: Norton, 1990. Print.

Serrano, Richard. *Against the Postcolonial*. Lanham: Lexington, 2005. Print.

Sheridan, Alan. *Michel Foucault: The Will to Truth*. London: Tavistock, 1980. Print.

Smith, Neil. *Uneven Development: Nature, Capital, and the Production of Space*. Athens: University of Georgia Press, 1984. Print.

Smock, Ann. *What Is There To Say?* Lincoln: University of Nebraska Press, 2003. Print.

Soja, Edward. *Postmodern Geographies: The Reassertion of Space in Critical Social Theory*. London: Verso, 1989. Print.

————. *Thirdspace: Journeys to Los Angeles and Other Real-and-Imagined Places.* Oxford: Blackwell, 1996. Print.

Sokal, Alan, and Jean Bricmont. *Fashionable Nonsense: Postmodern Intellectuals' Abuse of Science.* New York: Picador, 1998. Print.

Spivak, Gayatri. *A Critique of Postcolonial Reason.* Cambridge, MA: Harvard University Press, 1999. Print.

Tadjer, Akli. *Bel-avenir.* Paris: Flammarion, 2006. Print.

Taguieff, Pierre-André. *La force du préjugé.* Paris: La Découverte, 1988. Print.

Tanaka, Jiro. "Consilience, Cultural Evolution, and the Humanities." *Philosophy and Literature* 34.1 (2010): 32–47. Print.

Tarr, Carrie. *Reframing Difference: Beur and Banlieue Filmmaking in France.* Manchester: Manchester University Press, 2005. Print.

Tavernier, Bertrand and Nils Tavernier. Dirs. *De l'autre côté du périph.* Paris: Bibliothèque publique d'information, 2009. Film.

Terry, Don. "The Final Farewell at Cabrini-Green." *New York Times*, 9 Dec. 2010. Web. 9 Dec. 2010.

Tindall, Gillian. *Countries of the Mind: The Meaning of Place to Writers.* Boston: Northeastern University Press, 1991. Print.

Tönnies, Ferdinand, and Charles P. Loomis. *Community & Society (Gemeinschaft Und Gesellschaft).* East Lansing: Michigan State University Press, 1957. Print.

Tshimanga, Charles, Didier Gondola, and Peter J. Bloom. *Frenchness and the African Diaspora: Identity and Uprising in Contemporary France.* Bloomington: Indiana University Press, 2009. Print.

Tuan, Yi-Fu. "Humanistic Geography." *Annals of the Association of American Geographers* 66.2 (1976): 266–76. Print.

————. *Space and Place.* Minneapolis: University of Minnesota Press, 1997. Print.

————. "Space and Place: Humanistic Perspective." *Progress in Human Geography* 6 (1974). 211–52. Print.

————. *Topophilia: A Study of Environmental Perception, Attitudes, and Values.* With a new preface by the author. New York: Columbia, 1990. Print.

Turner, Victor. *The Ritual Process: Structure and Anti-structure.* Chicago: Aldine, 1969. Print.

Van Gennep, Arnold. *Les rites de passage: Étude systématique des rites de la porte et du seuil.* Paris: É. Nourry, 1909. Print.

Varela, Francisco, Evan Thompson, and Eleanor Rosch. *The Embodied Mind: Cognitive Science and Human Experience.* Cambridge, MA: The MIT Press, 1991. Print.

Veyne, Paul. *Writing History: Essay in Epistemology.* Middletown, CT: Wesleyan University Press, 1984. Print.

Von Hoffman, Nicholas. "Beware of the Robert Moses Revisionists." *The New York Observer*, 27 May 2007. Web. 10 Sept. 2012. http://observer.com/2007/05/beware-of-the-robert-moses-revisionists/.

Wacquant, Loïc. "Pour en finir avec le mythe des cités-ghettos: les différences entre la France et les Etats-Unis." *Les Annales de recherche urbaine* 54 (1992): 20–30. Print.

————. *Urban Outcasts.* Cambridge, UK: Polity, 2008. Print.

Walcott, Derek. "The Muse of History." *Is Massa Day Dead? Black Moods in the Caribbean.* Ed. Orde Coombs. New York: Anchor, 1974. 1–27. Print.

Westphal, Bertrand. *Géocritique; réel, fiction, espace.* Paris: Minuit, 2007. Print.

Williams, Raymond. *The Country and the City.* London: Chatto and Windus, 1973. Print.

Wilson, Edward O. *Consilience: The Unity of Knowledge.* New York: Knopf, 1998. Print.

Zemmouri, Mahmoud, dir. *100% Arabica.* Fennec Production. Polygram Video. France, 1997. Film.

Index

Traité du Tout-monde (Glissant), 174, 177–79
Trinidad, 155
Tropiques (journal), 154
Tuan, Yi-Fu, 4, 17–18, 77

unemployment, 135
United States, 184, 202n10
  racial segregation in, 108, 134
universalism, 110, 127, 134, 149
The Unnamable (Beckett), 38–39, 44–45, 51, 59–60, 62, 66
urbanism, 166, 199, 201n9
urban renewal, 2–4, 6–7, 129–30, 202n10
urban-rural hybrid culture, 166–67
utopianism, 2, 80, 178, 196

Van Gennep, Arnold, 85
Varela, Francisco, 39, 50–55, 56, 67–68, 94, 188, 197
  reterritorialization and, 197

Veyne, Paul, 20
Vietnam, 140
Villepin, Dominique de, 133

Wacquant, Loïc, 108, 134, 188
Walcott, Derek, 141
"Walking in the City" (Certeau), 97–98, 100–101
Wallerstein, Immanuel, 145
wandering (in Beckett), 46–48, 59
Watt (Beckett), 40, 44, 46
Weyl, Hermann, 94
Whitehead, A. N., 24, 29
Williams, Raymond, 3, 155
Wilson, E. O., 198
Wittgenstein, Ludwig, 27
Words and Music (Beckett), 59
World Bank, 142
World Systems Theory, 145
Worstward Ho (Beckett), 46, 48, 61–62, 66